Big Data Analytics in Smart Manufacturing

The significant objective of this edited book is to bridge the gap between smart manufacturing and big data by exploring the challenges and limitations. Companies employ big data technology in the manufacturing field to acquire data about the products. Manufacturing companies could gain a deep business insight by tracking customer details, monitoring fuel consumption, detecting product defects, and supply chain management. Moreover, the convergence of smart manufacturing and big data analytics currently suffers due to data privacy concern, short of qualified personnel, inadequate investment, long-term storage management of high-quality data. The technological advancement makes the data storage more accessible, cheaper and the convergence of these technologies seems to be more promising in the recent era. This book identified the innovative challenges in the industrial domains by integrating heterogeneous data sources such as structured data, semi-structures data, geo-spatial data, textual information, multimedia data, social networking data, etc. It promotes data-driven business modelling processes by adopting big data technologies in the manufacturing industry. Big data analytics is emerging as a promising discipline in the manufacturing industry to build the rigid industrial data platforms. Moreover, big data facilitates process automation in the complete lifecycle of product design and tracking. This book is an essential guide and reference since it synthesizes interdisciplinary theoretical concepts, definitions, and models, involved in smart manufacturing domain. It also provides real-world scenarios and applications, making it accessible to a wider interdisciplinary audience.

Features

- The readers will get an overview about the smart manufacturing system which enables optimized manufacturing processes and benefits the users by increasing overall profit.
- The researchers will get insight about how the big data technology leverages in finding new associations, factors and patterns through data stream observations in real time smart manufacturing systems.
- The industrialist can get an overview about the detection of defects in design, rapid response to market, innovative products to meet the customer requirement which can benefit their per capita income in better way.
- Discusses technical viewpoints, concepts, theories, and underlying assumptions that are used in smart manufacturing.
- Information delivered in a user-friendly manner for students, researchers, industrial experts, and business innovators, as well as for professionals and practitioners.

Big Data Analytics in Smart Manufacturing

Principles and Practices

Edited by
P Suresh, T Poongodi, B Balamurugan,
and Meenakshi Sharma

CRC Press

Taylor & Francis Group
Boca Raton London New York

CRC Press is an imprint of the
Taylor & Francis Group, an **informa** business

A CHAPMAN & HALL BOOK

First edition published 2022
by CRC Press
6000 Broken Sound Parkway NW, Suite 300, Boca Raton, FL 33487-2742

and by CRC Press
4 Park Square, Milton Park, Abingdon, Oxon, OX14 4RN

CRC Press is an imprint of Taylor & Francis Group, LLC

Library of Congress Cataloguing-in-Publication Data
Names: Suresh, P., 1983- editor.
Title: Big data analytics in smart manufacturing : principles and practices / edited by P. Suresh, T. Poongodi, B. Balamurugan, Meenakshi Sharma.
Description: First edition. | Boca Raton : Chapman & Hall/CRC Press, 2023. | Includes bibliographical references and index.
Identifiers: LCCN 2022032387 (print) | LCCN 2022032388 (ebook) | ISBN 9781032065519 (hbk) | ISBN 9781032065533 (pbk) | ISBN 9781003202776 (ebk)
Subjects: LCSH: Manufacturing processes--Data processing. | Big data. | Machine learning. | Artificial intelligence.
Classification: LCC TS183 .B54 2023 (print) | LCC TS183 (ebook) | DDC 670.285--dc23/eng/20220901
LC record available at https://lccn.loc.gov/2022032387
LC ebook record available at https://lccn.loc.gov/2022032388

ISBN: 978-1-032-06551-9 (hbk)
ISBN: 978-1-032-06553-3 (pbk)
ISBN: 978-1-003-20277-6 (ebk)

DOI: 10.1201/9781003202776

Typeset in Palatino
by MPS Limited, Dehradun

Contents

Preface

Smart manufacturing analytics explores recent trends and affords a roadmap to adopt big data analytics for promoting various applications that range from fault detection processes to predictive maintenance activities. Big data analytics has significantly changed and automated the data exchange processes with advanced manufacturing technologies. To remain competitive in the industrial domain, new methodologies of manufacturing, innovation, procurement, and logistics are adopted. This book covers the novel research work contribution of various pervasive applications from the authors in smart manufacturing. The main objective of this book is to gather relevant contributions for analyzing historical perspectives focusing on technological revolutions. Furthermore, theoretical concepts, principles, and practices of big data analytics in smart manufacturing are investigated with the original research analysis of different case studies. The characteristics, benefits, impacts, challenges, and opportunities of big data in design and manufacturing are also presented.

Editors

Prof. (Dr.) P Suresh is currently serving as Academic Coordinator and Professor in the Department of Mechanical Engineering at Galgotias University, Greater Noida, India. He received his Ph.D. degree in the Faculty of Mechanical Engineering, from Anna University, Tamil Nadu, in 2014. He completed a Master of Engineering in Engineering Design from Bharathiar University, Coimbatore, Tamil Nadu in 2001 and a Bachelor of Engineering in University of Madras, Chennai, Tamil Nadu in 2000. He has about 21 years of working experience in academics and research. He has published more than 55 publications in various international journals, conferences, and book chapters, in Elsevier, Springer, IET, etc. Dr. P Suresh is also associated with various professional bodies such as the Institution of Engineers of India (IEI), IAENG, International Association of Engineers, Life Member of ISTE (Indian Society for Technical Education), and he is the Senior Member of IRED.

Prof. (Dr.) T Poongodi is a Professor in the Department of Computer Science and Engineering at the Galgotias University, Delhi-NCR, India. She received her Ph.D. degree in Information Technology (Information and Communication Engineering) from Anna University, Tamil Nadu, India. She has more than 15 years of experience working in teaching and research. Her current research interests include network security, wireless ad hoc and sensor networks, Internet of Things (IoT), computer networks, and blockchain technology for emerging communication networks. Dr. T Poongodi is the author of over 40+ book chapters including some reputed publishers such as Springer, Elsevier, Wiley, De-Gruyter, CRC Press, IGI global, and 30+ international journals and conferences. She has published 10+ books in the areas of Internet of Things, data analytics, blockchain technology, Artificial Intelligence, machine learning, and healthcare informatics, published by reputed publishers such as Springer, IET, Wiley, CRC Taylor & Francis, and Apple Academic Press.

Prof. (Dr.) B Balamurugan is currently working as Associate Dean-Student Engagement, Shiv Nadar University, Delhi-NCR, India. His contributions focus on engineering education, blockchain, and data sciences. His academic degrees and 12 years of experience working as a faculty in a global university like VIT University, Vellore have made him more receptive and prominent in his domain. He does have 200+ high impact factor papers in Springer, Elsevier, and IEEE. He has done more than 50 edited and authored books and collaborated with eminent professors across the world from top QS ranked universities. He has served up to the position of Associate Professor in his stint of 12 years of experience with VIT University, Vellore. He had completed his bachelor's, master's, and Ph.D. degrees from top premier institutions in India. His passion is teaching and adapting different design thinking principles while delivering his lectures. He has published 30+ books on various technologies and visited 15 plus countries for his technical course. He has several top-notch conferences in his resume and has published over 200 quality journals, conferences, and book chapters. He serves on the advisory committee for several start-ups and forums and does consultancy work for the industry on industrial IoT. He has given over 175 talks at various events and symposiums. He is currently working as a Professor and Chief Research Coordinator at Galgotias University and teaches faculty and students about research, and does research on blockchain and IoT.

Prof. (Dr.) Meenakshi Sharma is Professor Dean R&D in Galgotias University, Greater Noida, India. She completed her M. Tech in Computer Science and Engineering from Kurukshetra University in 2006. She has been awarded Ph.D. in Computer Science from Kurukshetra University in 2011. She has 15+ years of experience in teaching and research. Her research interests include machine learning, image processing, big data analytics, data compression, and digital and data warehousing. She has a total of 50+ research publications in *IEEE Transaction*, *SCIE*, *SCI*, and *Scopus*. She got the Best Research and Teacher Award in 2017 and 2018. She attended as Session Chair in Many International Conferences and gave Guest Lecture on machine learning and big data in many engineering colleges. She works as a Reviewer in many SCI and Scopus Indexed Journals. She is the GUEST editor (*Scopus* Journal). She is also Guest Editor (CRC Press) Taylor Francis. She had guided two Ph.D. candidates, one thesis submitted, and five are under guidance.

Contributors

K. P. Arjun
Department of Computer Science and
  Engineering
GITAM University
Bengaluru, Karnataka, India

R. Mohammed Harun Babu
iNurture Education Solutions
Bangalore, Karnataka, India

Mukti Chaturvedi
Dayananda Sagar University Innovation
  Campus
Bengaluru, Karnataka, India

Satish Chinchorkar
Symbiosis Skills and Professional
  University
Pune, Maharashtra, India

S. Janarthanan
School of Computing Science and
  Engineering
Galgotias University
Delhi-NCR, India

Maya Shankar Jha
School of computer Science and
  Enginering
Galgotias University
Greater Noida, Uttar Pradesh, India

S. Karthikeyan
Department of Aerospace Engineering
B.S. Abdur Rahman Crescent Institute of
  Science and Technology
Vandalor, Tamil Nadu, India

K. Arun Kumar
SNS College of Engineering
Anna University
Coimbatore, Tamil Nadu, India

R. Satheesh Kumar
Department of CSE
Sahrdaya College of Engineering and
  Technology
Thrissur, Kerala, India

Vishwanadham Mandala
Enterprise Architect
Greenwood, Indiana, USA

Nirdhum Narayan
Galgotias University
Delhi-NCR, India

K. Nivitha
Department of IT
Rajalakshmi Engineering College
Chennai, Tamil Nadu, India

R. Poorvadevi
Department of Computer Science and
  Engineering
Sri Chandrasekharendra Saraswathi
  Viswa Mahavidyalaya
Kanchipuram, Tamil Nadu, India

C.D. Premkumar
Department of IT
Hindustan College of Engineering and
  Technology
Coimbatore, Tamil Nadu, India

S. Ramamoorthy
Department of Computing Technologies
SRM Institute of Science and Technology
Kattankulathur, Tamil Nadu, India

Puja Saha
Department of CSE
PSG College of Technology
Anna University
Coimbatore, Tamil Nadu, India

Aradhna Saini
G L Bajaj Institute of Engineering and
  Management
Department of Computer Science and
  Engineering
Greater Noida, Uttar Pradesh, India

S. Sharanya
Department of Data Science and Business
  Systems
SRM Institute of Science and Technology
Kattankulathur, Tamil Nadu, India

M. Shebana
Rathinam College of Arts and Science
Bharathiyar University
Coimbatore, Tamil Nadu, India

Roohi Sille
School of Computer Science
University of Petroleum & Energy Studies
Dehradun, Uttarakhand, India

Divyansh Singhal
School of Computer Science
University of Petroleum & Energy Studies
Dehradun, Uttarakhand, India

P. Sivaprakash
Rathinam Technical Campus
Affiliated to Anna University
Coimbatore, Tamil Nadu, India

S. Gnana Sowndharya
Rathinam College of Arts and Science
Bharathiyar University
Coimbatore, Tamil Nadu, India

N. M. Sreenarayanan
School of computer Science and Enginering
Galgotias University
Greater Noida, Uttar Pradesh, India

K. Udayakumar
Department of Computing Technologies
SRM Institute of Science and Technology
Chengalpattu, Tamil Nadu, India

S. Arungalai Vendan
Dayananda Sagar University Innovation
  Campus
Bengaluru, Karnataka, India

Santhi Venkatraman
Department of CSE
PSG College of Technology
Anna University
Coimbatore, Tamil Nadu, India

1

Machine Learning Techniques and Big Data Analytics for Smart Manufacturing

Nirdhum Narayan

Galgotias University, Delhi-NCR, India

Aradhna Saini

G.L. Bajaj Institute of Technology and Management, Greater Noida, Uttar Pradesh, India

S. Janarthanan

Galgotias University, Delhi-NCR, India

CONTENTS

DOI: 10.1201/9781003202776-1

1.1 An Overview of Smart Manufacturing

Smart manufacturing (SM) is an innovation-driven methodology that uses Internet-associated hardware to screen the creation cycle. The objective of SM is to recognize openings for robotizing activities and use information investigation to further develop fabricating execution. SM is a particular utilization of the Industrial Internet of Things (IIoT) [1]. Organizations include implanting sensors in assembling machines to gather information on their functional status and execution. Earlier, data were ordinarily kept in nearby information bases on individual gadgets and were utilized uniquely to survey the reason for gear disappointments after they happened. As SM turns out to be more normal, more machines become organized through the IoT, they will be better ready to speak with one another, possibly supporting more prominent degrees of mechanization.

Nowadays, SM is the capacity to ceaselessly keep up with and further develop execution, with escalated utilization of data, because of the evolving conditions. Advancements for making brilliant assembling frameworks or production lines are turning out to be progressively plentiful. Therefore, producers, enormous and little, need to accurately choose and focus on these advancements effectively. Likewise, different upgrades might be important to get the best advantage from the chosen innovation. For instance, SM frameworks could possibly naturally arrange more crude materials as the provisions, allot other hardware to creation occupations on a case-by-case basis to finish orders and get ready appropriation networks whenever orders are finished.

Notwithstanding the IoT, there are various innovations that will assist with empowering shrewd assembling, which include the following:

- **Computerized reasoning (AI)/AI** – It empowers programmed dynamic dependent on the reams of information that assembling organizations gather. Simulated intelligence/AI can investigate this information and settle on keen choices dependent on the inputted data.

- **Robots and driverless vehicles** – It can be useful by reducing the repetitive undertakings bylaborers, such as moving vehicles across an office.

- **Blockchain** – Its advantages, including permanence, discernibility, and disintermediation, can give a quick and productive approach to record and store information.

- **Edge registering (edge computing)** – Edge figuring assists makers with transforming huge measures of machine-produced information into noteworthy information to acquire experiences to further develop dynamic. To achieve this, it utilizes assets associated with an organization, such as cautions or temperature sensors, empowering information investigation to occur at the information source.

- **Prescient examination (predictive analytics)** – Organizations can dissect the utilization of tremendous measures of information they gather from each of their information sources to anticipate issues.

- **Computerized twins** – Organizations can utilize advanced twins to demonstrate their cycles, organizations, and machines in a virtual climate, and then, at that point, use them to foresee issues before they occur such as lift effectiveness and usefulness (Figure 1.1).

FIGURE 1.1
Smart manufacturing.

1.1.1 Upsides and Downsides of Smart Manufacturing

SM offers various advantages, including further developed effectiveness, expanded usefulness, and long-haul cost investment funds. In a keen manufacturing plant, efficiency is ceaselessly improved. On the off chance that a machine is dialing back creation, for instance, the information will feature it, and the man-made reasoning frameworks will attempt to determine the issue. These amazingly versatile frameworks empower more prominent adaptability.

As far as effectiveness is concerned, one of the primary reserve funds comes from the decreased underway vacation. Current machines are frequently furnished with distant sensors and diagnostics to make administrators aware of issues as they occur. Prescient AI innovation can feature issues before they happen and find ways to alleviate the monetary expenses. A well-planned brilliant processing plant incorporates mechanization just as human-machine joint effort, which empowers functional effectiveness.

A major disadvantage to SM is the forthright expense of execution. Accordingly, numerous little-to-moderate-sized organizations will not have the option to bear the impressive cost of the innovation, especially on the off chance that they take on a transient way of thinking.

Be that as it may, since reserve funds over the drawn out will offset the startup costs, associations need to anticipate the future regardless of whether they can't carry out brilliant production lines right away. Another disservice is that the innovation is exceptionally mind boggling, which implies that frameworks that are inadequately planned or not sufficient for a specific activity could cut into benefits.

The objective of smart manufacturing is to enhance the assembling system utilizing an innovation-driven methodology that uses Internet-associated apparatus to screen the creation interaction. SM empowers associations to recognize openings for computerizing activities and use information investigation to further develop fabricating execution.

1.2 Machine Learning in Smart Manufacturing

Machine learning (ML) discerned expanded utilization in commercial enterprise in the course of last many years. Two floods in the utilization of ML happened in assembling. Initial during in 1980s, in the company of the enterprise and second at present in progress. While ML saw critical consideration during the 1980s, business reception was not high in light of the fact that the strategies were hard to execute and in the presence of the innovation accessible at that point. Many organizations and analysts in industry are returning to past work, zeroing in principally on area explicit models.

ML has stayed "depot" in each period of the item existence pattern: origination, plan, assembling, attribute, and preserve. With the expanded reception of the Industrial Internet of Things (IIoT), Industry 4.0, and Smart Assembling, significantly more information is being created. ML is turning into the main strategy that is utilized for anticipating and ordering the trouble taking care of issues inside the creation frameworks [2]. ML utilizes expanded registering power and different programming for acquiring the significant data and information from the huge information, which are gathered from the climate, yet additionally has capacity to gain from that information by getting the fake/computational insight.

The main strategies that are utilized for learning, grouped by the accessible input, are directed, solo, and support learning techniques. Additionally, the complement is put on future patterns of ML in fabricating applications where the essential objective lies behind the use of large information to achieve cost-effective, issue free what's more, ideal quality assembling measure. The fast improvement of innovations interconnected with ICT and the web of things empowers the development of assembling which has prompted industry 4.0. The execution of Cyber-Physical System (CPS) joined with IoT can give canny, adaptable frameworks fit for self-realizing which presents the center of Industry 4.0. To accomplish astute and adaptable frameworks, large information is required. In information revelation in data sets (KDD) of large information, AI assumes a significant part alongside information mining, measurement, design acknowledgment, and different strategies. ML, as a piece of keen framework in Industry 4.0, is comprehensively carried out in different fields of assembling where its strategies are intended to remove information out of existing information [3]. The new information (data) upholds the course of dynamic or making forecast of assembling framework. Yet, the ultimate objective of the ML procedures is the discovery of the examples among the informational collections or consistencies that portray the connections and design between those sets. ML framework, which maps a contribution to a yield, should be prepared to learn. The framework preparing is accomplished by giving information and its relating yield while deciding the design in the machine so that planning can be learned. Distinctive investigations have various ways to deal with the structure of the field of AI; however, the design that is most generally utilized is ordered by learning measures, and that is managed, unaided, and supports learning (Figure 1.2).

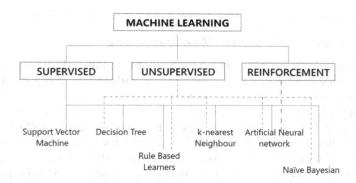

FIGURE 1.2
Machine learning techniques in smart manufacturing.

1.2.1 Supervised Machine Learning in Smart Manufacturing

The supervised learning is AI method, indicated for a huge measure of information (preparing sets), which are applied to the frameworks where the right reaction is given by the educated master. In supervised learning, a framework is prepared with information that has been named. The names order every information point into at least one gathering. Then, at that point, the framework figures out how this preparation information is organized and utilizes this to anticipate in which classifications to group new yield information. The last objective of finished managed learning measure is that the yields are sufficiently close to be helpful for all specified info place [4]. The bulk widely recognized managed machine learning assignments are order and relapse. In order tasks, the program needs to figure out how to anticipate the most expected classification, class, or mark for discrete yield esteems from at least one input informational collection. Like characterization, relapse issue likewise requires regulated learning procedures. The distinction in relapse issues is that projects should predict and foresee the worth of a constant yield by themselves. The administered learning is the most generally utilized ML strategy since larger part of uses can give named information.

1.2.2 Unsupervised Machine Learning in Smart Manufacturing

The unsupervised learning addresses the clever realizing where assessment of the activity isn't reliant, given nor directed, in light of the fact that there is no learned master. In contrast to regulated learning, the unaided taking in doesn't gain from marked information. Rather than that, it finds designs among the information. The task of unaided learning is to find gatherings of related perceptions of the info information, to be specific groups. Such perceptions inside bunches have relation dependent on some comparatively estimations where comparative focuses are assembled together. The primary objective of unaided learning is to find the obscure connections between classes utilizing the bunching investigation. As per Jordan and Mitchell and Hackeling another unaided learning task is dimensionality decrease. It addresses the most common way of finding the connections between input informational indexes and can be utilized for envisioning. [4] Taking into account that a few issues may contain a great many info information, issue with large information becomes difficult to picture.

1.3 Big Data Analysis in Smart Manufacturing

The mechanical development gives rise to a brought together (Industrial) IOT network, where approximately conjugated savvy fabricating gadgets assemble shrewd fabricating frameworks and empower exhaustive coordinated effort prospects that expand the dynamic and instability of their environments. From one viewpoint, this advancement produces a gigantic field for abuse, however then again additionally builds intricacy including new difficulties and necessities requesting for new methodologies in a few issues. One test is the examination of such frameworks that create colossal measures of (consistently produced) information, possibly containing important data helpful for a few use cases, such as information age, key execution marker (KPI) enhancement, conclusion, predication, criticism to plan or choice help.

Smart manufacturing frameworks are presently not progressive physical and intelligent encapsulated frameworks, yet heterogeneous, approximately coupled, non-progressive organized, digital actual frameworks of frameworks with occasion-based correspondence, teaming up in brought together organizations [5]. Aggregately seen, such new biological systems produce new mechanical conceivable outcomes possibly reasonable to fulfill complex client requests, assumptions, and wants. This implies for example new KPIs (for example, eco-effectiveness), creation adaptability, item and creation perceivability, or waste effectiveness; just as new (sorts of) impacting factors as adaptable items, incentive stamped patterns, online media criticism, store network variations, encompassing state, or exchanges in item, framework or request life-process. The intricacy of brilliant assembling frameworks creates new difficulties for exploration, advancement, and improvement exercises. New methodologies, even somewhat for conventional applications with respect to control, checking, perception, or enhancement are required, to deal with such new frameworks in a compelling and productive manner.

Smart manufacturing frameworks are creating an assortment of information; join blended also, totaled with information from interconnected frameworks, conceivably situated in a few layers and spaces. Discovering new affiliations, impacting cause and designs in this information, and noticing such discoveries through Big Data stream perception (additionally continuously) is one of the fundamental goals of enormous information investigation in SM. As a rule, Big Data examination is unequivocally associated with old-style information investigation also, mining draws near, and applied to a lot of information. Information typically comes from an assortment of sources and needs to go through a progression of techniques, for example, testing and questioning. Identified with smart manufacturing, further contemplations should be made, for example, enormous measures of multi-trademark information, designs, and mining in unique streamed information or (chronicled) information pails.

Enormous information by and large means an informational index that is improper to be utilized by customary information measure strategies because of their wide reach, complex construction, and size. Thusly, specialized and extraordinary frameworks, and philosophies, such as examination, catch, information curation, search, sharing, capacity, move, representation, and data protection, are needed to perform prescient examination, extricate esteem from information, and sometimes to a specific assort of informational index, among others. The acknowledgment of SM necessitates successful representation, investigation, and mutuality of different information emerging from item improvement and commercial enterprise system designing cycles to assembling destinations to be used for forecasts and displaying.

The dynamical patterns of large information climate in assembling administrations and the status of keen prescient information science instruments for huge information the executives in the viewpoint of Industry 4.0 acknowledgment. They focused on that the mindfulness and self-upkeep of a machine should be accomplished in an IoT-supported CPS climate, and that the choice help examination for machine well-being mindfulness investigation and self-support dependent on self-learning information foundation were needed to be created and applied. An exploration gathered information from different profane that comprised fabricating frameworks in a CPS climate and removed significant information from the enormous information utilizing calculations, for example, (1) signal handling, (2) highlight extraction, (3) well-being evaluation, (4) execution expectation, and (5) deficiency finding, of a prescient examination, for example, Watchdog Agent® was additionally directed. The outcomes were applied to modern bots and virtual artillery units. Shahbaz et al. proposed applied strategies and stages for different methods, such as measurable procedures, neural organization, choice trees, and hereditary calculation, to be sufficiently used on an item fabricating life cycle. Nagorny et al. presented a choice direction system that utilized Sustainable Process Analytics Formalism (SPAF) created by NIST [5].

Many investigations proposed huge information examination as an answer for different assembling issues. A methodology that performed constant checking and control in progressive degrees of perception plane, and clump level through measure production among information excavation approaches in biopharmaceutical producing ventures. Played out a venture that helped dynamic by changing incorporated fab information over to significant information in semiconductor fabricating businesses. The undertaking perceived and anticipated the vital factor of a process duration by constructing Machine Learning and Data Mining (MLDM) in view of the Selective Naïve Bayesian Classifier (SNBC) and restrictive common data expansion for include choice. Essentially, investigated information of a semiconducting material fab by utilizing advancements, for example, information mining, measure follow information investigation, stochastic recreation, and creation streamlining through an examination undertaking of IBM. They further developed creation productivity through better arranging and asset planning. Groger Mitschang directed explores on sign-based and pattern-based producing measure streamlining, as original information mining approaches gave through the Advanced Manufacturing Analytics Platform. Çiflikli and Kahya-Özyirmidokuz proposed an approach to identify disconnected machine breakdowns of floor covering fabricating through a choice tree. Shin et al. continued to direct an examination that played out the (1) distinguishing proof of assembling information to be dissected, (2) plan of a practical design for inferring logical models, and (3) plan of a scientific model to anticipate the manageability = execution, especially the force utilization, through enormous information foundation for power utilization productivity in assembling enterprises [5]. They fostered a model framework through MapReduce, Hadoop Distributed File System (HDFS), and an AI device. An examination that pictured the huge information identified with the coordinations of a shop floor by means of Radio Frequency Identification (RFID) connected with cloud fabricating was led in the point of view of SM acknowledgment.

1.3.1 Infrastructure

The alleged fourth mechanical insurgency depicts chiefly the double-dealing of the pattern those gadgets are getting more modest, quicker, less expensive, and portable; and that the Information Technology Foundation (WLAN, LAN, MAN, WAN, and so on letting associated workers, information bases, application programming) is extending around the world, turning out to be quicker and empower hardware to associate with this foundation. Accomplishments of the tertiary transformation as GPS, superior exact robots, new sorts of exceptionally exact detectors and entertainers, and so on are the reason for the fourth mechanical transformation. Models along these lines are intended, for example, arising third stage innovations with between conditions between online media, versatile and distributed computing, and (large) information examination to open possibilities of traditional IT advancements; or the arrangement of development gas pedals as IoT, 3D printing, what's more, mechanical technology, combined with the incorporation of activity advances (OT). Future savvy fabricating frameworks need to empower the abuse of these latest chances. Indeed, even today, individuals are encircled by associated computerized conditions consistently creating more collaborations with associated gadgets and programming. Such a development happens additionally in the assembling space (Figure 1.3).

Future smart manufacturing foundations are stood up to with the digitalization and hypervisor of (physiologic) objects upgraded with detectors, processors, recollection, and specialized gadgets, ready to impart coactively and to trade data freely through a receptive, prescient, social, mindful, or potentially independent conduct. A pre-owned term for such keen actual items is CPS which is conveyed in IIoT organizations.

SM frameworks must be founded on network advancements which empower a protected (encryption, validation, vigor, security), upended, and even cross-space and cross-layer correspondence among fixed and portable items (such as virtual articles, sensors, entertainers, gadgets, things, or frameworks). Organization innovations need to follow explicit prerequisites identified with, for example, ongoing, wellbeing, security, information sums, wired or remote, uninvolved or on the other hand dynamic, and so on. Bunk field levels necessitate time period capacities of seconds or milliseconds for reaction, dependability, goal, and fix (for example, command or real-time measurements of the cycle), while more significant levels just necessitate time spans of weeks or months (for example, for creation arranging or bookkeeping). Potential appropriate innovations are, for example, 6LowPan, ZigBee, (Industrial) Ethernet, Wi-Fi, or Bluetooth (Figure 1.4).

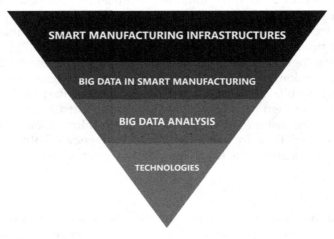

FIGURE 1.3
Smart manufacturing analysis.

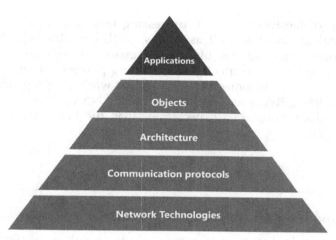

FIGURE 1.4
Smart manufacturing infrastructure (layers).

1.3.2 Architecture

Architecture, as a rule, are depicting mixes of parts/modules furthermore, their collaboration, and ought to give a bound together design and phrasing for utilized terms. Engineering ought to incorporate a consistent turn of events, an interaction furthermore, an approval sees, and ought to give situations to an approval engineering perspective model [5]. A keen assembling design ought to likewise give a bound together construction and phrasing covering required angles in brilliant assembling as item, framework or request life cycles, esteem streams, data streams, or progressive layers. Such structures are at present a work in progress.

1.4 Comparative Study of Smart Manufacturing

Instrument wear is the most normally noticed exhibition in assembling processes, such as boring, processing, and turning. The pace of hardware wear is impacted by many cycle boundaries, for example, cutting velocity and advancement speed, cutting apparatus calculation, and possessions of duties and device stuff. With the quick progression of detecting innovation and expanding counting of sensors prepared on present-day CNC instruments, it is feasible to foresee apparatus eroding all the additional precisely utilizing different estimation information. The most famous information-driven ways to deal with prognostics incorporate ANNs, choice trees, and SVMs with regard to frameworks wellbeing the executives. ANNs are a group of data processing models dependent on organic neural organizations which are utilized to gauge compound connections among data sources and results. The contributions of the ANN model incorporate workpiece hardness, cutting velocity, feed rate, hub cutting extent, and mean upsides of three power parts. Exploratory outcomes have to be visible that the representation prepared by ANNs gives precise forecasts of facet harshness and instrument flank wear.

The expectation of hardware wear in processing tasks was directed utilizing three well-known AI calculations, as well as ANNs, SVR, and RFs [6]. The presentation measures incorporate mean squared blunder, R-squared, and preparing time. A bunch of measurable highlights was extricated from cutting powers, vibrations, and acoustic outflows. The exploratory outcomes have shown that while the preparation time on the specific dataset utilizing RFs is longer than the FFBP ANNs with a solitary secret layer and SVR, RFs produce more exact expectations than the FFBP ANNs with a solitary secret layer and SVR.

1.5 Applications Used in Smart Manufacturing

Any place there is a cycle, a creation resource, and surprisingly a completed item, IoT can bring seriousness by empowering information assortment from various frameworks and cycles. The information is examined and changed into signs to further develop effectiveness, manageability, and usefulness. Probably the most well-known use instances of shrewd assembling incorporate Digital Factory, Maintenance preventive/prescient, Facility the executives, Automation enablement, Work wellbeing and expanded insight, and so on.

Computational knowledge is a fundamental piece of brilliant assembling to empower exact experiences for better direction. AI has been broadly researched in various stages of fabricating lifecycle covering idea, plan, assessment, creation, activity, and sustainment as displayed in Figure 1.5. The uses of information mining in assembling designing are

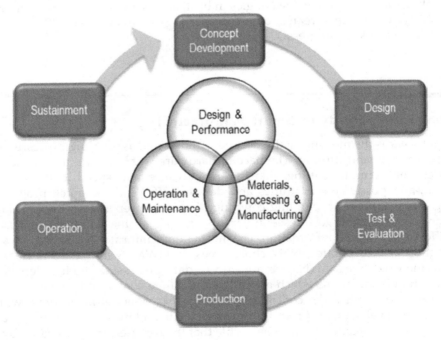

FIGURE 1.5
Various stages of fabricating lifecycle.

evaluated covering various classes of creation processes, tasks, shortcoming identification, upkeep, choice support, and item quality improvement.

1.5.1 Distinct Examination for Item Quality Assessment

Surface coordination examination is normally reviewed utilizing machine vision and picture handling methods to distinguish surface deformity for upgraded item quality in assembling. Customary AI has gained surprising headway and yields dependable outcomes much of the time yet unique pre-handling proceeds toward underlying build, factual build, channel-build, and mock-up-build procedures are expected to separate agent highlights with master information. Profound research has been explored to study undeniable level conventional highlights and put in a wide scope of surfaces or hard to recognize absconds instances. Convolutional neural network, initially intended for picture examination, is very much fit for robotized deformity recognizable proof in surface incorporation review. Profound convolutional neural network engineering is planned and the hyper-boundaries are improved dependent on backpropagation and stochastic angle plunge calculations. The exploratory outcomes show that CNN works appropriately with various sorts of imperfections on finished or non-finished surfaces. A nonexclusive methodology dependent on CNN is to separate fix highlight and anticipate deformity regions by means of thresholding and fragmenting. The outcomes appear the pre-trained CNN model functions admirably on a little dataset with further developed exactness for mechanized surface examination framework.

1.5.2 Symptomatic Investigation for Shortcoming Appraisal

Producing frameworks are generally dependent upon disappointments brought about by debasement or unusual working conditions, prompting exorbitant burden, surrender, crack, overheating, consumption, and wear. The disappointment might bring about higher working expenses, lower efficiency, more excluded part squander, and surprisingly startling personal time. To execute brilliant assembling, it is essential for a shrewd industrial facility to screen hardware conditions, recognize the nascent deformities, analyze the underlying driver of disappointments, and afterward join the data into assembling creation and control [3]. With amassed information from savvy tangible and mechanization frameworks, increasingly more profound learning strategies have been broadly researched for apparatus issue conclusion and order.

The results show that stacked Auto Encoder plays out marvelous. It might be derived that the significant learning models outflank standard AI systems with planned features, for instance, support vector machine, and BP neural network similarly as to arrange accuracy.

1.5.3 Prescient Examination for Deformity Anticipation

To expand fabricating usefulness while diminishing upkeep cost, it is pivotal to create and execute a canny support technique that permits producers to decide the state of in-administration frameworks to anticipate when upkeep ought to be performed. The transient conduct in the chronicled information is significant for forecast, and profound repetitive neural organization has shown its capacity to demonstrate fleeting example. As of late, an overall intermittent neural organization, named long momentary memory, has been researched to anticipate imperfection proliferation and gauge staying helpful life

(RUL) of mechanical frameworks or parts. A cutthroat study-based RNN has been put forward for long haul visualization of moving comportment wellbeing ranking. Profound Trusted Criss-cross is researched to show the complicated connection in the middle of substance evacuation tariff and synthetic mechanical cleaning procedure boundaries in semiconductor fabricating. An integrable methodology of Deep trusted, Criss-cross and molecule channel for the RUL presents a forecast of clay carriage. By collecting the result of group DBNs, Support Vector Regression model is researched to foresee power load interest. To foresee the asset demand in distributed computing, DBN is proposed to streamline work timetable and equilibrate the computational burden.

1.6 Challenges of Machine Learning in Smart Manufacturing

Securing information is the most well-known test when AI is applied in brilliant assembling. This is likewise an impediment as the accessibility, quality, and piece (e.g., Are meta-information included? Are information named?) of the assembling information close by impacting the exhibition of ML calculations. A few difficulties the informational index can contain are, for example, high-dimensional information can address for few ML calculations, that is, it can carry a serious level of superfluous and repetitive data which might affect the presentation of learning calculations. Today, most AI methods handle just information with persistent and ostensible qualities. How huge the impact is, relies upon different variables including the actual calculation and the boundary settings. It tends to be viewed as quite difficult for most exploration in assembling and not just ML appeal, to get clasp of any information due to, for example, certainty treat or an essential absence of information catching through the cycle.

Despite the fact that by and large ML permits the extricating of information and creates preferable outcomes over most customary techniques with less prerequisites toward accessible information, certain angles concerning the accessible information that can forestall the fruitful application actually must be thought of. Along with the following tip, this features the expanded along to comprehend the information to try ML. Contrasted with conventional techniques where a ton of time is consumed to remove data, in ML a ton of time is consumed on setting up the information.

After the accessible information is gotten, the information regularly must be pre-handled relying upon the necessities of the calculation of decision. Pre-handling of information basically affects the outcomes. In any case, there are many normalized devices accessible which hold up the most widely recognized pre-handling procedures such as normalizing and separating the data [7]. Also, it must be checked whether the preparation information is uneven. This can introduce a test for the preparation of specific calculations. In assembling practice, it is not an unexpected issue that upsides of specific ascribes are not accessible or missing in the informational index. These supposed missing qualities present a test for the utilization of ML calculations.

Notwithstanding, every issue and later applied ML calculation have explicit necessities with regard to supplanting missing qualities. By supplanting missing qualities, the first informational collection is impacted. The objective is to lessen the inclination and other negative impact however much as could reasonably be expected in regard to the investigation objective. As this issue addresses an exceptionally normal test, there is a lot of writing and viable arrangements accessible.

A significant test of expanding significance is the issue of what ML method and calculation to pick (determination of ML calculation). Considering all things, there were endeavors to seek after the meaning of "general ML procedures," the assorted issues and their necessities feature the requirement for particular calculations with specific strengths and shortcomings. Particularly because of the expanded consideration of experts and specialists for the field of ML in assembling, an enormous number of ML calculations or if nothing else varieties of ML calculations are accessible. Adding to this all-around existing intricacy, blends of various calculations, supposed "mixture draws near," are turning out to be an ever-increasing number of normal promising preferred outcomes over "individual" single calculation application.

Many investigations are accessible featuring an effective utilization of ML strategies for explicit issues. Simultaneously the test information is not freely accessible as a rule. This makes a nonpartisan and unprejudiced evaluation of the outcomes and accordingly the last examination testing. Starting today, for the most part, acknowledged way to deal with selecting an appropriate ML calculation for a specific issue is as follows: one glances at the accessible information and how it is portrayed (named, unlabeled, accessible master information, and so on) to pick between a managed, solo, or RL approach. The overall relevance of accessible calculations with respect to the examination issue prerequisites (for example, ready to deal with high dimensionality) must be analyzed [8]. A particular spotlight must be laid on the construction, the information types, and in general measure of the accessible information, which can be utilized for preparation and assessment. Past uses of the calculations on comparative issues are to be explored to distinguish an appropriate calculation. The term "comparable" for this situation implies, research issues with equivalent prerequisites for example in different disciplines or spaces. One more test is the understanding of the outcomes. It must be considered that not just the organization or delineation of the result is important for the understanding yet in addition the particulars of the picked calculation itself, the boundary settings, the "planed result," and furthermore the information including its pre-handling. Inside the understanding of the outcomes, certain more unmistakable constraints (again relying upon the picked calculation) can have an enormous effect.

1.7 Advantage of Machine Learning in Smart Manufacturing

1.7.1 Deep Learning Model for Smart Manufacturing

For smart manufacturing, a deep learning model is needed [9] with Industry 4.0 both supervised and unsupervised with analysis regress trees, artificial neural networks, and Bayes network. And mainly focused on deep learning autoencoders, convolutional neural networks, and recurrent neural networks increasing more important in smart manufacturing applications in the research area. In CNN model with layer 1 and in convolution, pooling and fully connected layerwith input and output data of feature extraction process. In LSTM neural networks with the connection of neurons with input data in direct cycle. Two memory cell components – like the long and short term with gate controls like input, output, and forget gates.

In LSTM input uses a convolution operation for connection with hidden to hidden, visual 2d matrix as input convolution LSTM layers for encoding layers with 128 filters dropout and afterward 64 filters dropout. Flatten with repeat vector dropout of 10 filters and in decoding part bidirectional LSTM 200 filters Bi-LSTM layers finally fully connected prediction. And for calculating the root mean square error (RMSE) of the loss functionwith epochs and training with number iteration process with optimizer to minimize the loss function.

1.7.2 Smart Manufacturing of Industrial IoT Robotics

Smart manufacturing for industries, which is more important for robotics [10] process automation, will improve the human-level interaction reduced and with industrial growth rate increased; and there are some industries that require human-less process such as biohazards processing and chemical industries; most involvement of human will impact their lives mostly their health problems such as cancer and skin disease, breathing issues, lungs related, etc. (Figure 1.6).

In context awareness is required to recognize and analyze with all users connected to various domains and actions to be taken. Making sub-components with system-level configuration is most cost-effective for industrial growth rate in terms of manufacture. Making all the users or a system level interaction with internal organization only not outside the organization involvement uses completely self-optimization and healing function. Large-scale industrial engineering data to create more intelligent decision-making with shifting both internal and external conditions.

1.7.3 Smart Factory Production

Smart factory and production were more important for industrial growth rate with economic development [11] in rapid advancement in latest technologies increasing production rate and data enrichment more complex. Regular methodologies for handling manual and traditional mechanisms will increase the time delay, and increase in the cost for scheduling will reduce this type of delay by smart factory production system with reinforcement learning and rewards to help to achieve multiple agendas and scheduling in smart manufacturing. In some cases, short period of work orders and machine not working in case of fault, frequent maintenance is required for that to overcome it. As a result, large capacity work will be handled parallel and readily available.

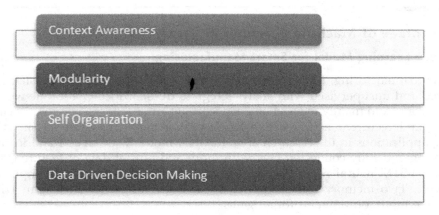

FIGURE 1.6
Smart system functions.

This is a once-in-a-lifetime opportunity to increase manufacturing system performance. Big data from smart factories, on the other hand, is multidimensional and based on real-time operations operations. The development of analytical algorithms to boost manufacturing's "smartness" operations is critical to reaching big data's full potential. Production scheduling, for example, is a difficult combinatorial problem that is generally solved by employing static and predictable assumptions in a centralized manner.

1.7.4 Data Clustering-Based ML

Another significant benefit of using a machine learning model is data clustering [12]. Adverse manufacturing conditions, on the other hand, can make precise detection of such manufacturing issues difficult. And, in machine learning (ML) methods and models for predicting during the SPM process, the thickness of the material can be measured such that the cost of in-process thickness measuring may be drastically lowered and it is possible to produce high-quality steel plates. Data clustering and machine learning with supervised learning algorithm, in steel industry development can be used to calculate the precision of thickness prediction. The most advanced revolution, Industry 4.0, often known as the fourth industrial revolution, spreads, modern production gets smarter, utilizing cutting-edge technology AI, cloud computing, the IoT, CPS, and big data are just a few examples. These technologies make smart manufacturing possible.

1.7.5 Imbalanced Data and Comparative Analysis in Smart Manufacturing

The IoT paradigm is transforming manufacturing into smart manufacturing; Industry 4.0 is a term that is frequently used [13]. Smart manufacturing's central pillar is to use IoT data and machine learning (ML) to automate defect prediction, reducing maintenance time and costs while also enhancing product quality. However, in real-world sectors, flaws are vastly overwhelmed by instances of excellent performance (flawless samples); this bias is reflected in data collected by IoT devices.

1.7.6 Human to Machine Applications for Smart Industry

Recent developments in low-latency communication network trends and technology are largely data driven by smart industry applications in IoT. Tactile Internet allows users to manipulate items from afar and incorporates bidirectional video, audio, and tactile data transmission, which is being accustomed to implement such applications. The end-to-end propagation latency, on the other hand, is a persistent bottleneck that can be eased by employing application layer and network layer prediction techniques based on artificial intelligence [14]. Human-machine interaction is based on virtual reality. Moreover, proposed modern edge technology drive server master and slave devices with supervised binary classifier for forecasting various feedback samples. In smart industrial evolution process of IoT, remotely accessing, receiving input from the environment, and performing action toward perceiving input requires supervised and reinforcement learning steps with critic and self-learning state. And human to master interface with communication channel network to slave interface with remote operated robot.

1.8 Future of Smart Manufacturing

1.8.1 Smart 3D Printing Techniques Using AI and Cloud

AI-based cloud 3D smart printing in manufacturing industries for both academic and industrial development has been taken up with more gain in 3D printing [15]. Specifically, to maximize smart manufacturing assistance for diverse manufacturing industry development around the country. The projected concept of in-house smart manufacturing is stressed and matched with future ongoing development to assist country households that were becoming more productive and to promote national economic prosperity. 3D printed wooden furniture, shoes, and dress items are the most popular things for households, whereas circuit boards for electronics, leather goods, and medical equipment are among others. With mutual benefits and agreements, the objects stated above can be imaginatively and as in-house items, they're created in a unique way (can be organized in recent technologies of smart contracts). To design smart contracting between the parties of the business owner's policies and agreements, a significant amount of effort is required.

1.8.2 Blockchain Secured Industry 4.0

Blockchain is another age of secure data innovation that is changing the manner in which organizations and enterprises carry on with work. A few examinations have been directed on significant empowering innovations for asset association and framework activity in blockchain got shrewd assembling in Industry 4.0 [16]. Square chain application issues in adaptability and versatility, just as network safety issues (CSIs), have all been explored. Future examination bearings for blockchain got shrewd assembling are given in view of the discoveries of this investigation, which may assist with controlling exploration on squeezing network protection issues for in the period of Industry 4.0, insight is an absolute necessity to requests for savvy modern improvement like digital, cloud, and social assembling. Blockchain, a progressive worldview that is newly evolved and adjusting, adding another apparatus to the security and adequacy of frameworks in the advanced world, is one method for tending to this security issue. In both business and industry, as an establishment for dispersed records, the blockchain gives straightforward and conveyed implication for going through with exchanges (i.e., computational trust).

1.8.3 Smart Transportation System

The Internet of Vehicles (IoV) is a brand-new idea that is intended to help achieve the objective of intelligent transportation systems (ITSs) [17]. IoV integrates smart vehicles with different environments, different platforms like industry infrastructure with various sensors, computer network nodes with exchange data platform which create a suitable environment and social space for the public and enhance the safety for all the road pedestrians. Resource sharing and vehicle management to increase the efficiency and capability of blockchain utilize the more secured resource sharing without privacy of the entities. The sharing technique and the proposed consensus mechanism are combined for trust management by employing vehicle reputation scores. Smart parking and vehicle platooning are two popular vehicle management concepts. Vehicle users can utilize the smart parking management system to find out about available parking spaces and make reservations in advance. Vehicle-generated data such as traffic data and accident incidences will make traffic management-related services easier to deliver than before, as well as sharing the information with others for effective management services and safety for smart transportation system.

1.8.3.1 Safety and Security in Autonomous Vehicles

Primary need and importance in safety and security for autonomous vehicle with all types of environments like roads, signals, sign boards for traveling are required to ensure the safety with sensors and GPS for transportation with one location to another location. Most importantly digital twin analysis [18]. When radar sensor values are modified in an attempt to produce a collision, the vehicle follower model is examined and sensor, VANET, GPS spoofing, operational (Figure 1.7).

However, during the entire development process, including functionality, system integration, verification, and validation, a complete profile of AV testing approaches is still required. As a result, digital twins can be used as a useful virtual testing environment.

1.8.4 Augmented Reality in AI-Based Education System

AR (Augmented Reality) in AI, which plays a critical role Kaviyaraj & Uma [19], Shang & You [20] in most industries, including the Army, education, medical domain, manufacturing domain, remote monitoring and navigation, and game world, was a new era of artificial intelligence-based education system in 2030. Improve virtual engagement in the classroom, as well as all subject expertise, through the use of an interactive learning process. In traditional way of class room teaching not being followable for all scenarios like the COVID-19 pandemic made to sit in one place to learn something without day-to-day teaching and learning process required to change by the new development and innovation in it. VR and AR in AI-based education system improve the teaching and learning process for the students and teachers.

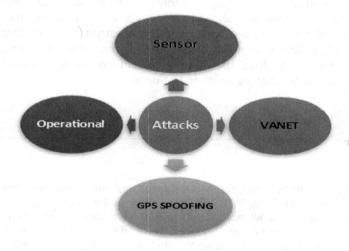

FIGURE 1.7
Types of attacks on autonomous vehicle.

Implementing smart innovation in regular classroom teaching instead of online pedagogy with smart devices is an alternative way of teaching all the courses either in augmented or virtual reality way for education system. Like 3D figures and much more processes, school level and higher studies program implemented for the students for future revolutionary changes required for the students and teachers knowledge to be upgraded.

1.9 Conclusion

This chapter presents the key ideas of information examination dependent on a contextual analysis. These ideas incorporate information understanding, information readiness, information pipeline, and information investigation innovations. To upgrade the functional proficiency top to bottom, enlightening and prescient examination were performed. In expansion, Overall Equipment Effectiveness (OEE) and the exhibition of the forecast strategy were extensively assessed. The outcomes have drawn consideration toward further developing the creation execution by diminishing the machine personal time. However, the forecasts made by the model are very adequate in terms of anticipating the impromptu stops, as spontaneous stops are one of the primary reasons of diminished creation execution. The use of ML is firmly identified with enormous information without which the turn of events and execution of ML strategies would not be conceivable because of the way that separating the information is the main activity that led to the accomplishment of imperfection-free and shortcoming-free processes. Additionally, the further improvement of ML application empowers the learning system where the fake/computational insight assumes the main part. Today, the ML calculations have a wide use in various fabricating regions such as advancement, control, investigating, security, and confirmation where the addition of straightforwardness of the whole assembling climate is gainful for cost decrease without influencing the nature of creation. Additionally, ML calculations have application in semiconductors just as in LEAN assembling conditions where the consequences of the trial show an improvement in process quality.

Nonetheless, still the greatest test furthermore is thefuture pattern that assembling is confronting today is reflected in the further turn of events and utilization of ML calculations, yet in addition finding the human specialists in information science and streamlining logical fields address another testing issue.

References

1. Burns, E. https://internetofthingsagenda.techtarget.com/definition/smart-manufacturing-SM
2. Sharp, M., Ak, R., & Hedberg Jr, T. (2018). A survey of the advancing use and development of machine learning in smart manufacturing. *Journal of Manufacturing Systems*, 48, 170–179.
3. Bajic, B., Cosic, I., Lazarevic, M., Sremcev, N., & Rikalovic, A. (2018). Machine learning techniques for smart manufacturing: applications and challenges in industry 4.0. Department of Industrial Engineering and Management Novi Sad, Serbia, 29.

4. Kang, H. S., Lee, J. Y., Choi, S., Kim, H., Park, J. H., Son, J. Y., ... & Do Noh, S. (2016). Smart manufacturing: past research, present findings, and future directions. *International Journal of Precision Engineering and Manufacturing-Green Technology*, 3(1), 111–128.

5. Nagorny, K., Lima-Monteiro, P., Barata, J., & Colombo, A. W. (2017). Big data analysis in smart manufacturing: a review. *International Journal of Communications, Network and System Sciences*, 10(3), 31–58.

6. Wu, D., Jennings, C., Terpenny, J., Gao, R. X., & Kumara, S. (2017). A comparative study on machine learning algorithms for smart manufacturing: tool wear prediction using random forests. *Journal of Manufacturing Science and Engineering*, 139(7), 1–3.

7. Wang, J., Ma, Y., Zhang, L., Gao, R. X., & Wu, D. (2018). Deep learning for smart manufacturing: methods and applications. *Journal of Manufacturing Systems*, 48, 144–156.

8. Wuest, T., Weimer, D., Irgens, C., & Thoben, K. D. (2016). Machine learning in manufacturing: advantages, challenges, and applications. *Production & Manufacturing Research*, 4(1), 23–45.

9. Essien, A., & Giannetti, C. (2020). A deep learning model for smart manufacturing using convolutional LSTM neural network autoencoders. *IEEE Transactions on Industrial Informatics*, 16(9), 6069–6078. doi:10.1109/TII.2020.2967556

10. Lins, R. G., & Givigi, S. N. (2021). Cooperative robotics and machine learning for smart manufacturing: platform design and trends within the context of industrial Internet of Things. *IEEE Access*, 9, 95444–95455. doi:10.1109/ACCESS.2021.3094374

11. Zhou, T., Tang, D., Zhu, H., & Wang, L. (2021). Reinforcement learning with composite rewards for production scheduling in a smart factory. *IEEE Access*, 9, 752–766. doi:10.1109/ACCESS.2020.3046784

12. Park, C. Y., Kim, J. W., Kim, B., & Lee, J. (2020). Prediction for manufacturing factors in a steel plate rolling smart factory using data clustering-based machine learning. *IEEE Access*, 8, 60890–60905. doi:10.1109/ACCESS.2020.2983188

13. Fathy, Y., Jaber, M., & Brintrup, A. (2021) Learning with imbalanced data in smart manufacturing: a comparative analysis. *IEEE Access*, 9, 2734–2757. doi:10.1109/ACCESS.2020.3047838

14. Mondal, S., Ruan, L., Maier, M., Larrabeiti, D., Das, G., & Wong, E. (2020). Enabling remote human-to-machine applications with AI-enhanced servers over access networks. *IEEE Open Journal of the Communications Society*, 1, 889–899. doi:10.1109/OJCOMS.2020.3009023

15. Jawad, M. S., Bezbradica, M., Crane, M., & Alijel, M. K. (2019) AI cloud-based smart manufacturing and 3D printing techniques for future in-house production. In 2019 International Conference on Artificial Intelligence and Advanced Manufacturing (AIAM), pp. 747–749. doi:10.1109/AIAM48774.2019.00154

16. Leng, J. et al. (2021) Blockchain-secured smart manufacturing in industry 4.0: a survey. *IEEE Transactions on Systems, Man, and Cybernetics: Systems*, 51(1), 237–252. doi:10.1109/TSMC.2020.3040789

17. Mollah, M. B. et al. (2021). Blockchain for the Internet of vehicles towards intelligent transportation systems: a survey. *IEEE Internet of Things Journal*, 8(6), 4157–4185. doi:10.1109/JIOT.2020.3028368

18. Almeaibed, S., Al-Rubaye, S., Tsourdos, A., & Avdelidis, N. P. (2021). Digital twin analysis to promote safety and security in autonomous vehicles. *IEEE Communications Standards Magazine*, 5(1), 40–46. doi:10.1109/MCOMSTD.011.2100004

19. Kaviyaraj, R., & Uma, M. (2021). A survey on future of augmented reality with AI in education. In 2021 International Conference on Artificial Intelligence and Smart Systems (ICAIS), pp. 47–52. doi:10.1109/ICAIS50930.2021.9395838

20. Shang, C., & You, F. (2019). Data analytics and machine learning for smart process manufacturing: recent advances and perspectives in the big data era. *Engineering*, 5(6), 1010–1016.

2

Data-Driven Paradigm for Smart Manufacturing in the Context of Big Data Analytics

Satish Chinchorkar

Ex-Professor Symbiosis Skills & Professional University, Pune, India

CONTENTS

2.1 Introduction

Manufacturing is considered a significant factor for the economy, social development, and growth. The impact of digitalization on these socioeconomic and financial factors is very high. There is a lot of potential while adopting Information and Communication Technology (ITC) and big data technologies to make manufacturing intelligent and more productive because huge data are being generated and consumed in this sector. The advantage of the adoption of technology such as big data enables generation of new revenue streams from information-based products and services while embedded intelligence contributes to improving productivity and profitability. Monetization of data from and about products, customers, and markets has been embedded in business strategy and becomes an important source of revenue and provides a competitive strength.

Smart manufacturing, which involves digital transformation of manufacturing and supply chain (SC) operations and processes, elucidates how the products are being engineered, designed, fabricated, used, and served digitally. Smart manufacturing comprises a number of emerging technologies and concepts such as the digital twin (DT), which yields enormous business benefits such as reliability, productivity, and quality improvement, better labor efficiency and resources utilization, energy-saving, maintenance cost and equipment downtime reduction, inventory optimization, and reduced worker injuries. These are few direct benefits of cyber-physical integration apart from competitive advantages obtained such as less time to market and transparency in business operations.

In view of these business benefits of smart manufacturing and because of the constantly diminishing cost of smart sensors and communication technology, there is a trend of increased migration to smart manufacturing. This trend reflected either value created by replacing old machinery (which might be expensive) or equipping the existing machines with smart sensors that collect and communicate data.

The deployment of all these technological data is treated as a fuel to run the smart factories. Industry often finds that challenges are shifted to organizational and cultural factors that are difficult to address than technical ones where the existing human intelligence and resources can be diverted.

Smart manufacturing can be also treated as a fully connected and agile system that provides responsive, adoptive, and connected manufacturing processes [1]. Over traditional linear or sequential SCs, interconnected SCs are being created by combining Operations Technology (OT) with Information Technology (IT). The integration of somatic, working, and human resources for production, maintenance, and stock control activities is carried out in cases where entire production operations are integrated to identify and cater the ever-fluctuating requirements.

Five key points that characterize the Smart Factory are connected, optimized, transparent, proactive, and agile with perceived benefits such as resource efficiency, value, lower production cost, and safety & durability. Internet of Things (IoT) enabled Smart Factory integrates the assets, operations, and business systems using technologies such as network (wireless) connectivity, CC (cloud computing), analytics, and application development with smart sensors deployed to obtain the business benefits such as asset visibility and reliability, product quality and traceability, resource efficiency and safety.

The application of innovative data analytics to match corporal science for refining the enactment and ability of decision-making at the workplace is known as smart manufacturing. The adoption of smart sensors and technology such as IoT in smart manufacturing shifted the challenges to manage the "big data," created on the shop floor, that are of bulk size, rapidly changing, and of diverse type. Subsequently, there is a high requirement of skilled resources to manage this big data implemented in smart manufacturing operations.

Increasing realization of the value of data specifically in this competitive world, the exponential growth of data, and availability and affordability of data and technology are rapidly transforming the traditional manufacturing operations into smart manufacturing operations. This gave birth to the concept of smart manufacturing. Data are treated as the lifeblood of the Smart Factory. Although entire digitalization and automation are aimed for making a Smart Factory, it does not aim to transform into a "murk" factory. Individuals are yet needed there at crucial operation, rather than freeing them to take up new challenges with better work conditions.

2.2 Historical Background

Conducting the literature review for upcoming and emerging technology such as "Smart Factory" is challenging because the literature availability in such evolving areas is less compared with other traditional areas and a highly cited paper may not necessarily give impactful information.

Hence the article [2] consolidates the literature of review specifically elaborating the subject "Smart Factory" with the help of a tool known as the "bibliometric" in which Systematic Literature Network Analysis (SLNA) is selected. In this tool, the conventional content-based reviews are supported by taking out the quantitative information from bibliographical networks used to detect the emerging and ever-changing field information along with related areas including research directions, critical areas, organizations, relations, politicians, and technology providers involved in translation toward implementing the Smart Factory. According to them, Smart Factory is a manufacturing plant where components of Industry 4.0 are applied. The static list of 10 most cited papers was generated using the methodologies such as SLR (Scope, Location, and Relevance), CNA (Citation Network Analysis), GCS (Global Citation Score), with AKA (Author Keyword Analysis). Cluster based on the topic "Smart Factory" is created and Kleinberg's burst detection algorithm was introduced to connect the topic with other pillars of Industry 4.0.

Mukherjee et al., in their article [3], explained the architecture of the Smart Factory with the following three layers for systematic understanding:

1. Physical Resources Layer: It consists of
   - Reconfigurable manufacturing unit: Modular manufacturing units, configurable controller.
   - Reconfigurable production line: Manufacturing resources based on XML.
   - Intelligent data acquisition: RFID, supervisory control and data acquisition (SCADA), DT, distributed control system (DCS), and process control system (PCS).
2. Network Layer: It consists of
   - Industrial Wireless Sensor Networks: IWSNs.
   - Related technologies: Component Object Model (COM), software defined industrial networks, device-to-device communication (D2D), edge computing.
3. Data Application Layer: It consists of
   - Ontology-based manufacturing model: Interoperable manufacturing system.
   - Implementation of big data in manufacturing: Predictive maintenance built on big data, product design optimization using the big data from production.

The application of Physical, Network, and Data Layers along with a case study of candy packing Smart Factory in which cyber-physical production system (CPPS) creates the connections of smart sensors, embedded terminal structures, smart control system, and communications infrastructure are explained well to illustrate the Smart Factory concept.

A comprehensive study of characteristics, technologies, and enabling factors of initiatives such as the fourth industrial revolution, CPPS, a system of digital manufacturing, smart factory, intelligent manufacturing, and advance manufacturing [4] creates a basis for analyzing the common factors. After refereeing about 83 papers relevant to smart manufacturing, a total of 5 characteristics, 11 technologies, and 3 enabling factors were identified to define the scope of smart manufacturing. Five characteristics identified are as follows: (1) context awareness, (2) modularity, (3) heterogeneity, (4) interoperability, and (5) compositionality. Eleven technical approaches identified are intelligent control, optimizing energy and efficiency, cyber security, cyber-physical manufacturing system, visual technology, IoT, application of cloud computing, 3D printing, use of smart material, data analytics, and IT-based productions. Three enabling factors are rules, regulations, and statutes, innovation in education and training and sharing of data.

Specifications of controlling environment specifically for data-driven orchestration of software services needed in smart manufacturing are explained [5] with a prediction that the next industrial revolution (Industry 4.0) will be driven by digitization which is reflected in the reference architecture RAMI 4.0 with IIRA. The data-oriented need is increased due to distributed intelligence integrated across diversified manufacturing operations. Description of DISRUPT project was adopted to analyze the multi-source, multi-scale, and multi-variant data of smart manufacturing. The role of cloud-based controller in the data life-cycle is explained for collection, preparation, processing, management, and distribution stages.

Manufacturing industries, such as Ford assembly line (1900), Toyota production system (1960), Flexible manufacturing (1980), cloud computing (2010), Industry 4.0 (2010), Smart Manufacturing Leadership Coalition (2011), and China Manufacturing (2015), are witness to many paradigm shifts. The manufacturing machines and equipment are gradually prepared with smart sensors and communication competences [6] for which data become the fuel. This chapter gives deep learning algorithm and its implementations toward transforming manufacturing smart. A comparison of advanced deep learning has been made with the traditional machine learning methods to increase the productivity and quality of the manufacturing systems. Future trends with challenges related to the adoption of deep learning in smart manufacturing were elaborated. According to them, around 82% of companies that adopted the smart manufacturing concepts realized an increase in efficiency, whereas nearly 45% of companies achieved customer satisfaction. Smart Factory is characterized as a factory in which all production units are integrated using wireless networks, activities are tracked by smart sensors, and operations are managed using computational power and intelligence to improve the quality of product, throughput of system, and resilience while optimizing the cost.

Three pillars for the Smart Factory are defined as Internet of Things (IoT), cloud computing (CC), and cyber-physical system (CPS) in which information is collected at various phases of Product Life Cycle (PLC) and activities such as raw material, machine operations, logistics and operators used for data-driven intelligence and advanced analytics. The data mining techniques applied can be viewed as five dimensions such as (1) identification and detailing, (2) correlation, (3) saggregation, (4) forecast, and (5) grouping, and progress analysis. Algorithms in machine learning specifically such as Artificial Neural Network (ANN), Classification and Regression with Support Vector Machine (SVM), and Random Forest or Bayesian Network for Instance-based Learning, whereas deep learning proposes advanced analytical tools for data-driven manufacturing applications specifically using big data.

Systematic mapping of big data in manufacturing [7] explains that manufacturing intelligence can be built using big data technology in a manufacturing environment.

Advancement and economic access to data storage and processing technology made it feasible to make decisions based on data (facts) rather than just intuition or guess. This trend is remarkable in the industry where big data and data analytics are enablers for the fourth industrial revolution [8]. Knowledge merging of Digital Technology and Manufacturing Processes for big data applications was illustrated and applied to four main design philosophies of Industry 4.0 such as integrated, information limpidity, distributed decisions, and technical support. Accordingly, six steps for the maturity index model were defined as computerization, connectivity, visibility (for collection of raw data), transparency (for data aggregation and correlation), predictive capacity, and adaptability. The third CPPS model with SC architecture explained consists of five stages: smart network, data to information transformation, computer-generated, cognition, and formation. Finally, big data and analytics play a central role while applying the algorithms to raw data.

A systematic literature review analyzing around 92 related publications [9] identified 13 characteristics of DT: (1) Physical Entity/Twin; (2) Virtual Entity/Twin; (3) Physical Environment; (4) Virtual Environment; (5) State; (6) Realization; (7) Metrology; (8) Twinning; (9) Twinning Rate; (10) Physical-to-Virtual Connection/Twinning; (11) Virtual-to-Physical Connection/Twinning; (12) Physical Processes; and (13) Virtual Processes. Further eight-dimensional model of DT explained (1) integration breadth; (2) connectivity mode; (3) update frequency; (4) CPS intelligence; (5) simulation capabilities; (6) digital model richness; (7) human interaction; and the (8) product life-cycle. The seven knowledge gaps in DT have been identified as (1) Business Benefits; (2) DT through the Product Life-Cycle Stages; (3) Applicable Use Cases; (4) Technical Applications; (5) Stages of Reliability; (6) Responsibility of Data; and (7) Association between corresponding Virtual Entities.

2.3 Smart Manufacturing

The National Institute of Standards and Technology (NIST) defines Smart Manufacturing as structures that are "completely connected, collective manufacturing systems that reply in instantaneous to reply to the varying requirement and situations on the shop floor, in the supply chain system, and also in customer requirements."

The SMLC definition states, "Smart Manufacturing in terms of the capability to resolve present and future issues through an open infrastructure that permits solutions to be employed at the rapidity of business while producing privileged value."

In smart production, the traditional manufacturing processes are transformed to leverage the opportunities of digitization such as:

- Manufacturing operations for additive manufacturing, advanced planning and scheduling, chatbots, and DT.
- Warehouse operations for technologies such as augmented reality, and robotics.
- Inventory Control using smart sensors and applying data analytics.
- Quality Control where optical analysis, real-time equipment, and part monitoring can be conducted.
- Maintenance where augmented reality and smart sensors can be used.
- Safety and sustainability wherein information from various sources is analyzed and used.

In the example of manufacturing processes above, the data are used to detect the errors in operation, provide user feedback, and envisage operational and resources inadequacies and variations of demands. This needs data measurement across production, environment, and product performance.

Fixtures including material handling equipment, tools, machines, pumps, and regulators in smart manufacturing are integrated with a central governing system.

Automation is a sole isolated activity or method in smart manufacturing, whereas in a Smart Factory shop-floor activities are integrated with SC and other relevant tasks that are performed through an interconnected IT-OT (Information Technology, Operations Technology) platform. This will transform the entire production scenario with an enhanced relationship with suppliers as well as customers.

Smart manufacturing models from Small and Middle Enterprises (SME) address the challenges in digital transformation which consists of the following three dimensions [10]:

1. Organization as a dimension includes money, resources, approach, process, and product.
2. Maturity as a dimension includes novice, beginner, learner, intermediate, and expert.
3. Tool-kit dimension suggests the list of applicable tools and technologies for these dimensions.

There is an increase in demand for product customization at a mass production scale that is profitable. Service-Oriented Architecture (SOA) in Smart Manufacturing System (SMS) to take up this challenge [11] provides additional agility, productivity, and quality. This SOA provides integration with different network technologies at a different level and also the integration with various activities as ecosystem dimensions such as Supply Chain Management (SCM), Customer Relationship Management (CRM), and Product Lifecycle Management (PLM).

The relationship among various Internet-based technologies in CPS in smart manufacturing [12] is defined as Relation ((SCPS (IoP, IoS, IoT), IoCK), factory).

SCPS: Smart Cyber-Physical System

IoP: Internet of People

IoS: Internet of Services

IoT: Internet of Things

IoCK: Internet of Content and Knowledge

Typical characteristics of smart manufacturing are varied resources, vibrant routing, complete connectivity, deep conjunction, self-involvement, and usage of big data.

2.4 The DT

Constantly changing demands, the need of reducing the cycle time needed to market, and the requirement of product development performance are conditions that created a need for DT. DT makes it possible for producers to accomplish the actual, reciprocal, and correlating corporeal object and its digital depiction. DT eliminates costly and time expensive physical mock-ups.

Analytical, storage, and management capabilities are needed to process the exponentially increasing volume and variety of the data sets during manufacturing operations. These data sets represent DT which is a feature of the Smart Factory configuration.

The DT, which is a system of sophisticated virtual product models, addresses all stages of product realization. To connect between design and production, simulated models of manufacturing goods are needed. DT reflects the real and virtual world. The "Skin Model Shapes" concept elaborates the DT of corporeal product in design and manufacturing [13] which considers conversion, composition, decomposition, and evaluation as major operation stages catering the following properties:

- Fidelity: Capability to define the intimacy to the physical product.
- Expansibility: Capability to connect, attach, or substitute models.
- Interoperability: Capability to transform, consolidate, and create similarity between various models.
- Scalability: Capability to deliver insight at various scales.

The data-driven activities that specifically include operations tracking and improvement, design and development of inventive products & services, and diversified value proposition with the business model are possible using DT with intelligent algorithm [14]. Machine learning, cloud computing, and wireless communication are major enablers of DT. DT can be treated as the next-generation simulation that provides elements and dynamics of convergence between physical and virtual spaces. Around 85% of DT models are developed for the "manufacturing assets" category, whereas 11% of DT models are developed for "factories." There is still scope for developing the DT models for "people," and for "production network."

Various standards in the area of design, planning for manufacturing, planning for inspection, manufacturing, and inspection are analyzed, which is required for DT. Different industrial communication protocols are mapped to seven layers of the OSI model applicable to DT. Challenges in developing the DT models are identified as architecture patterns, communication latency, data capturing, standards, functionality, version management, and the human factor. Big data analysis is useful in DT specifically for analyzing the hidden meaning in data for getting data processing results on time and high-quality data.

There is a strong need for future production systems to become more independent to be capable to respond fast to unforeseen events locally [15]. Three aspects of DT, modularity, connectivity, and autonomy, are significant for future manufacturing systems. In the shop-floor scenario on the arrival of new orders, in case of changed order priorities and faced hindrances during operations, production system and production units are expected to react autonomously; for this entire knowledge of the present state of production along with its own capabilities is essential. A realistic model with an autonomous system that interacts with the physical and virtual world is known as DT.

Implementation of DT is suggested in SMEs where around 74% of the time is consumed in the acquisition of process information and development of feasible layout options [16]. DT contributes to the development of CPPS required for smart SMEs.

DT is a classic example of advanced digitalization applicable in many areas specifically in smart manufacturing [17]. Different kinds of enormous data need are constantly gathered, processed, and consolidated in DT. For this several approaches and techniques are needed to manage the data with operations. Digitalization evolved over a period from digital enablement to digitalization aided to digitally control to cyber-physical integration. The tools and techniques used also evolved from the use of computers to computer-aided software to the Internet and automation to emerging technologies such as IoT, CC, big data, and DT. Five-dimensional DT model proposed with the following five dimensions of DT:

1. PE – Physical Entity
2. VM – Virtual Models
3. SS – Services
4. DT – Data
5. CN – Connections.

Connectivity is established within the following five dimensions:

- Connectivity between services and data
- Connectivity between physical entity and data
- Connectivity between data and simulated models
- Connectivity between physical entity and cyber models
- Connectivity between virtual models and services
- Connectivity between physical entity and services.

This five-dimensional DT model enables collection and transmission, storage and processing, and fusion and visualization of data used for smart manufacturing.

2.5 Big Data

Effective understanding and use of a new wealth of raw data created in manufacturing can be managed effectively using technology such as big data. There is a need to manage the bulk, diversity, pace, and reliability of constantly increasing information through six subsystems: data creation, data consolidation, data transportation, data processing, data storage, and data analysis using big data. Big data has the capability to transform traditional manufacturing into smart manufacturing using this increasing volume of data [18]. The application of big data to data-life-cycle stages in manufacturing can convert the product life-cycle data into manufacturing intelligence. Big data in smart manufacturing enables smart factories to make appropriate decisions independently.

There is increasing data volume, variety, and complexity from handcraft era to machine era and from an information era to big data era in the area of production and engineering. Accordingly, the medium used for storage, analysis, and communication of the data also changed from paper documents to databases to cloud and Internet. Big data is classified into information system data, smart equipment data, product data, user data, and public data categories.

Emerging technologies including the Internet, the Internet of Things, and cloud computing had led to the exponential growth of data in manufacturing. To control the volume and variety of data the scope, features, and value delivered by big data got evolved [19]. Big data broadly connects and integrates the physical world, human society, and cyberspace. The contribution of big data is significant in the area of national development, industrial upgrades, scientific research, and the developing interdisciplinary research to perceive and present things better and predict the future based on facts.

Big data possesses the traditional key traits such as volume, velocity, and variety [20], and added traits such as exhaustively, perseverance, indexicality, relationality, extensionality, and scalability make big data significant.

Information System Management (ISM) in any organization consists of three major elements [21]: hardware, software, and data. Hardware and software achieved their maturity level to some extent; however, the third element, data, is still struggling with challenges such as heterogeneity, scale, timeliness complexity, and privacy issues that are further exaggerated due to the continuous explosion of information. The adoption of big data approach creates value from data to make ISM more effective.

Five dimensions of business value generation [22] from big data are as follows:

- Generating the transparency
- Enabling the experimentation
- Segmenting the population
- Supporting or replacing the human decision-making
- Innovating the new business models.

However, while obtaining these business values big data also faces some challenges such as forming data policies, adoption of technology, resistance to organizational changes, access to data, and map the structure of an industry.

Big data gives visibility into market trends, customer buying patterns, maintenance cycles, and specifically Logistics and Supply Chain related data that are one of the major pillars of smart manufacturing [23]. Descriptive, predictive, and prescriptive analytics using big data contribute to making effective decisions on the strategic direction of an organization. Specifically, in the field of Logistics and Supply Chain Management, the approach such as big data analytics is applicable for operations such as strategic sourcing, development of Supply Chain Networks, product design, and development, demand planning, procurement, production operations, controlling inventory, and logistics management. There are different types of big data applicable in various SC strategies used in smart manufacturing such as sustainable SC, agile SC, collaborative SC, process-based SC, and functional SC.

Big data analytics has proven very effective specifically in energy-intensive industries [24] using two major technologies: energy-big-data acquisition and energy-big-data mining. Interdisciplinary research areas in the sector of energy, manufacturing, and big data are production-energy intake, energy-big-data application, manufacturing-big-data application, and consolidated big data-driven analytics infrastructure for energy-demanding production industries. Energy, spatial, and time dimensions are the dimensions of three-dimensional model. Examples of IoT devices applied for energy dimensions are smart electricity meters; smart water, gas, and quality meters; temperature sensors; pressure sensors; and RFID readers/tags whereas equipment, machines, workstations, factory, and industries are examples of spatial dimensions. Minutes, hours, days, weeks, and months units are examples of time dimensions.

A sum of objects connected to the Internet has exceeded the total population on the planet [25] and major concerns about data collection efficiency, the volume of data processing, analytics, and security are raised due to the constant expansion of the network and connecting devices. Big data analytics offers many opportunities to resolve these concerns while implementing the IoT for smart manufacturing. There is a revolutionary change in business processes by data integration and big data analytics. A huge volume of sensor-generated data are being captured, integrated, stored, preprocessed, mapped, transformed, cleansed, explored, stored, analyzed, shared, and utilized using big data. Connectivity, storage, quality of services, real-time analysis, and benchmarking are the specific requirements of smart manufacturing; big data is an appropriate resolution for these requirements.

2.6 Data-Driven Paradigm

Digitization is just conversion of data, whereas digitalization includes a total transformation that consists of collection, analysis, and usage of data for making better decisions or having better results.

Manufacturers are realizing the strategic importance of data in manufacturing operations. The data-driven strategies can make the companies more competitive; in fact, it becomes the necessary condition for smart manufacturing.

Scheduling and sequencing of the job is a very complex process in manufacturing. Generally, the following two approaches are adopted for scheduling the jobs [26]:

1. Computing a complete production schedule ahead of time.
2. Applying dispatching rules for constantly changing priorities of jobs waiting for operations.

The first approach is time-consuming and rigid, and does not cater the uncertainties in manufacturing due to fluctuations in processing time and machine breakdowns.

The second approach of "dispatching rules" is highly flexible which optimizes idle machine time. After the changes in the system state, revised schedules need to be prepared every time using the dispatching rules strategy. This sensor-equipped collaborating machine enables to collection of the data and further data-driven simulation-based optimized job scheduling decisions for smart manufacturing can be taken.

The CPS already existed in the earlier Industrial Revolution (i.e. Industry 3.0) but the fourth industrial revolution (also called Industry 4.0) provides interoperability by effective storage, analysis, and communication of data. The capability of learning from real-time data is being enhanced to make the processes more agile, productive, preemptive, and prognostic.

Digital transformation is performed in three major stages: digitization (where data conversion takes place), digitalization (where adoption of the process is being done), and transformation (where value creation for business objectives is fulfilled).

Data-driven smart manufacturing can be classified into four major modules: modules for manufacturing, data-driven module, real-time tracking module, and module for processing the problems [18]. These modules can be applied to in smart design, intelligent planning, effective process, material delivery and monitoring, production process monitoring, product quality, and smart tools with machine maintenance. Data life-cycle stages in all these areas are commonly classified as follows:

- Identification of data sources
- Collection of data
- Storage of data
- Processing of data
- Visualization of data
- Transmission of data
- Application of data.

For better understanding and management, the data in manufacturing are being classified into three major categories:

- Design: For an application such as market forecast, demand analysis, and smart product/service design.
- Manufacturing: For an application such as decision support, equipment supervision, and product quality control.
- Maintenance and repairs: For an application such as operations monitoring, fault prediction, and smart maintenance.

In manufacturing sector, the evolution of data from handicraft era to machine era to information age to big data era [18] is characterized as volume (huge quantity), variety (different forms), velocity (constant changes), veracity (biasness), and value (hidden in data).

Response Surface Methodology (RSM) is applied for observational data [27] for data-driven decision-making and management in smart manufacturing. From a potential variable set of data, the candidate variable subset of data is determined and after application of the response modeling the parameters are used in RSM.

The data in IoT promote the deployment of sensors, in CC promote networked data storage and analysis, and in AI promote timely decisions without human interferences.

Various techniques are being deployed in data-driven smart manufacturing that include pattern recognition, neural networks, automation, complex algorithms, artificial intelligence, activity scheduling, data mining, and problem solving.

Traditional SC phases such as develop, plan, source, make, deliver, and support which are sequential are integrated and centrally controlled by data-driven digital hub in Smart Factory.

2.7 Conclusion

Decisions based on the data (facts) leave no room for interpretation, correct the information, enhance the ability to evaluate the state, organize action, and improve the quality and efficiency. This gives more assurance that the choice made is correct for the

human as well as machines, and this confidence is a key toward a successful implementation. Hence, it might be worth paying the premium required for managing the
raw data around. The manufacturing sector is not an exception to this. Lots of hidden
opportunities are getting uncovered with application and productive usage of the information in production.

The data generated in manufacturing systems will have explosive growth. Big data
enables organizations to implement data-driven strategies to be sustainable.
Considering the increasing implementations of connected devices, emerging technologies, and automation in the sector, data-driven manufacturing becomes the essential
environment for intelligent production. Hence, information is the crucial component
for improving production performance. Implementation of Industry 4.0 and thereby
transformation of traditional manufacturing in the smart manufacturing enables a
factory to produce customized and small-lot products speedily and economically,
which becomes essential in the current competitive market. Obtaining the required
results from data-driven manufacturing of the network with three types of integrations
is expected [28] as follows:

a. Horizontal assimilation through value connections.

b. Vertical assimilation with connected production systems.

c. Complete digital integration of manufacturing through the complete value chain.

Data, which are also known as facts, the tiniest part, rather than fuel in this cyber-physical
integrated environment, provide the required intelligence to smart manufacturing.
Enabling technologies involved in the fourth industrial revolution keeping data as a focal
point are the facilitators to transform traditional manufacturing into smart manufacturing
(Figures 2.1 and 2.2).

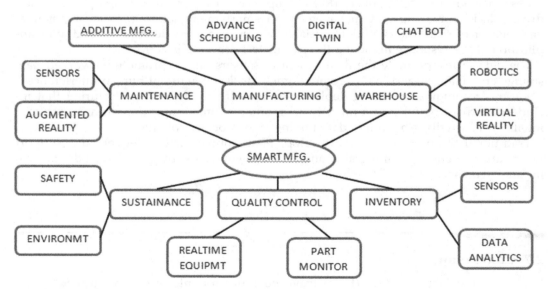

FIGURE 2.1
Data-driven paradigm for smart manufacturing.

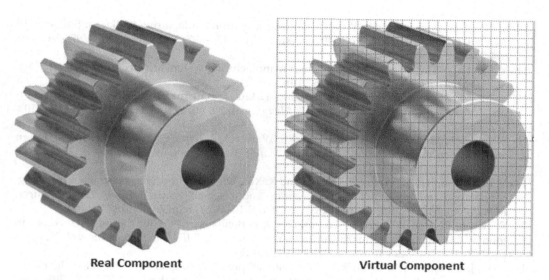

Real Component   **Virtual Component**

FIGURE 2.2
Comparison between conventional manufacturing and smart manufacturing workflow.

References

1. Deloitte University Press, "The smart factory," *Smart Fact. Responsive, Adapt. Connect. Manuf.*, p. 24, 2017 [Online]. http://media.daimler.com/marsMediaSite/en/instance/ko.xhtml?oid=9905147
2. F. Strozzi et al., "Literature review on the 'Smart Factory' concept using bibliometric tools," no. May, pp. 1–32, 2017.
3. M. Mukherjee, B. Yin, B. Chen, J. Wan, L. Shu, and P. Li, "Smart factory of industry 4.0: key technologies, application case, and challenges," *IEEE Access*, vol. 6, pp. 6505–6519, 2018. doi:10.1109/ACCESS.2017.2783682
4. S. Mittal, M. A. Khan, D. Romero, and T. Wuest, "Smart manufacturing: characteristics, technologies and enabling factors," *Proc. Inst. Mech. Eng. Part B J. Eng. Manuf.*, vol. 233, no. 5, pp. 1342–1361, 2019. doi:10.1177/0954405417736547
5. V. Tountopoulos, E. Kavakli, and R. Sakellariou, "Towards a cloud-based controller for data-driven service orchestration in smart manufacturing," *Proc. 2018 6th Int. Conf. Enterp. Syst. ES 2018*, pp. 96–99, 2018. doi:10.1109/ES.2018.00022
6. J. Wang, Y. Ma, L. Zhang, R. X. Gao, and D. Wu, "Deep learning for smart manufacturing: methods and applications," *J. Manuf. Syst.*, vol. 48, pp. 144–156, 2018. doi:10.1016/j.jmsy.2018.01.003
7. P. O'Donovan, K. Leahy, K. Bruton, and D. T. J. O'Sullivan, "Big data in manufacturing: a systematic mapping study," *J. Big Data*, vol. 2, no. 1, 2015. doi:10.1186/s40537-015-0028-x
8. M. Åkerman et al., "Challenges building a data value chain to enable data-driven decisions: a predictive maintenance case in 5G-enabled manufacturing," *Procedia Manuf.*, vol. 17, pp. 411–418, 2018. doi:10.1016/j.promfg.2018.10.064
9. D. Jones, C. Snider, A. Nassehi, J. Yon, and B. Hicks, "Characterising the digital twin: a systematic literature review," *CIRP J. Manuf. Sci. Technol.*, vol. 29, pp. 36–52, 2020. doi:10.1016/j.cirpj.2020.02.002

10. S. Mittal, D. Romero, and T. Wuest, "Towards a smart manufacturing toolkit for SMEs," *IFIP Adv. Inf. Commun. Technol.*, vol. 540, no. August, pp. 476–487, 2018. doi:10.1007/978-3-030-01 614-2_44

11. Y. Lu et al., "The paradigm shift in smart manufacturing system architecture," *IFIP Int. Conf. Adv. Prod. Manag. Syst.*, pp. 767–776, 2016.

12. X. Yao, J. Zhou, Y. Lin, Y. Li, H. Yu, and Y. Liu, "Smart manufacturing based on cyber-physical systems and beyond," *J. Intell. Manuf.*, vol. 30, no. 8, pp. 2805–2817, 2019. doi:10.1 007/s10845-017-1384-5

13. B. Schleich, N. Anwer, L. Mathieu, and S. Wartzack, "Shaping the digital twin for design and production engineering," *CIRP Ann. Manuf. Technol.*, vol. 66, no. 1, pp. 141–144, 2017. doi:10.1016/j.cirp.2017.04.040

14. Y. Lu, C. Liu, K. I. K. Wang, H. Huang, and X. Xu, "Digital twin-driven smart manufacturing: connotation, reference model, applications and research issues," *Robot. Comput. Integr. Manuf.*, vol. 61, no. August, p. 101837, 2020. doi:10.1016/j.rcim.2019.101837

15. R. Rosen, G. Von Wichert, G. Lo, and K. D. Bettenhausen, "About the importance of autonomy and digital twins for the future of manufacturing," *IFAC-PapersOnLine*, vol. 28, no. 3, pp. 567–572, 2015. doi:10.1016/j.ifacol.2015.06.141

16. T. H. J. Uhlemann, C. Lehmann, and R. Steinhilper, "The digital twin: realizing the cyber-physical production system for industry 4.0," *Procedia CIRP*, vol. 61, pp. 335–340, 2017. doi: 10.1016/j.procir.2016.11.152

17. Q. Qi et al., "Enabling technologies and tools for digital twin," *J. Manuf. Syst.*, vol. 58, no. October 2019, pp. 3–21, 2021. doi:10.1016/j.jmsy.2019.10.001

18. F. Tao, Q. Qi, A. Liu, and A. Kusiak, "Data-driven smart manufacturing," *J. Manuf. Syst.*, vol. 48, no. January, pp. 157–169, 2018. doi:10.1016/j.jmsy.2018.01.006

19. X. Jin, B. W. Wah, X. Cheng, and Y. Wang, "Significance and challenges of big data research," *Big Data Res.*, vol. 2, no. 2, pp. 59–64, 2015. doi:10.1016/j.bdr.2015.01.006

20. R. Kitchin and G. McArdle, "What makes big data, big data? Exploring the ontological characteristics of 26 datasets," *Big Data Soc.*, vol. 3, no. 1, pp. 1–10, 2016. doi:10.1177/2053951 716631130

21. S. Chinchorkar and Shrigiriwar, "Making information system management better with big data," *Manthan*, pp. 23–28, 2016.

22. S. Fosso Wamba, S. Akter, A. Edwards, G. Chopin, and D. Gnanzou, "How 'big data' can make big impact: findings from a systematic review and a longitudinal case study," *Int. J. Prod. Econ.*, vol. 165, no. January, pp. 234–246, 2015. doi:10.1016/j.ijpe.2014.12.031

23. N. Subramanian, A. Gunasekaran, T. Papadopoulos, and P. Nie, "4th party logistics service providers and industrial cluster competitiveness," *Ind. Manag. Data Syst.*, vol. 116, no. 7, pp. 1303–1330, 2016. doi:10.1108/imds-06-2015-0248

24. Y. Zhang, S. Ma, H. Yang, J. Lv, and Y. Liu, "A big data driven analytical framework for energy-intensive manufacturing industries," *J. Clean. Prod.*, vol. 197, pp. 57–72, 2018. doi: 10.1016/j.jclepro.2018.06.170

25. E. Ahmed et al., "The role of big data analytics in internet of things," *Comput. Networks*, vol. 129, pp. 459–471, 2017. doi:10.1016/j.comnet.2017.06.013

26. E. M. Frazzon, M. Kück, and M. Freitag, "Data-driven production control for complex and dynamic manufacturing systems," *CIRP Ann.*, vol. 67, no. 1, pp. 515–518, 2018. doi:10.1016/ j.cirp.2018.04.033

27. N. Sadati, R. B. Chinnam, and M. Z. Nezhad, "Observational data-driven modeling and optimization of manufacturing processes," *Expert Syst. Appl.*, vol. 93, pp. 456–464, 2018. doi:10.1016/j.eswa.2017.10.028

28. S. Wang, J. Wan, D. Li, and C. Zhang, "Implementing smart factory of industrie 4.0: an outlook," *Int. J. Distrib. Sens. Networks*, vol. 2016, 2016. doi:10.1155/2016/3159805

3

Data-Driven Models in Machine Learning: An Enabler of Smart Manufacturing

Mukti Chaturvedi and S. Arungalai Vendan

Dept. of ECE, School of Engineering, Dayananda Sagar University, Bengaluru, Karnataka, India

CONTENTS

DOI: 10.1201/9781003202776-3

3.1 Introduction

Several industries have adopted big data analysis for process efficiency. Data-driven modeling is made mandatory to avoid part and process failures. The data-driven models use the existing data sets for pattern recognition and regression analysis without the need for solving the complex mathematical relations which describe the process. Machine learning (ML) has made a transforming impact on the industry in product design and manufacturing and is projected to have greater demand in Industry 4.0. Modern industrial paradigm is experiencing a transition into digital manufacturing with 3D printing due to its exceptional advantages over conventional subtractive techniques. Adaptation to additive manufacturing (AM) has the advantages of making complex shapes and topologically optimized structures. However, its adoption in industry is restricted due to less exposure in working with design software, limited reference data and material library availability, process defects, and inconsistent product quality.

Sporadically, the AM parts show incomplete fused parts and trapped gases causing porosity, anisotropic microstructure, and distortion due to residual stresses. Addressing these issues necessitates in-depth understanding of the complex relationship of material properties, process parameters, and microstructural and mechanical properties of 3D printed parts. Dependency of material properties on the process parameters has been attempted with physical models and is found to be complex and non-linear.

The data-driven models showing promising performance in classification, clustering, and regression have found increasing attention in AM systems. ML algorithms help to optimize process parameters by learning the inter-intra dependencies from the previous data and also enable design corrections with in-process defect monitoring systems. Besides assessment and control of the product quality, product design planning is also supported by these algorithms. Artificial neural network (ANN) in ML is a strong computational model with capacity to analyze large data sets. Integration of Artificial Intelligence (AI) techniques to AM processes can allow better control of the process properties.

Figure 3.1 shows the classification of various domains of AM and the tested ML techniques that have been applied in each domain by researchers.

The state-of-art ML is used for AM for advanced research. Scope of extrapolating this study, challenges, and addressal mechanisms are presented in the following sections.

3.2 3D Printing Process

3D printing is one form of AM technique and is in the phase of increased adoption in the manufacturing industry. It is an automated process based on the principle of layered manufacturing, in contrast to subtractive or formative manufacturing. This principle

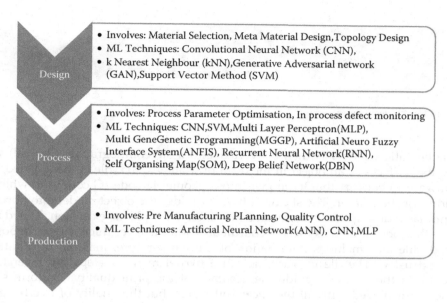

FIGURE 3.1
AM process classification and applicable ML techniques.

enables manufacturing a 3D object from layered material deposition of equal thickness based upon the CAD file created for the part to be manufactured.

The advent of AM in 1987 marked it as a method for rapid prototyping and generative manufacturing. With time, there have been significant advances in the field which have brought different types of machines under the layered manufacturing category. All the different processes have different principles of manufacturing appropriate for different tasks and a wide variety of materials. Some of the materials include metals and polymers. This technology provides freedom of design with no requirement of expensive tooling and at the same time opens up opportunities for low-cost testing and minimum weight manufacturing. Manufacturing parts with complex geometries and mass customization are made possible with this technology. The AM process chain (Figure 3.2) involves creation of mathematical models using 3D software programs or with 3D scanners for digital representation of the objects.

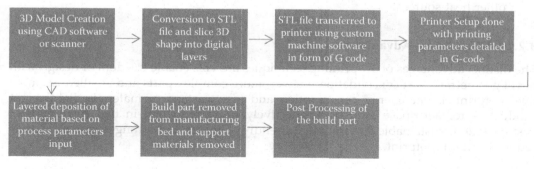

FIGURE 3.2
Additive manufacturing process chain.

FIGURE 3.3
Process chain for AM techniques.

The mathematical model is then converted into a stereolithographic file (.stl) which describes the surfaces of an object in the form of triangles. STL file is then loaded into a slicer software to convert the 3D model into a geometric code (G-code) file which has instructions for the printer. The slicing software divides the object model into horizontal layers and has a description of necessary movements for plastic extrusion. This data set consists of the contour data as the x–y coordinates and the layer thickness for deposition. The G-code file also includes information of the temperature, material flow rate, and speed of extrusion. The file instructions cause two elementary steps per layer for the manufacture of the part and guide the accuracy of the print quality. Uniform surface smoothness is achieved with all the slicer soft-wares, but the quality of overhangs and bridges depends on the performance of slicer. The process chain remains the same for different techniques with the difference in the processing of each layer and joining together of subsequent layers (Figure 3.3).

Several techniques of AM (Figure 3.4) enable the manufacturing of complex geometries with a wide variety of materials for catering to a range of applications in distinct industries. Materials are available in different physical forms and the same printing process cannot be used for all forms of materials. This describes the requirement of distinct 3D printing processes [1].

- Powder form – The materials utilize a light/heat source to compress and melt the layers of the powder and fuse them together in the required shape for an application.
- Resin form – Polymers used in resin form utilize a light beam or a laser beam to fuse the layers together.
- Filament – Material is jetted or melted droplets are extruded through a heated extruder; binder is used to fix the layers.
- Pellets, granules form – Granules of a powder are fused together using laser or other heat sources.

3.2.1 3D Printing – Advantages

The distinct advantages of 3D printing techniques are viz., enable freedom of design with novel geometries, part consolidation – fewer, more complex parts and smaller assembly line footprint, lower energy consumption and less wastage of materials, lightweight products – for aerospace industry – effectively cause reduction in fuel consumption, customization, sustainable/environment-friendly – lighter and stronger materials, thus reduced carbon footprint.

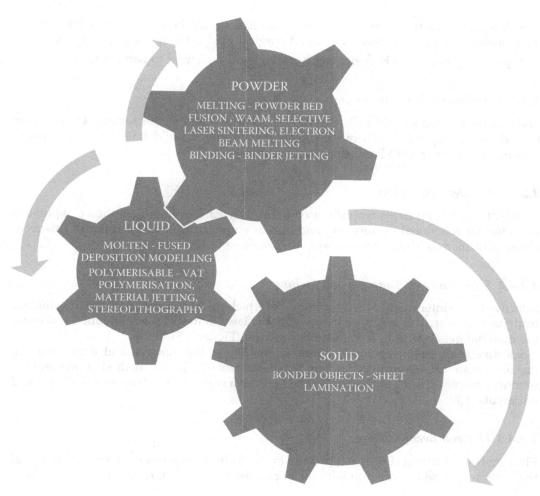

FIGURE 3.4
AM process techniques based on material state.

3.2.2 3D Printing – Disadvantages

- Limitations of size, raw material – currently nearly 100 materials available which is much lesser than conventional manufacturing,
- high cost of printing, having no cost reduction even with increased volume,
- need for post-processing of build parts and long cycle times.

3.2.3 3D Printing – Beneficiary Industries

AM has now moved into the following various industrial applications [1,2]:

- Aeronautics and aerospace industry: Structural parts of space vehicles, castings for complex gear cases and covers, fuel tanks, lightweight engine parts, and structural hinges.
- Automotive: Electrical components.

- Medical industry – Dental implant products, dental braces, hip and knee implants, hearing aids, prosthetics, and surgical guides for specific operations.
- Jewellery making – Forging, stone cutting, and polishing to name a few.

3.2.4 3D Printing Techniques

The process techniques and their derivatives are elaborated in this section. Experiments with different deposition schemes have shown improved build times or part strength depending on the material and the process parameters [3–5].

3.2.4.1 Powder Bed Fusion

Powder bed fusion (PBF) is typically used to produce smaller high-definition components intended for functional prototyping and also as engineering functional parts. This technique is further classified into sintering and melting techniques [6].

3.2.4.2 Selective Laser Sintering and Melting

Selective laser sintering (SLS) is a technique in which metal powdered material is sintered using laser power. This is caused by pointing the laser in the 3D model-defined space and the material gets bound to form a solid structure (Figure 3.5).

Selective laser melting involves complete melting of the material and thus results in products with different properties than SLS weldments [1,7]. This method allows making of more complex shapes as the powder bed acts as a support structure for overhangs and undercuts [1,8].

3.2.4.3 Electron Beam Melting

Electron beam melting (EBM) is a process in which heat source is the electron beam and the parts are formed in vacuum with metal powder (Figure 3.6). A variety of metal alloys

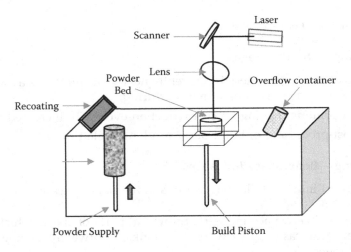

FIGURE 3.5
PBF schematic diagram.

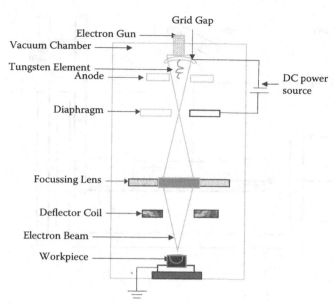

FIGURE 3.6
EBM schematic diagram.

can be used to produce fully dense parts with this technique. This is a requirement in medical industry, particularly for implants and aerospace and aviation industry products as well.

3.2.4.4 Photo-Polymerization

It is an AM process technique used for prototyping and yields parts with a good surface finish. It is further categorized into stereolithography (SLA) and digital light processing (DLP).

3.2.4.5 Stereolithography

Stereolithography (SLA) is the printing technique for making patterns, prototypes, and models, by the process of photo-polymerization. This process involves heated chaining together molecules to form a 3D polymer product [1]. SLA is the most accepted and accurate AM printing process with an excellent surface finish. This process requires a movable platform in which a vat holds the photopolymer resin (Figure 3.7). The resin gets hardened at the point where laser hits the surface. Limitations of this technique are post-processing steps and brittleness of materials affecting its stability [9].

3.2.4.6 Digital Light Processing

Digital light processing (DLP) is a process that uses a liquid crystal display panel with an arc lamp. In a single pass, the entire shallow polymer vat gets exposed to the arc (Figure 3.8). This process has less wastage and lower running costs [7,10].

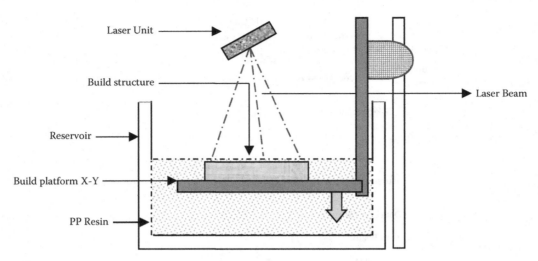

FIGURE 3.7
SLA schematic diagram.

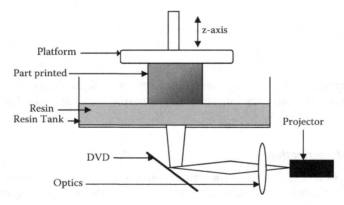

FIGURE 3.8
DLP schematic diagram.

3.2.4.7 Inkjet: Binder Jetting

The material used in this method of 3D printing is fused layer by layer with the binder material which is jetted and sprayed onto the powder bed. The powder bed lowers down fractionally after each layer and the bed surface is smoothened with a roller, before the process repeats for subsequent spraying of the binding material resulting in the fusion of the layers. Binder jetting has the advantage of powder bed providing the required support for overhangs and undercuts. On the contrary, parts produced are not as strong as SLA and require post-processing to ensure durability [11].

3.2.4.8 Inkjet: Material Jetting

The part material is selectively jetted through multiple jet heads, also another jet is used for jetting out the wax-like support material. The process is repeated after layer milling and UV light curing to form the complete product. Simultaneous deposition of a range of materials is possible in this technique [2,7].

3.2.4.9 Material Extrusion

This method is also known as free form fabrication (FFF). Parts are manufactured by layered deposition by extrusion of small beads of molten plastic filaments. The layers of material deposited on a heated bed harden and form a structure. Extrusion head is moved in the vertical and horizontal directions and the material flow is adjusted with the help of the stepper motors. Microcontroller controls the entire printing process with the computer-aided manufacturing (CAM) package [1,12].

Improper layer-to-layer adhesion may result in porous products. Post-processing using acetone is done to resolve this problem [13,14].

3.2.4.10 Selective Deposition Lamination (SDL)

This process uses standard copier paper for layer-by-layer printing. Successive layers are fixed to the previous layers with the help of adhesive. Adhesive is applied selectively based on the 3D model detail of actual and supporting parts. Paper feed mechanism is used to feed new paper into the printer. Movement of the build plate is then allowed to reach up to the heat plate and application of pressure enables the surface bond. The edges of the product are then created by cutting the excess sheets of paper with an adjustable blade made of tungsten carbide. After the cutting sequence, a layer of adhesive is deposited and this process continues to create the 3D printed part [1]. The process can produce fully color 3D printed parts, with no post-processing requirement and is safe and ecofriendly.

The different 3D printing techniques with specific processes, applications with some process parameters of importance, are listed in Table 3.1 [1,3,9–11,15–18].

3.3 Need for Parametric Analysis and Optimization in 3D Printing

The different techniques of 3D printing involve control of the build quality on the many process variables. Improved part quality may be achieved by analysis and appropriate selection of process parameters in the fabrication stage. The different manufacturing techniques have different parameters affecting the build properties with varying significance levels. These parameters are listed in Table 3.1. Establishing the relation between the mechanical properties and the process parameters requires deriving empirical model using conventional statistical tools or by adopting ML techniques. The combination of a number of process parameters makes the parametric analysis an essential step in assuring desired build properties. Optimization in the manufacturing process would result in reduction of product development cycle time and also improve the product quality, thus enabling relevance in the competitive manufacturing industry. ML techniques can be employed to arrive at an empirical model for establishing dependencies between the process and build parameters. Material properties in such behavioral studies can be manipulated with a combination of building parameters and their various levels to arrive at the optimum levels of build parameters. In this chapter on application of ML for parametric analysis and optimization of process parameters,

TABLE 3.1

AM Process Techniques

3D Printing Technique	Process	Popular Material	Parameters of Importance	Application
Material Extrusion	FDM	• ABS • Nylon • PLA • Laywood (WPC) • Bio Materials • Polycarbonate • PolyPhenyl Sulphone • Elastomers • Thermoplastics	• Infill Density and Pattern • Build Orientation • Deposition Rate • Shell Thickness • Layer Thickness • Raster Width • Raster Angle • Extruder Temperature • Build Bed Temperature • Air gap • Build Orientation • Printing Speed	Rapid tooling patterns jigs and fixtures, Small detailed parts Presentation models Patient and food applications High heat applications lightweight durable products Aerospace Architecture Automobiles- concept models and functional prototypes Sporting goods
Powder Bed Fusion (PBF)	SLS, SLM	• Nylon (Polyamide) • Alumide (nylon+Aluminum) • Stainless Steel • Aluminum and Cobalt Derivatives • Gold, Silver • Titanium • Polystyrene • Elastomer Composites • Bio-Materials (Bone Tissue)	• Exposure time • Interval time • Point Distance • Spot Size • Scanning Speed • Scanning mode • Part Bed Temperature • Part Orientation • Hatch spacing • Scan Pattern Laser • Beam Diameter • Laser Power	Jewellery making Rapid tooling patterns Less detailed parts Parts with snap-fits living hinges High heat applications
	EBM	• Stainless Steel • Titanium • Polymers • Ceramics • Metal Matrix composites		Aerospace Medical Implants Tooling

Process	Technology	Material	Parameters	Applications
Vat Photopolymerization	SLA	Photopolymer, Ceramics, PLA, Bio-Materials (bone Tissue)	Layer Thickness, Hatch spacing, Hatch Depth, Post Curing Time	Rapid tooling patterns, Snap fits, Presentation models, High heat applications
	DLP	PLA	Layer Thickness, Exposure time, Shutter speed, Horizontal Resolution, Base Exposure Time	
InkJet	Polyjet - Liquid in cartridge form	Photopolymer, Waxes resin	Saturation Level, Power Level, Drying time, Spread Speed, Layer Thickness	Very detailed parts, Rapid tooling patterns, Presentation models Jewelry and fine items, Architecture Consumer electronics Sporting goods with colors Toys
	Material Jetting - Liquid	Acrylic based thermo polymeric Plastic, Natural and Synthetic Waxes, Fatty Esters, Ceramics, Bio Materials	Powder Spread, Print Speed, Heater Power Ratio, Print Orientation	Very detailed parts, Rapid tooling patterns, Jewelry and fine items, Medical devices, jigs and fixtures for machine shops
	Binder Jetting-Liquid – binder, powder-material	Metals, Polymers, Ceramics		Modeling, Prototyping, sandmoulds and cores for casting
Sheet Lamination	SDL-Sheets	Paper	Sheet Thickness, Direction of Travel, Sonotrode Normal Force, Oscillation amplitude	Prototyping
	LOM	Metals, PVC, Paper		Less detailed parts, Rapid tooling patterns

(Continued)

TABLE 3.1 (Continued)

AM Process Techniques

3D Printing Technique	Process	Popular Material	Parameters of Importance	Application
	Ultrasonic Consolidation	• Metal	• Travel speed temperature	Structures with complex internal geometries, Multi-material structures, Embedded Fibers within metal matrices, Smart structures with sensors, actuators
Directed Energy Deposition	WAAM - Filament	• Metals and composites in wire form	• Wire feed orientation • Tool Speed • Deposit Rate • Wire feed rate • Arc Energy • Angle of Inclination • Travel Speed • Amperage • Supply Frequency • Operating voltage • Wire Batch Variability • Inter-pass temperature	Hostile Environment manufacturing, aerostructure components, Lattice Structures, Functionally graded materials
	Directed Metal Laser Sintering	• Stainless Steel • Aluminum • Bronze and Cobalt Derivatives • Titanium • Ceramics, • Biomaterials (boneTissue)	• Laser power • Scanning Speed • Layer Thickness • Hatch Spacing	Rapid tooling, High heat applications, Medical implants, Aerospace parts

ANN algorithms have been used to arrive at the parametric importance on the build parameters [19,20].

Several researchers have focused their work on finding the optimum range of a selection of parameters to identify their impact on the build properties. The collection of various results gives partial knowledge of feature importance and optimum parameter ranges which would result in an efficient AM process. This results in incomplete establishment and understanding of process parameter dependencies. Further research work can be directed to have an inclusive study of inferences drawn from independent studies of parameter optimization. Topology optimization is performed considering material anisotropy and deposition orientation in the process considered. Best indicators can be obtained by a balance of various process parameters [21].

3.4 ML Technique – Overview

ML algorithms encapsulate the technologies from various streams such as data science, statistics, sensing technologies, image processing, mathematical functions, and computational processes to give solutions for industrial automation. Industries of varying interests and applications like e-tailing, security systems, search engines, banking transactions, fashion, and manufacturing are experiencing the integration of ML concepts into their everyday transactions. It provides predictability to the processes that originally would be practiced based only upon trial and error and the expertise of the executive in charge. ML algorithms are a step toward powering intelligent applications which work autonomously in the decision-making and giving predictions or classifications [22–24].

ML algorithms do not directly involve intensive manual mathematical calculations, but use several libraries incorporating various functionalities that can be applied to data of different forms and sequences. Computational libraries like NumPy are used for implementing the required functionalities. The ML domain of AI makes this possible with the definitions of a number of algorithms which help train the systems for causing near-natural decision-making in the required processes.

Several classifications of algorithms have been made depending on different forms of data sets (Figure 3.9).

Different categories of ML algorithms find applications in different domains and applications as listed in Figure 3.10.

3.4.1 Reasons for Adoption of ML in 21st Century

Efficient data processing with ML algorithms helps in developing predictive models which enable building of smart systems. Minimum time to market and customizations are the essential requirements of the 21st century and the smart systems help in meeting these requirements.

ML finds applications in the following domains viz., image recognition, speech recognition, medical diagnosis, statistical arbitrage, learning associations, classification predictions, extraction, and regression.

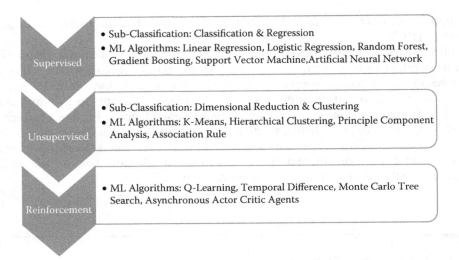

FIGURE 3.9
Classification of ML algorithms and factors of selection.

FIGURE 3.10
ML applications.

3.4.2 Popular Techniques of ML Applied in AM

3.4.2.1 Linear Regression

This is a supervised ML model used in data analytics for various utilities and the prediction made by this model are observed to have a constant slope indicating the linear relation of the output with the control variables and are continuous. This algorithm can be applied to single or multiple variables for both the control and the controlled parameters. The prediction function used in the linear regression model outputs the target variable predictions based upon the independent process parameters.

This predicted output takes the form of a regression line having certain weight and bias, similar to the equation of a straight line. The correct values of weight and bias are learned based upon the input data set and with this training, the regression equation will approximate the line of best fit. Mean squared error (MSE) of the actual and the predicted output is used as a cost function for the purpose of optimizing the weight value for getting results closer to the line of best fit.

With the increasing process and control parameters increased, the model complexity and the iterations required also increase. Linear regression algorithm can be used to find the feature significance indicating the impact that each independent variable has on the target parameter/s. Covariance matrix showing the correlation values between all parameters is generated with a prediction function. A sample covariance matrix is shown in Table 3.2.

Heat map can then be generated to visualize the covariance values. Figure 3.11 shows a sample feature importance chart and heat map showing the covariance values and their impact as color grades.

The part distortion in the 3D printing process is attributed to defects like porosity, anisotropy which results from the residual stresses. Rapid heating and slow conduction are understood to be the causes for residual stresses. Layer thickness, laser power, scan speed, hatch distance, raster width, and part orientation are some of the parameters which control the 3D printing process and the build properties [20]. ML techniques are capable of finding abstract correlations in a process and also develop mathematical

TABLE 3.2

Sample Covariance Matrix

Parameters	IV1	IV2	IV3	IV4	IV5	IV6	DV1	DV2	DV3
IV1	1	0	0	0	0	0	−0.6905	−0.5597	−0.3763
IV2	0	1	0	0	0	0	−0.5341	0.65606	0.45712
IV3	0	0	1	0	0	0	0.15008	0.16906	0.32399
IV4	0	0	0	1	0	0	−0.0127	0.01721	0.07729
IV5	0	0	0	0	1	0	0.08803	−0.0851	−0.032
IV6	0	0	0	0	0	1	−0.2752	0.02715	−0.4767
DV1	−0.69	−0.534	0.15008	−0.01	0.0880	−0.275	1	−0.0763	0.15773
DV2	−0.55	0.6560	0.1690	0.017	−0.085	0.027	−0.0763	1	0.64168
DV3	−0.37	0.4571	0.3239	0.077	−0.032	−0.476	0.1577	0.6416	1

IV – independent variable; DV – dependent variable.

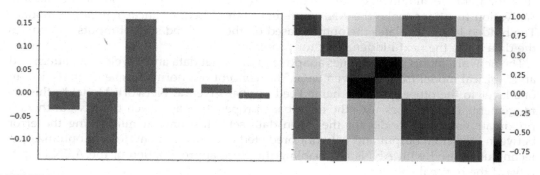

FIGURE 3.11
Example of a feature importance chart and a heat map.

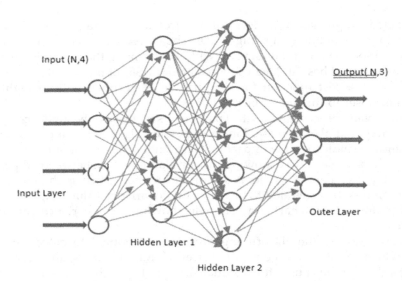

FIGURE 3.12
ANN architecture showing all the layers with corresponding weights for four input and three output system.

models for the processes having conditions closer to real-time manufacturing, which manually are not feasible.

3.4.2.2 Artificial Neural Networks

These are a set of algorithms that imitate the structure and functioning of human brain and are widely used in AI applications. These applications are classified as regression analysis, pattern recognition, classifications, and control systems [25–27].

An artificial neural network (ANN) is a supervised ML technique that is a non-linear model and is used to communicate output to the given inputs. The architecture of ANN is described in terms of sequential layers – input, hidden, and the output layers (Figure 3.12). Layers are formed of complex interconnection of functional units called neurons which are capable of learning the data, generalizing it, and deriving results from the complete training data set. ANN model consists of three entities: weights, learning rule for iterative modification of weights, and the activation function of the neuron. Activation functions make the ANN different with respect to linear regression models. The hidden layer calculates the output based on the weighted sum of inputs and passes the data on to the next hidden layer for processing.

The network in this way becomes adaptive to the input data and develops a pattern and an empirical model from the given data. This concept of information being passed from one layer to the other gives the name Feed Forward Neural Network Model to this arrangement. This network uses the error back-propagation approach to arrive at the approximate empirical model for the given data set. This aims at minimizing the error between the actual output and network predicted output. Gradient descent optimization technique is used with ANNs for enabling the close approximation of the ANN output toward the optimal solution.

A number of hyperparameters can be varied over several trials and these result in difference in the cost function value. The number of layers assumed in a model and the corresponding number of neurons in each hidden layer, and the number of epochs (trials), are some of the hyperparameters. Optimal selection of the number of neurons is required to avoid over- or underfitting in the given dataset. Overfitting previous observations by researchers suggest having the number of neurons between 5 and 10. These along with some other network parameters are called hyperparameters of the ANN and several mechanisms are described in the ML libraries for hyperparameter tuning. Underfitting means an acceptable relation between the data and the model is not developed.

3.4.3 Applications of ANN in 3D Printing

Data-driven designing using ANN technique enables feature recommendations to existing CAD models and also speeds up the design process. Printability analysis of products is ensured and it results in reduction of support material requirement. A variant of ANN using hierarchical clustering for design feature classification and Support Vector Machine (SVM) concept to enhance the clustering can be used for the process design. The trained ANN models when incorporated into finite element simulation and may be analyzed for structural performance of built parts.

The 3D printing process is monitored in various ways to acquire information about the printing condition. Defect detection is done with optical camera, near-IR thermal CMOS camera, X-Ray phase contrast imaging, or X-Ray CT of entire workpiece. Pyrometers are used for obtaining melt pool temperature. Several varying quality parts are produced for obtaining data sets for training and testing. ML in this way allows defect identification and prediction through an extensive data of as-required and failed printing samples relying on computer vision capabilities. The data sources can be of the following types and dimensions: (i) Spectra – 1D; (ii) graphs and images; and (iii) morphologies. The ANN algorithms in various configurations can be used to detect the defects such as porosity defect, under-melting, keyholing, and balling.

3.5 ML in Additive Manufacturing Industry – State of Art

Research advancements have been made in this field in an effort of making generalizations from the limited data sets, which aids in establishing dependencies of the build geometry and mechanical properties on the process parameters and various manufacturing conditions.

Chowdhury and Anand [27] utilized a finite element simulation for the AM process with design specific set of parameters. This simulation output and the build surface data from the CAD model are used as the training data set for the ANN model. Simulation with modified geometry and the results indicate the performance of the method in obtaining accurate builds compensating the thermal effects of the AM process.

Iuganson [25] proposed algorithms for enabling computer vision systems with scanning cameras and computer tomography for collecting printing information. In the proposed AI-based algorithm, the problematic layers identified by the computer vision system are removed.

Paraskevoudis et al. [28] described techniques for quality assessment of 3D printed parts using neural networks using the video captured during the manufacturing process. Images captured with the stringing effect were subjected to scaling, horizontal flipping, 90° rotation,

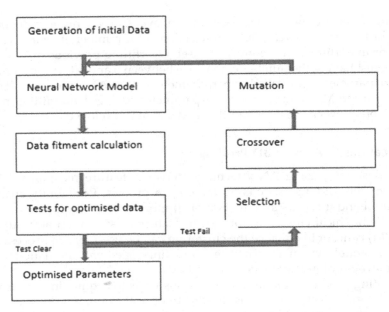

FIGURE 3.13
Flow chart of genetic algorithm.

and change of brightness for the purpose of data augmentation. Kim et al. [29] and Cui et al. [30] developed an in situ monitoring and failure detection method by deep learning techniques using convolutional neural network. They used the Visual Geometry Group Network (VGGNet) model to train the sample images and that resulted in 97% accuracy. This pre-trained model could detect 96% of the spaghetti-shaped errors with a printer monitoring system. High learning accuracy was obtained but the test evaluation showed overfitting because of limited data sets, which then required data augmentation in the image data sets. Sood et al. [31,32] employed ANN to confirm the nonlinear relationship of process parameters of the complex Fused Deposition Modeling process. Empirical model of this process for the study of dependency was built based upon face-centered central composite design (FCCCD) with half factorial 2k design. Rong-Ji et al. [33] and Wang et al. [34] suggested the use of NN-based genetic algorithm to determine optimized parameters for the non-linear complex multivariable SLS 3D printing process. They proposed the use of genetic algorithm (GA) for process parameter optimization. Flowchart of the algorithm is given in Figure 3.13.

Based on the literature understandings, attempts have been made to illustrate the utility of ML for 3D printing with some case studies.

3.6 Case Studies for the Experimental Data

3.6.1 Case Study I

Experimental data sets obtained from FCCCD were used to arrive at the generic model for compressive strength and assess the effect of independent variables on the strength [32]. ABS P400 is the material used for test fabrication using an FDM machine. FDM process involves a number of interrelated process parameter factors which govern the output

TABLE 3.3

Control Factors for the FDM Machine

Symbol	Control Factors (Predictors)	Low Level (−1)	Centre Level (0)	High Level (1)	Unit
A	Layer Thickness	0.127	0.178	0.254	mm
B	Orientation	0	15	30	Degree
C	Raster Angle	0	30	60	Degree
D	Raster Width	0.4064	0.4564	0.5064	mm
E	Air Gap	0	0.004	0.008	mm

characteristics. ANN with backward propagation is considered for the correlation and predictive analysis. Table 3.3 lists five predictor variables and their values considered for analysis. Table 3.4 lists the dataset with normalized values of control factors and the target variable, i.e., the compressive stress values.

This data was used to train ANN model with the following details:

```
AM_data = pd.read_csv("CompStrength.csv")
X = dataset[:,0:5]
Y = dataset[:,5]
```

```
# Split X and y into train and test data
X_train, X_val_test, Y_train, Y_val_test = train_test_split(X, Y, test_size=0.40)
X_val, X_test, Y_val, Y_test = train_test_split(X_val_test, Y_val_test, test_size=0.5)
```

```
print(X_train.shape, X_val.shape, X_test.shape, Y_train.shape, Y_val.shape, Y_test.shape)
#Create Model
model = Sequential([Dense(32, activation='relu', input_shape=(5,)), Dense(32, activation='relu'),Dense(1, activation='linear'),])
model.compile(optimizer='sgd',loss='mean_squared_error', metrics=['mse','mae'])
hist = model.fit(X_train, Y_train,batch_size=32, epochs=100, validation_data=(X_val, Y_val), verbose = 0)
```

The trained model was evaluated for the MSE and the error is found to be reduced Figure 3.14 with the number of iterations based on the back-propagation concept

```
#Print f score
#f1s = f1_score(Y_test,y_pred)
print('f1 score is ', f1s)
```

```
#Print R2 score
r2 = r2_score(Y_test,Y_pred)
print('R2 score is ', r2)
R2 score is 0.6517637681179421
```

Table 3.5 shows the comparison of actual and predicted output values. Fig. 3.15 and Table 3.6 represents the regression line and the regression statistics respectively.

```
#plot predicted against actual values
fig, ax = plt.subplots()
ax.scatter(Y_test, Y_pred)
```

TABLE 3.4

Dataset for Five Process Parameters and one Target Variable

A	B	C	D	E	Stress
−1	−1	−1	−1	1	15.21
1	−1	−1	−1	−1	12.41
−1	1	−1	−1	−1	10.16
1	1	−1	−1	1	10.78
−1	−1	1	−1	−1	14.28
1	−1	1	−1	1	15.83
−1	1	1	−1	1	74.48
1	1	1	−1	−1	16.98
−1	−1	−1	1	−1	13.89
1	−1	−1	1	1	16.18
−1	1	−1	1	1	11.13
1	1	−1	1	−1	10.44
−1	−1	1	1	1	13.58
1	−1	1	1	−1	16.29
−1	1	1	1	−1	11.83
1	1	1	1	1	10.78
−1	0	0	0	0	12.49
1	0	0	0	0	12.34
0	−1	0	0	0	14.98
0	1	0	0	0	12.28
0	0	−1	0	0	11.95
0	0	1	0	0	11.87
0	0	0	−1	0	11.56
0	0	0	1	0	11.25
0	0	0	0	−1	12.26
0	0	0	0	1	11.09
0	0	0	0	0	11.72
0	0	0	0	0	12.48
0	0	0	0	0	12.67
0	0	0	0	0	11.31
0	0	0	0	0	11.01
0	0	0	0	0	12.88

```
ax.plot([Y_test.min(), Y_test.max()], [Y_pred.min(), Y_pred.max()], 'k--', lw=4)
ax.set_xlabel('Measured')
ax.set_ylabel('Predicted')
plt.show()

# performing the regression and fitting the model
result = sm.OLS(Y, X).fit()
# printing the summary table
print(result.summary())
```

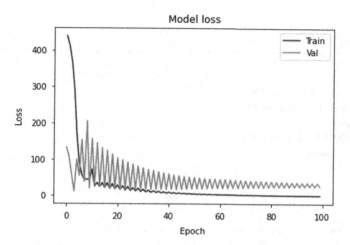

FIGURE 3.14
Reduction of mean squared error with the number of epochs.

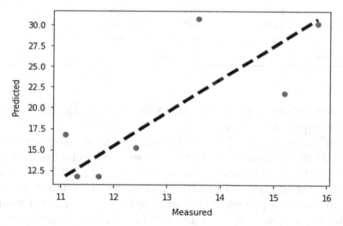

FIGURE 3.15
Regression line indicating distribution of values.

TABLE 3.5

Comparison of Actual and Predicted Value

Actual Value	ANN Predicted Value
11.44314	11.01
18.073174	15.83
13.372294	13.89
18.44802	14.28
14.642846	16.18

TABLE 3.6

Regression Results

OLS Regression Results

==

Dep. Variable: y R-squared (uncentered):	0.093
Model: OLS Adj. R-squared (uncentered):	0.075
Method: Least Squares F-statistic:	0.5537
Date: Wed, 24 Mar 2021 Prob (F-statistic):	0.734
Time: 10:54:05 Log-Likelihood:	−136.78
No. Observations: 32 AIC:	283.6
Df Residuals: 27 BIC:	290.9
Df Model:	5
Covariance Type:	Nonrobust

==

	Coef	std err	t	P>|t|	[0.025	0.975]
x1	−3.0567	4.460	−0.685	0.499	−12.207	6.094
x2	2.0117	4.460	0.451	0.656	−7.139	11.162
x3	4.0983	4.460	0.919	0.366	−5.052	13.249
x4	−3.6844	4.460	−0.826	0.416	−12.835	5.466
x5	3.3622	4.460	0.754	0.457	−5.789	12.513

==

The coefficients mentioned as "coef" in Table 3.6 indicate the significance of each parameter to the compressive stress.

Hyperparameter tuning of ANN network was used to make observations in the error calculations for different numbers of hidden layers and neurons in the hidden layers. This feature can also be used to assess the best performing activation functions and the performance metric for the trained model. The results of variation of hyperparameters show variation in the loss parameter of the model. Best model parameters are thus accessed from these results and used therein for making correlation and predictive analyses. Below mentioned are the results for hyperparameter tuning of various parameters:

    1. Batch Size and Epochs:

```
# define the grid search parameters
batch_size = [10, 15, 20, 25, 32]
epochs = [10, 50, 100]
param_grid = dict(batch_size=batch_size, epochs=epochs)
```

OUTPUT:

Best Score: −5.242857 using {'batch_size': 10, 'epochs': 50}
MAE: −3.943
Mean: −3.970985 Stdev (4.112636) with: {'batch_size': 10, 'epochs': 10}
Mean: −1.418258 Stdev (0.872121) with: {'batch_size': 10, 'epochs': 50}

Mean: −1.418258 Stdev (0.872121) with: {'batch_size': 10, 'epochs': 100}
Mean: −4.010448 Stdev (4.089970) with: {'batch_size': 15, 'epochs': 10}
Mean: −1.418258 Stdev (0.872121) with: {'batch_size': 15, 'epochs': 50}
Mean: −1.418258 Stdev (0.872121) with: {'batch_size': 15, 'epochs': 100}
Mean: −3.388574 Stdev (3.247933) with: {'batch_size': 20, 'epochs': 10}
Mean: −1.418258 Stdev (0.872121) with: {'batch_size': 20, 'epochs': 50}
Mean: −1.418258 Stdev (0.872121) with: {'batch_size': 20, 'epochs': 100}
Mean: −3.093424 Stdev (3.074959) with: {'batch_size': 25, 'epochs': 10}
Mean: −1.742354 Stdev (1.252545) with: {'batch_size': 25, 'epochs': 50}
Mean: −1.418258 Stdev (0.872121) with: {'batch_size': 25, 'epochs': 100}
Mean: −3.222438 Stdev (3.020104) with: {'batch_size': 32, 'epochs': 10}
Mean: −1.418258 Stdev (0.872121) with: {'batch_size': 32, 'epochs': 50}
Mean: −1.418258 Stdev (0.872121) with: {'batch_size': 32, 'epochs': 100}

2. Neurons in the Hidden Layer:

neurons = [1, 5, 10, 15, 20, 25, 30]
param_grid = dict(neurons=neurons)

OUTPUT:

Best Score: −5.109524 using {'neurons': 1}
MAE: −5.110
Mean: −1.418258 Stdev (0.872121) with: {'neurons': 1}
Mean: −1.418258 Stdev (0.872121) with: {'neurons': 5}
Mean: −1.418258 Stdev (0.872121) with: {'neurons': 10}
Mean: −1.418258 Stdev (0.872121) with: {'neurons': 15}
Mean: −1.418258 Stdev (0.872121) with: {'neurons': 20}
Mean: −1.418258 Stdev (0.872121) with: {'neurons': 25}
Mean: −1.418258 Stdev (0.872121) with: {'neurons': 30}

- **REMARK:** Change in the number of neurons did not show any variation in the model performance

3. Optimizer:

optimizer = ['sgd', 'RMSprop', 'Adagrad', 'Adadelta', 'Adam', 'Adamax', 'Nadam']
param_grid = dict(optimizer=optimizer)

OUTPUT:

MAE: −1.418
Config: {'optimizer': 'sgd'}
Best Score: −1.418258 using {'optimizer': 'sgd'}
PARAMS [{'optimizer': 'sgd'}, {'optimizer': 'RMSprop'}, {'optimizer': 'Adagrad'}, {'optimizer': 'Adadelta'}, {'optimizer': 'Adam'}, {'optimizer': 'Adamax'}, {'optimizer': 'Nadam'}]
Mean: −1.418258 Stdev (0.872121) with: {'optimizer': 'sgd'}
Mean: −1.418258 Stdev (0.872121) with: {'optimizer': 'RMSprop'}

Mean: −2.111519 Stdev (1.544026) with: {'optimizer': 'Adagrad'}
Mean: −4.010448 Stdev (4.089970) with: {'optimizer': 'Adadelta'}
Mean: −1.418258 Stdev (0.872121) with: {'optimizer': 'Adam'}
Mean: −1.418258 Stdev (0.872121) with: {'optimizer': 'Adamax'}
Mean: −1.418258 Stdev (0.872121) with: {'optimizer': 'Nadam'}

4. Learning Rate and Momentum:

learn_rate = [0.001, 0.01, 0.1, 0.2, 0.3]
momentum = [0.0, 0.2, 0.4, 0.6, 0.8, 0.9]
param_grid = dict(learn_rate=learn_rate, momentum=momentum)

OUTPUT:

MAE: −1.418

Config: {'learn_rate': 0.001, 'momentum': 0.0}
Best Score: −1.418258 using {'learn_rate': 0.001, 'momentum': 0.0}

5. Finding the Model Performance Score with Hyperparameter Tuning:

grid = GridSearchCV(estimator=model, param_grid=param_grid, n_jobs=−1, cv=3, scoring= 'neg_mean_absolute_error')
grid_result = grid.fit(X_train,Y_train)
 # summarize results
print("Best Score: %f using %s" % (grid_result.best_score_, grid_result.best_params_))
means = grid_result.cv_results_['mean_test_score']
stds = grid_result.cv_results_['std_test_score']
params = grid_result.cv_results_['params']
print('PARAMS', params)
for mean, stdev, param in zip(means, stds, params):
**   print("Mean: %f Stdev (%f) with: %r" % (mean, stdev, param))**

3.6.2 Case Study II

Rong-Ji et al. [33] modeled the SLS for predicting the density as a function of layer thickness, hatch spacing, laser power, scanning speed, temperature of working environment, interval time, and scanning mode. The parameter values and the density (controlled variable) values are given in Table 3.7.
   The ANN was created with the following design:
   No. of hidden layers – 2
   No. of neurons in the 1st layer – 5
   No. of neurons in the 2nd layer – 2

 # Defining the Input layer and FIRST hidden layer, both are same!
model.add(Dense(units=5, input_dim=7, kernel_initializer='normal', activation='relu'))

 # Defining the Second layer of the model

TABLE 3.7

Dataset for ANN Model

Thickness (mm)	Power (W)	Scan Speed (mm/s)	Hatch (mm)	Interval Time (s)	Temp (°C)	Scan Mode	Density (g/mm³)
0.32	16	2600	0.2	0	95	1	0.8
0.2	24	6000	0.16	0	83	2	0.12
0.32	24	6000	0.28	2	93	1	0.52
0.24	23	3600	0.2	3	93	1	0.69
0.32	40	6000	0.28	2	80	1	0.42
0.48	40	6000	0.28	0	93	2	0.4
0.48	40	6000	0.2	3	85	1	0.48
0.48	21	3600	0.28	2	93	1	0.45
0.48	20	3600	0.2	0	78	2	0.42
0.48	30	6000	0.16	1	93	2	0.49
0.48	18	2600	0.28	1	80	2	0.4
0.48	27	2600	0.16	0	93	1	0.45
0.32	30	4000	0.24	4	84	2	0.5
0.32	30	4000	0.30	3	89	1	0.42
0.32	30	4800	0.24	3	84	1	0.41
0.32	36	4000	0.24	4	87	1	0.54
0.32	36	4800	0.24	4	87	2	0.52
0.32	36	4800	0.30	3	86	1	0.45
0.4	36	4800	0.30	4	87	1	0.42
0.4	36	4800	0.24	3	84	2	0.48
0.4	36	4000	0.24	4	84	1	0.5
0.4	30	4800	0.30	4	86	2	0.42
0.4	30	4800	0.24	3	87	1	0.43
0.4	30	4000	0.30	3	84	1	0.43
0.4	30	4000	0.24	4	87	2	0.52
0.4	25	4000	0.2	0	95	1	0.43
0.2	16	2600	0.16	4	78	1	0.58
0.32	22	3600	0.28	0	80	1	0.42
0.24	40	6000	0.2	0	93	1	0.63
0.32	30	4800	0.30	3	87	2	0.42
0.32	36	4000	0.30	2	84	2	0.4
0.4	36	4000	0.30	3	87	2	0.45

```
# after the first layer we don't have to specify input_dim as keras configure it
automatically
model.add(Dense(units=2, kernel_initializer='normal', activation='tanh'))
```

```
# The output neuron is a single fully connected node
model.add(Dense(1, kernel_initializer='normal'))
```

The multiple layers get connected to the other with certain weights which get decided by the back-propagation concept. The measure of interconnecting weights is found in the below lines of code:

```
#Finding Weights
weights = model.get_weights()
```

OUTPUT:

dense_21

WEIGHTS FOR LAYER 1 – 7inputs ∗ 5 neurons: [array([

```
[−0.36204544, −0.36208114, 0.36885086, 0.03851277, 0.23564498],
[−0.10825093, −0.02018934, −0.17444763, −0.04192852, 0.23968516],
[ 0.02120862, 0.06449796, −0.20412943, −0.02532344, 0.1630645],
[−0.37449473, −0.30774152, 0.10682095, 0.3750077, 0.38300142],
[−0.22842225, −0.1606261, −0.20222077, 0.1736857, 0.18182755],
[ 0.20892677, 0.19011547, 0.01022853, −0.27780172, −0.12249029],
[ 0.07912945, 0.04905066, 0.10865683, −0.1383193, −0.00704578]],
```

BIAS VALUE FOR 5 NEURONS dtype=float32), array([0.24244791, 0.16890904, 0.21753025, 0.22347008, 0.29469186], dtype=float32)] dense_22

WEIGHTS FOR LAYER 2 – 5inputs ∗ 2 neurons: [array([

```
[ 0.2692027, 0.38504666],
[ 0.30670962, 0.31413823],
[−0.301856, −0.27893597],
[−0.3458042, −0.24571447],
[−0.35720497, −0.38640118]], dtype=float32),
```

BIAS VALUE FOR 2 NEURONS array([0.03617259, 0.02524469], dtype=float32)]

dense_23

WEIGHTS FOR LAYER 3 – 2inputs ∗ 1 output: [array[[0.44301498],

[0.36199534]], dtype=float32),

BIAS VALUE FOR LAYER 3 array[0.03590777], dtype=float32)]

The weights and the bias associated with the layers in the ANN describe the regression function that the network builds for the interconnection of various layers of deep network. These values change with every iteration (epoch) of the model training process and are based upon the concept of back-propagation; the error function is assessed and the weights get updated accordingly. This process repeats till the error is within acceptable limits as regulated by the statistical methods.

Best configuration parameters can be found by assessing the accuracy in a range of certain parameters (Figure 3.16).

The parameters considered are batch size and the number of epochs.

```
def FunctionFindBestParams(X_train, y_train, X_test, y_test):
    # Defining the list of hyper parameters to try
    batch_size_list=[5, 10, 15, 20]
    epochs_list = [5, 10, 15, 20]
SearchResultsData=pd.DataFrame(columns=['TrialNumber', 'Parameters', 'Accuracy'])

# initializing the trials
TrialNumber=0
```

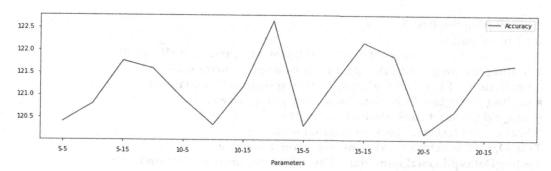

FIGURE 3.16
Accuracy vs. number of parameters.

```
for batch_size_trial in batch_size_list:
  for epochs_trial in epochs_list:
    TrialNumber+=1
```

Once the optimum value of hyperparameters are found, then the following steps are performed:
ANN MODEL CREATION, ANN MODEL COMPILE, ANN MODEL FITTING INTO TRAINING SET

```
MAPE = np.mean(100 * (np.abs(y_test-model.predict(X_test))/y_test))
  # printing the results of the current iteration
  #print(TrialNumber, 'Parameters:','batch_size:', batch_size_trial,'-", 'epochs:',epochs_trial,
  'Accuracy:', 100-MAPE)
print(TrialNumber, 'Parameters:','batch_size:', batch_size_trial,'-', 'epochs:',epochs_trial,
'MAPE:', MAPE)

SearchResultsData=SearchResultsData.append(pd.DataFrame(data=[[TrialNumber, str
(batch_size_trial)+''+str(epochs_trial), MAPE]], columns=['TrialNumber', 'Parameters',
'MAPE']))
  return(SearchResultsData)
```

OUTPUT:

1. Parameters: batch_size: 4 – epochs: 50 MAPE: −29.781453837220702
2. Parameters: batch_size: 4 – epochs: 100 MAPE: 1.7170211519753429
3. Parameters: batch_size: 8 – epochs: 50 MAPE: −9.665216023077832
4. Parameters: batch_size: 8 – epochs: 100 MAPE: −16.11087217349149

```
# Calling the function
ResultsData=FunctionFindBestParams(X_train, y_train, X_test, y_test)
%matplotlib inline
ResultsData.plot(x='Parameters', y='Accuracy', figsize=(15,4), kind='line')
```

Generating predictions and finding accuracy:
```
# Generating Predictions on testing data
Predictions=model.predict(X_test)
```

```
# summarize the first 5 cases
for i in range(5):
    print('%s => %d (expected %d)' % (X[i].tolist(), predictions[i], y[i]))
# Scaling the predicted Price data back to original price scale
    Predictions=TargetVarScalerFit.inverse_transform(Predictions)
# Scaling the y_test Price data back to original price scale
y_test_orig=TargetVarScalerFit.inverse_transform(y_test)
# Scaling the test data back to original scale
Test_Data=PredictorScalerFit.inverse_transform(X_test)
TestingData=pd.DataFrame(data=Test_Data, columns=Predictors)
TestingData['Density']=y_test_orig
TestingData['PredictedDensity']=Predictions
TestingData.head()
# Computing the absolute percent error
APE=100*(abs(TestingData['Density']-TestingData['PredictedDensity'])/TestingData
['Density'])
TestingData['APE']=APE
print('The Accuracy of ANN model is:', 100-np.mean(APE))
TestingData.head()
```

OUTPUT: On training the model and using the functions for different functionalities, the results are obtained in Tables 3.8 and 3.9 and Figure 3.28. The accuracy of ANN model is 89.10132919664483.

TABLE 3.8

Predictions of Test Data and Absolute Percentage Error (APE)

Thickness (mm)	Power (W)	Scan Speed (mm/s)	Hatch (mm)	Interval Time (s)	Temp (°C)	Scan Mode	Test Density (g/mm³)	Predicted Density (g/mm³)	APE
0.16	15	2400	0.15	3	87	2	0.42	0.45544	8.438006
0.16	18	2000	0.12	3	87	1	0.54	0.484564	10.26597
0.2	15	2000	0.12	4	87	2	0.52	0.476254	8.412649
0.16	18	2400	0.15	3	84	1	0.45	0.419894	6.690319
0.24	10	1800	0.1	0	78	2	0.42	0.446154	6.227242

TABLE 3.9

Correlation Matrix

	Thickness	Power	Hatch	Scan Speed	Interval Time	Temp	Scan Mode	Density
Thickness	1	0.028752	−0.05541	0.093669	−0.03486	0.136468	0.0306	−0.57792
Power	0.028752	1	0.669299	0.276294	0.486099	−0.04852	0.025168	−0.05349
Hatch	−0.05542	0.669299	1	−0.02172	0.037323	0.051946	0.058799	0.098381
Scan Speed	0.093669	0.276294	−0.02172	1	0.468156	−0.04457	0.052778	−0.57594
Interval Time	−0.03486	0.486099	0.037323	0.468156	1	−0.18641	0	−0.15689
Temp	0.136468	−0.04852	0.051946	−0.04458	−0.18641	1	−0.10329	0.174405
Scan Mode	0.0306	0.025168	0.058799	0.052778	0	−0.10329	1	0.004452
Density	−0.57792	−0.05348	0.098381	−0.57594	−0.15688	0.174405	0.004452	1

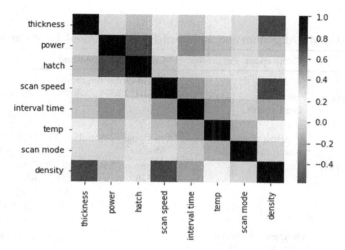

FIGURE 3.17
Heat map showing dependencies of control and target variables.

Feature importance of process parameters in controlling the target parameter – density is numerated in Table 3.9 in the form of correlation matrix.

The correlation matrix and the resulting heat map in Figure 3.17 indicate the significance of each process parameter on governing the output. It also yields the interdependency of process parameters on each other.

3.7 Comparison of ML Analysis to Statistical Analysis Tools

A comparison of conventional statistical and neural network analysis results is shown in Table 3.10. It may be observed that the ANN method of predictions for any process gives better performance parameters in terms of lower mean of errors, better predictability, higher R^2 measure, and lower absolute average deviation. The non-linear characteristics of the 3D printing process parameters and the build properties are also found to be appropriately captured by the ANN models.

However, the application of ML techniques has certain limitations in their implementation to various types of processes, having various datasets. This may require further advancements in the design of the ML models using the different algorithms. Some of these constraints are as follows:

- Repeatability of the learning model for making predictions is lesser. It is observed that repeating the same test does not produce similar result.
- These models have a variety of hyperparameters which can be tuned for generating low model losses. This requires a detailed knowledge of the hyperparameters and also several parameter combinations need to be evaluated for getting results within acceptable limits.
- Normalization of input data is essential to have uniformity in the application of weights and biases to the neurons.

TABLE 3.10

Comparison Between ML Algorithm and Statistical Tools for Various Error Parameters

Target Variable	Comparison Parameter	Conventional Method	ANN Configuration
Bead geometry during single-track melting [35]	Error for bead height, bead width	Second Order Regression Model, 2.633%, 2.308%	4-12-2 ANN: 1.922%, 2.104%
Dynamic modulus of elasticity [35]	R^2 value, average absolute deviation	Fractional Factorial Model	Higher R^2, lower absolute deviation
Wear characteristics [35]		Regression Model – 0.9516	5-8-1 ANN R^2 value 0.9902
Compressive strength [32]			5-8-1 minimum performance function value $3.73334*10^{-32}$
Part density [34]	Difference between simulation and experimental values		0.0119 g/cm^3

- Selection of optimum number of input parameters is essential to avoid overfit and underfit of the ANN model and may also cause excessive computational time.

3.8 Challenges Associated for Ml Applications to 3D Printing

The application of ANNs to manufacturing has its constraints of results being reported in a unmetrical format, which need an interpretation pertaining to the process and the corresponding training data in contrast to a process-specific system. Trial and error method of finding the appropriate neural network model for a process is the cause for low-performance metrics leading to lower reliability. The system model design based on ANN concept has the drawback of lacking reproducibility in repeated iterations owing to the difference in initial weights, data set used for training the model, and the normalization method applied to each model [36].

Limited training data sets pose the problem of high prediction errors with new process parameters. The higher dataset availability for different processes can help improve the prediction accuracy.

3.8.1 Big Data Challenges

The application of ML algorithms to the datasets needs appropriate deciding factors for best fit. Some of the key factors to be considered in application of ML algorithms to any process are described in this section.

- *Data Collection and Usage*
  - Need to understand the kind of data needed and its usage.
  - Data collection and anomaly detection using in situ monitoring techniques have limitations due to the constraints of the sensors in the harsh printing conditions.

- Data should be in a format and the parameter levels should be such which ensure appropriate training of the model and can help to predict the output or to develop the regression model. Redundant data will cause more computational time.

- *Data Validation* – Source of data collection should be credible and in the expected format without anomalies. This is of importance for the results to be having significance. The data input for the ML algorithms may also need pre-processing to enable the efficient and reliable ML process.

- *Algorithm Selection* – Selection of algorithm needs to be appropriate according to the type of data and the insights that are expected from the ML. For example, according to the availability of labeled or unlabeled data, supervised or unsupervised algorithms selection is needed. Depending on the type of data processing required, linear or logistic regression algorithms need to be selected.

- *Training Dataset* – For the considered algorithm to accurately identify any pattern and to extract insights from the data, the data set should be considerably large. Small data set may not give desired performance of the algorithm and may yield unreliable results.

- *Data Noise* – Irrelevant or redundant data can induce errors in the algorithm usage and consequently reduces the efficiency of the algorithm.

3.8.2 Scope of Issue Addressal/Advanced Techniques

3.8.2.1 Data Augmentation

The performance of any deep learning model depends entirely on the form, range, and amount of data. Inappropriate data which may mean insufficient or less diversified data may result in underfitting or overfitting of the model, respectively [37].

Data augmentation is creating different versions of the given input data to artificially increase the dataset size and consequently enhance the learning model performance. It can be applied to the training data set at the time of data generation, after pre-processing and before training. Data in the form of audio, text, images, or other formats can all be augmented using various techniques.

3.8.2.2 Transfer Learning

This method of ML is the reuse of a trained model on another task. This can enable deep neural network training with lesser available data. In transfer learning, the learning enabled from a previous task, common to features of another task, is used for categorizing another data set [38,39]. Benefits from a successful application of transfer learning can be seen in Figure 3.18. Red dotted line is the high-performance curve with transfer learning as compared with the darker line indicating performance without transfer learning.

3.8.3 Few-Shot Learning

With a small data set, there may be discrepancies in the ML predictions which may misguide the design, process or production of AM systems [40]. Few-shot learning is an

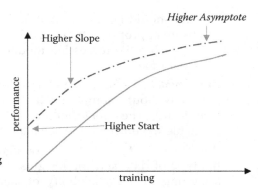

FIGURE 3.18
Benefits of transfer learning.

Higher Slope – Steeper rate of skill improvement during source model training.

algorithm used in cases where training data set has limited information. It helps build accurate ML models with lesser training data. It enables learning for rare cases for appropriate classification even on exposure to less rare data. Few-shot learning finds application in image classification, semantic segmentation, image generation, object detection, and NLP. Few-shot learning is based upon two approaches:

i. Data-Level approach – It utilizes data augmentation techniques to add random noise to the available data set, thus creating new data. New data samples in image format may also be produced using Generative Adversarial Networks.

ii. Parameter Level approach – Few-shot learning samples have high dimensional space due to inadequate data. Parameter space can be appropriately limited to address the possible overfitting issues. Regularization techniques or loss functions are employed to solve such ML problems. Meta-learning techniques are also employed where the algorithm is directed to the best route in the parameter space to generate optimal prediction results.

3.9 Conclusions

There is significant scope for the utilization of ML concepts and models in various stages of the AM system, from the Design for AM, to parametric analysis and process monitoring for anomaly detection and sample quality control. The use of data-driven models is more computationally efficient as compared to other simulation methods. ML techniques offer data-driven solutions that demand large data set or the application of advanced techniques to generate the required data set. Identification of significant set of control and process parameters can help simplify the challenges associated with limited manufacturing data sets. The case studies record that ML techniques have capability for efficient prediction and identification of feature importance in the AM processes. Big data analytics can be considered as a feasible solution to the optimization and parametric analysis challenges faced in the AM process techniques. Based on the identified challenges, advanced techniques of the data-driven models can be explored to generate the required datasets which can lead to enhanced ML efficiency in the domain of AM.

References

1. Gokhare, V. G., Raut, D. N., & Shinde, D. K. (2017). A review paper on 3D-printing aspects and various processes used in the 3D-printing. *International Journal of Engineering Research & Technology*, 6(06), 953–958.

2. Ramya, A., & Vanapalli, S. L. (2016). 3D printing technologies in various applications. *International Journal of Mechanical Engineering and Technology*, 7(3), 396–409.

3. https://www.xometry.com/blog/3d-printing-processes

4. https://www.lboro.ac.uk/research/amrg/about/the7categoriesofadditivemanufacturing/

5. https://www.additivemanufacturing.media/blog/post/what-is-directed-energy-deposition(2)

6. Lu, Q. Y., & Wong, C. H. (2017). Applications of non-destructive testing techniques for post-process control of additively manufactured parts. *Virtual and Physical Prototyping*, 12(4), 301–321.

7. The free beginners guide to 3D printing. https://3dprintingindustry.com/3d-printing-basics-free-beginners-guide

8. Sung Ha Hanyang Structures and Composites Lab. (HSCL) dept. of mechanical engineering Hanyang university, KOREA Stanford Composite Design Team.

9. Roysarkar, K. P., Banerjee, P. S., Sinha, A., & Banerjee, M. K. Optimization of stereo-lithography process parameters for quality characteristics improvement.

10. Ibrahim, A., Sa'ude, N., & Ibrahim, M. (2017). Optimization of process parameter for digital light processing (DLP) 3d printing. Faculty of Mechanical Engineering (p. 86400). UniversitiTun Hussein Onn (UTHM), Malaysia.

11. Mostafaei, A., Elliott, A. M., Barnes, J. E., Li, F., Tan, W., Cramer, C. L., … & Chmielus, M. (2021). Binder jet 3D printing—process parameters, materials, properties, modeling, and challenges. *Progress in Materials Science*, 119, 100707. doi:10.1016/j.pmatsci.2020.100707

12. Kumbhar, N. N., & Mulay, A. V. (2016, December). Finishing of fused deposition modelling (FDM) printed parts by CO2 laser. In *Proceedings of 6th International & 27th All India Manufacturing Technology, Design and Research Conference* (pp. 63–67).

13. Dey, A., & Yodo, N. (2019). A systematic survey of FDM process parameter optimization and their influence on part characteristics. *Journal of Manufacturing and Materials Processing*, 3(3), 64.

14. Gonabadi, H., Yadav, A., & Bull, S. J. (2020). The effect of processing parameters on the mechanical characteristics of PLA produced by a 3D FFF printer. *The International Journal of Advanced Manufacturing Technology*, 111(3), 695–709.

15. Gajera, H. M., Dave, K. G., Darji, V. P., & Abhishek, K. (2019). Optimization of process parameters of direct metal laser Sintering process using fuzzy-based desirability function approach. *Journal of the Brazilian Society of Mechanical Sciences and Engineering*, 41(3), 124.

16. Gibson, I., Rosen, D. W., & Stucker, B. (2010). Sheet lamination processes. In *Additive Manufacturing Technologies* (pp. 223–252). Springer, Boston, MA.

17. https://amfg.ai/2018/09/27/metal-3d-printing-what-is-direct-energy-deposition/

18. https://omnexus.specialchem.com/selection-guide/acrylonitrile-butadiene-styrene-abs-plastic, viewed on 31/12/20.

19. Sood, A. K., Ohdar, R. K., & Mahapatra, S. S. (2010). Parametric appraisal of mechanical property of fused deposition modelling processed parts. *Materials & Design*, 31(1), 287–295.

20. Haq, R. H. A. et al. (2019). *IOP Conf. Ser.: Mater. Sci. Eng.* 607, 012001.

21. Shirmohammadi, M., Goushchi, S. J., & Keshtiban, P. M. (2021). Optimization of 3D printing process parameters to minimize surface roughness with hybrid artificial neural network model and particle swarm algorithm. *Progress in Additive Manufacturing*, 6(2), 199–215.

22. https://www.analyticsvidhya.com/blog/2019/10/mathematics-behind-machine-learning/, viewed on 04/04/21.

23. https://data-flair.training/blogs/types-of-machine-learning-algorithms/, viewed on 04/04/21.

24. https://huspi.com/blog-open/guide-to-machine-learning-algorithms, viewed on 05/04/21.

25. Iuganson, R. (2018). Artificial intelligence in 3D printing: real-time 3D printing control.
26. Mahmood, M. A., Visan, A. I., Ristoscu, C., & Mihailescu, I. N. (2021). Artificial neural network algorithms for 3D printing. *Materials*, 14(1), 163.
27. Chowdhury, S., & Anand, S. (2016, June). Artificial neural network based geometric compensation for thermal deformation in additive manufacturing processes. In *International Manufacturing Science and Engineering Conference* (Vol. 49910, p. V003T08A006). American Society of Mechanical Engineers.
28. Paraskevoudis, K., Karayannis, P., & Koumoulos, E. P. (2020). Real-time 3D printing remote defect detection (stringing) with computer vision and artificial intelligence. *Processes*, 8(11), 1464.
29. Kim, H., Lee, H., Kim, J. S., & Ahn, S. H. (2020). Image-based failure detection for material extrusion process using a convolutional neural network. *The International Journal of Advanced Manufacturing Technology*, 111(5), 1291–1302.
30. Cui, W., Zhang, Y., Zhang, X., Li, L., & Liou, F. (2020). Metal additive manufacturing parts inspection using convolutional neural network. *Applied Sciences*, 10(2), 545.
31. Sood, A. K., Equbal, A., Toppo, V., Ohdar, R. K., & Mahapatra, S. S. (2012). An investigation on sliding wear of FDM built parts. *CIRP Journal of Manufacturing Science and Technology*, 5(1), 48–54.
32. Sood, A. K., Ohdar, R. K., & Mahapatra, S. S. (2012). Experimental investigation and empirical modelling of FDM process for compressive strength improvement. *Journal of Advanced Research*, 3(1), 81–90.
33. Rong-Ji, W., Xin-Hua, L., Qing-Ding, W., & Lingling, W. (2009). Optimizing process parameters for selective laser Sintering based on neural network and genetic algorithm. *The International Journal of Advanced Manufacturing Technology*, 42(11), 1035–1042.
34. Wang, R. J., Li, J., Wang, F., Li, X., & Wu, Q. (2009). ANN model for the prediction of density in selective laser Sintering. *International Journal of Manufacturing Research*, 4(3), 362–373.
35. Baturynska, I. (2019). Application of machine learning techniques to predict the mechanical properties of Polyamide 2200 (PA12) in additive manufacturing. *Applied Sciences*, 9(6), 1060.
36. Munguía, J., Ciurana, J., & Riba, C. (2009). Neural-network-based model for build-time estimation in selective laser Sintering. *Proceedings of the Institution of Mechanical Engineers, Part B: Journal of Engineering Manufacture*, 223(8), 995–1003.
37. https://neptune.ai/blog/data-augmentation-in-python, viewed on 12/04/21.
38. https://machinelearningmastery.com/transfer-learning-for-deep-learning, viewed on 11/04/21.
39. https://builtin.com/data-science/transfer-learning, viewed on 11/04/21.
40. https://medium.com/quick-code/understanding-few-shot-learning-in-machine-learning-bede251a0f67, viewed on 10/04/21.

4

Local Time Invariant Learning from Industrial Big Data for Predictive Maintenance in Smart Manufacturing

S. Sharanya

Department of Data Science and Business Systems, SRM Institute of Science and Technology, Kattankulathur, Tamil Nadu, India

S. Karthikeyan

Department of Aerospace Engineering, B. S. Abdur Rahman Crescent Institute of Science and Technology, Vandalur, Tamil Nadu, India

CONTENTS

4.1 Portfolio of Predictive Maintenance and Condition Monitoring

Equipment failure prediction in industries has a long-term history in the industrial development. The notion of Industry 4.0 shifts the paradigm of manufacturing industries from physical elements to cyber-physical systems with intense automation and acute data exchange to achieve the aspiration of "smart factory." This dramatic excrescence is facilitated by digital transformation, innovations, supporting technologies, and business goals.

DOI: 10.1201/9781003202776-4

Intelligent networking of automation inside the industries is nurtured by technologies such as Internet of Things (IoT), cognitive computing, cloud computing, Artificial Intelligence, additive manufacturing, etc.

4.1.1 Characteristics of Industry 4.0

The envelope of Industry 4.0 is characterized by the following traits:

i. Interfacing the physical assets and digital world
ii. Deploying intense automation than the previous generations
iii. Closed loop data exchange
iv. Development of customized products
v. Intelligent production/assembly line.

Attaining these objectives fosters intelligent and autonomous decision-making to develop a more connected industry value chain.

4.1.2 Industry 4.0: Revolution or Evolution?

Production and manufacturing industries have an incredibly old history. The swift transition between various industrial revolutions has brought momentous changes in production and decision-making process. Each revolution is thought as replacement of legacy technologies by modern versions. But the reality is that it is the gradual and incremental developments resulted in the next revolutionary elements. Figure 4.1 shows the key features of each revolution.

Industry 1.0: This is witnessed around 1784 after the invention of mechanical looms. Another milestone during this era is design of steam-driven engines. The textile industry and factories were mechanized by alternate power sources.

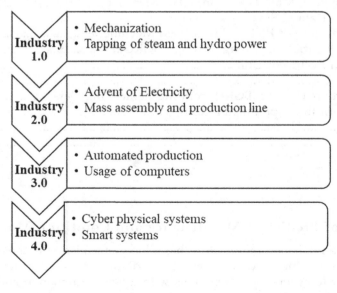

FIGURE 4.1
Prominent features that characterize each industrial revolution.

Industry 2.0: The first revolution focused on mechanization of industries whereas the next revolution is triggered by electrical power. Around 1870, the generation of huge amount of electrical power led to the notion of mass production. Humans were employed in large numbers to scale up the production. Indigenous Ford assembly line is a noted example for mass production with increased efficiency at decreased operational costs.

Industry 3.0: This era is the electronic revolution which was fostered by development of computers and its deployment in various phases of industrial automation. Another milestone of data exchange is achieved in the year 1969 by the design of ARPANET, a forerunner of today's World Wide Web (WWW). The main characteristics of this period were highly automated assembly lines and influence of high-end technologies in productions.

Industry 4.0: This is featured by the notion of building cyber world. This is a multi-faceted era which is a culmination of emerging technologies such as IoT, big data analytics, machine learning, Artificial Intelligence, edge computing, cloud computing, 3D printing, additive manufacturing, etc. This era can be easily distinguished by the following traits visualized in industries: speed, wholesomeness, and pervasive nature.

4.2 Condition Monitoring and Predictive Maintenance

Condition monitoring (CM) is the process of uninterrupted surveillance of any system. The micro-level activities include system monitoring, fault detection, fault diagnostics, and fault prognostics. The results of the CM process are quantified by monitoring the vital parameters that characterize the health state of the system [1]. A fault is detected when the values deviate from their normal operational range.

Figure 4.2 gives an overview of the condition monitoring and its various sub-tasks. A brief description of these tasks is provided in the following:

i. Condition monitoring: The continuous process of monitoring the parameters of any system to detect any meaningful change in the values.

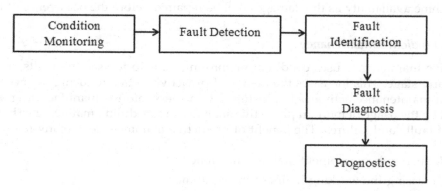

FIGURE 4.2
Sequence of steps in condition monitoring and fault diagnosis.

    ii. Fault detection: Fault detection is done by the diagnostic module to detect the presence of faults.

   iii. Fault identification: Characterizing the faults is done in fault identification phase. The severity of the fault and all failure modes are analyzed in this phase.

   iv. Fault diagnosis: The detailed investigation on the fault causes is done in this module.

    v. Fault prognosis: This is an advanced phase where a prognostic model is activated to assess the likelihood of fault occurrence is predicted [2]. This phase also includes the fault recovery actions to restore the system to safe state.

4.2.1 Taxonomy of Maintenance Activities in Industries

The primary goal of CM is to reduce the failure effect on the system, and to increase the productive operational time of the equipment. The machine availability gives the fraction of time the equipment functions for its full capacity termed as operational time and its mathematical estimation is governed by Equation 4.1.

$$\text{Availability} = \frac{\text{Operational time}}{\text{Operational time} + \text{down time}} \tag{4.1}$$

Downtime is the duration in which the machine does not meet its recommended performance. All the maintenance strategies followed by the industries are grounded on the machine availability. Every industry will have its own unique maintenance policies categorized under the umbrellas of reactive and proactive maintenance. The maintenance activities that are conducted after the onset of fault will be labeled as reactive while the activities that are taken by anticipating the occurrence of faults are termed as proactive maintenance. Smart manufacturing industries deploy proactive maintenance which are again forked as preventive and predictive maintenance.

4.2.1.1 Preventive Maintenance

The maintenance activities are scheduled periodically in regular intervals. The equipment is inspected and checked for any wear and tear. Based on the utility or on timescale, maintenance procedures will be rolled on. The preventive maintenance activities will increase the machine availability as the damages will be repaired before the occurrence of failure.

4.2.1.2 Predictive Maintenance

Predictive maintenance uses condition monitoring tools to foresee the faults at exceedingly early stage. This increases the degree of proactivity, thus reducing the necessity of frequent maintenance activities [3]. Instilling smartness into the manufacturing sector is inflated by the usage of modern predictive analytics in scheduling maintenance before the onset of faults and failures. The benefit of predictive maintenance is many folds:

    i. Reducing the equipment maintenance time

   ii. Increasing the working hours of the equipment

   iii. Minimizing the cost of spare parts and supplies

   iv. Ensuring operator safety.

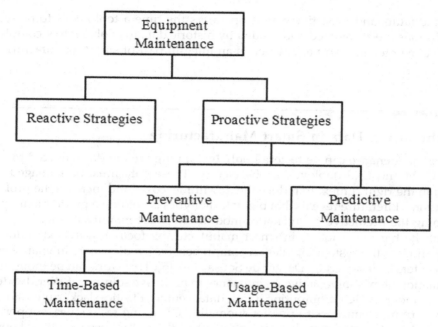

FIGURE 4.3
A comprehensive taxonomy of equipment maintenance strategies.

The taxonomy of equipment maintenance policies is given in Figure 4.3.

4.3 Role of Predictive Maintenance in Smart Manufacturing

The predictive maintenance in industries comprehends the degree of degradation and anticipate the damages sourced by failures, wear and tear, and other hidden elements in the entire industrial ecosystem. By leveraging the techniques such as IoT, ML, AI, big data, the manufacturers instill smartness in the maintenance domain [4]. As most of the equipment in smart factories are connected, deploying predictive maintenance solutions by anchoring big data, enterprise applications and intelligent algorithms will be a wise choice to render timely solutions.

Condition monitoring and predictive maintenance are two solutions to completely understand the maintenance policies for use cases in smart manufacturing. To mitigate the risks, the manufacturing ecosystem should formulate equipment maintenance schedules and asset monitoring process. This resource-intensive process is expensive. Providing proactive maintenance solutions by installing proper sensors and integrating them will avoid machine failures, unplanned maintenance activities, and their costs.

Smart manufacturing environment provides a lot of data that can be tapped to predict the optimal maintenance time with clean and consistent data. Predicting machine failures by exploiting the streaming data from smart manufacturing can label the failure state before the complete collapse of the equipment. The copious amounts of data sourced by the sensors integrated with human effort can train predictive maintenance models to identify the faults and proactively alert operators the time a tool needs to be replaced. These solutions are automated and guided by historic data to evolve into a complete and sustainable maintenance strategy which is an integral part of smart manufacturing.

4.4 Niche of Big Data in Smart Manufacturing

Predictive maintenance can be fostered only by tapping the big data sourced by various sensors, CRM and ERP deployed in the factory. These data must be managed and interpreted in the right context to reduce the downtime, costs, and increase the profitability of institutions. Literature reveals that big data analytics is holding a predominant position in designing the predictive maintenance modules in smart manufacturing.

Most of the big data models in smart manufacturing focus toward extracting useful information from the system log files. A comprehensive predictive maintenance solution for data centers is designed by Decker de Sousa et al. [5]. This work can be thought of as a transformation of existing reactive maintenance to proactive solution at Worldwide Large Hadron Collider (LHC) Computing Grid data center. Elastic slack suite, supervised machine learning techniques to predict anomalies, clustering techniques, support vector machines (SVM) to detect novel events are some of the techniques to extract knowledge from big data log files. Predictive maintenance in hardware is also quite common. An adaptation of predictive maintenance solution by integrating cloud platform for quality monitoring of wind turbines is proposed by Canizo [6]. Random forest is used to predict the maintenance status for every 10 minutes which can be visualized using a dashboard. A variety of big data supporting frameworks such as Apache Kafka, Apache Spark, Apache Mesos, and HDFS are used to implement this.

A big data-based predictive maintenance framework for machine tool linear axis avoids unplanned downtime of equipment [7]. This work builds many statistical failure models and condition-based maintenance activities from dataset derived from 29 homogeneous machines. A detailed analysis of Key Process Indicators (KPIs) to investigate the long-term effects through optimal time-based approach is done. A complete big data ecosystem for condition monitoring and predictive maintenance is implemented in large-scale manufacturing plants [8]. This work addresses the issues in acquiring big data, integration, storage, transformation, visualization, and analytics from the data. This system also includes data security frameworks and transformation protocols.

Tao et al. elaborated the scope and deployment of big data in smart manufacturing [9]. This work gives detailed insight to evolution of big data from classic handicrafted data. In addition to this, this work presents a generic framework depicting the lifecycle of manufacturing data. The key technologies in big data and smart manufacturing are discussed in this chapter. A deep neural network to predict fault in train bogies with high degree of accuracy is proposed by Hu et al. [10]. This self-adaptive does not depend on complex signal processing or sampling size. This is a novel method to manage mechanical big data.

Reducing energy consumption is a major focus area of Industry 4.0. A big data-driven predictive analytical framework for reducing the consumption of energy is suggested by Zhang et al. [11]. Two main modules implemented in this work are energy acquisition through big data and mining useful knowledge through data mining techniques. The proposed idea is implemented in ball mill industry and was found to reduce the total energy consumption by 3%. An integrated system that monitors the logistics along with

RFID-enabled big data was observed to improve the managerial decision-making [12,13]. The big data is stored in the form of tuples from which the operations and logics are explored in the form of cuboids. A map table is used to reduce the dimensions of the cuboid and spatio-temporal relations were also found in this work. Another notable work in amalgamating smart manufacturing objects and wireless technologies to aid decision-making in logistics is proposed by Hu et al. [14]. The data are captured through RFID tags and intelligent shop floors are managed through big data.

The brief literature suggests that smart manufacturing has already headed toward tapping big data. Many notable works are found in logistics tracking, implementing intelligent shop floors, and managing energy consumption. The study reveals that there is a gap in implementing big data-based solutions in predictive maintenance. This work focuses on developing a predictive analytic framework by building a bidirectional gated recurrent unit (BGRU) for predicting the remaining useful life (RUL) of bearings by using mechanical big data.

4.4.1 Significance of RUL in Mechanical Machineries

RUL of any equipment is an estimate of the remaining unit of time that will function to its assured performance. The most common methods to estimate the RUL based on the mechanical big data are as follows:

- Lifetime data that represents the time of failure of similar equipment
- Run-to-failure histories
- Health indicator values.

Figure 4.4 shows an example for analyzing the breaking point of bearings based on vibration signals. Point A is the moment at which a defect has initiated in the bearing. A noticeable change in the vibration can be observed only after the defect progresses which is indicated by point B. Point C is the time at which a defect was found by classical methods of fault diagnosis and Point D is reached when the bearing fails completely. The time to failure or RUL is the duration between points B and D. Equation 4.2 shows the calculation of RUL.

$$RUL = \text{Time of complete failure} - \text{time at which defect is noticeable} \quad (4.2)$$

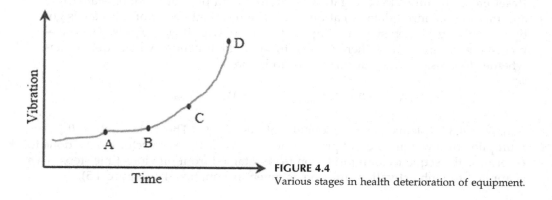

FIGURE 4.4
Various stages in health deterioration of equipment.

The main objective of RUL prediction is improving operational efficiency by reducing the downtime of the components. Many machine learning and deep learning algorithms are extensively used in industries to estimate the RUL [14]. But processing complex mechanical big data in more reliable way is the greatest challenge faced by machine learning algorithms. To alleviate this issue, deep learning algorithms capable of learning the patterns and trends from mechanical big data are now dominating the domain of predictive maintenance.

4.5 Local Time Invariant Learning Through BGRU

BGRU is a flavor of recurrent neural networks that can tap temporal information from the input data [15,16]. The proposed work focuses on predicting the RUL of industrial bearings whose health state is monitored by recording the vibration signals which is a mechanical big data, through accelerometers installed at various locations [17,18].

4.5.1 Gated Recurrent Unit

RNNs are immensely powerful in learning invariable length signals. But the major drawbacks are vanishing and exploding gradient problems. Hence, long short-term memory (LSTM) and gated recurrent unit (GRU) that can capture long-term information through complex activation functions came into existence [19]. This work deploys bidirectional GRU that updates weights in forward as well as backward directions. In a GRU cell, two vectors are combined into a single one. A gate controller controls the update and reset gates. The output of these gates updates the hidden state and the output of the GRU cell.

The clear distinction between GRU and LSTM is that the former holds long-term or short-term dependencies within a single cell state, whereas the LSTM uses cell state to hold long-term memory and hidden state to hold short-term memory. The computations in GRU make it feasible to transfer the single hidden state to be transferred between time [20].

The major components of a GRU are update and reset gates that are trained selectively to wade off irrelevant data. These gates can be thought of as vectors that take values within the range [0,1], which acts as weights to be updated on hidden units. If the gate value is taken as 0, then the data will not play any role in updating the hidden states.

The roles of the gates are as follows:

i. **Reset gate:** The input for this gate arrives from both previous hidden state (h_{t-1}) and the original input data (x_t) at time "t." The resultant vector of this gate is got by multiplying hidden state and input at time "t" with their weights. These elements are summed and then passed to sigmoid function, which determines whether to consider this information or to ignore it.

$$\text{Gate}_{reset} = \text{sigmoid}(W_{input\_reset}.x_t + W_{hidden\_reset}.h_{t-1}) \qquad (4.3)$$

Equation 4.3 explains the functionality of reset gate. The hidden state (h_{t-1}) is multiplied by a weight and dot product of the same with reset vector will be done to determine the sequence of information to be retained from previous time steps. This is applied to tanh activation function as given in Equation 4.4 (Figure 4.5).

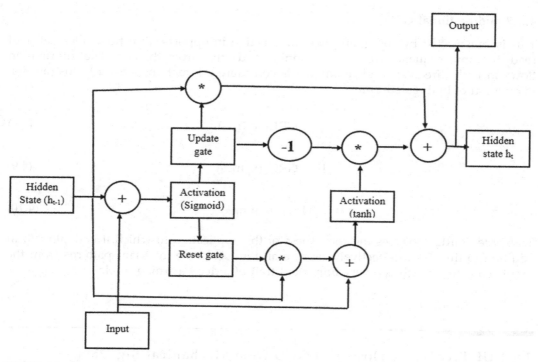

FIGURE 4.5
GPU cell showing all the gates with activation functions.

$$\text{result} = \tanh(\text{gate}_{\text{reset}} \bullet (W_{h1}.h_{t-1}) + W_{x1}.x_t) \tag{4.4}$$

ii. **Update gate:** The operation is same as reset gate, but each gate will have its unique weight as mentioned in Equation 4.5.

$$\text{Gate}_{\text{update}} = \text{sigmoid}(W_{\text{input\_up}}.x_t + W_{\text{hidden\_up}}.h_{t-1}) \tag{4.5}$$

Dot product of previous hidden state and update vector is used to compute a partial output result 1 and is given in Equation 4.6. The output of update gate determines how much of previous information is retained by GRU.

$$\text{result1} = \text{gate}_{\text{update}} \bullet h_{t-1} \tag{4.6}$$

Element-wise inversion of the update gate (−1) is done, and the result is multiplied with the output of tanh to update the added information in the current hidden state (h_t). The final output of the GRU is obtained by summing the previous hidden state with result1. Equation 4.7 shows this operation.

$$h_t = \text{result} \bullet \left(\frac{1}{\text{gate}_{\text{update}}}\right) + u \tag{4.7}$$

4.5.2 Bidirectional GRU

This is constructed by combining two GRU acting in opposite directions. One cell will read the input sequence from the beginning and other from the end. The information flows in both directions and its impact is considered. Equations 4.8–4.10 illustrate the integration of both gated units.

$$\overrightarrow{h_t} = GRU_f(x_t, \overrightarrow{h_{t-1}}) \tag{4.8}$$

$$\overleftarrow{h_t} = GRU_b(x_t, \overleftarrow{h_{t-1}}) \tag{4.9}$$

$$h_t = \overrightarrow{h_t} \oplus \overleftarrow{h_t} \tag{4.10}$$

Thus, the BGRU enhances the robustness of the application to which it is deployed. In addition to this, it can effectively capture all the local time invariant patterns from the input sequence, which is a very important trait of a deep learning model.

4.6 RUL Prediction Through BGRU from Mechanical Big Data

The BGRU described in previous section can effectively capture monotonic and non-monotonic trends from the input data. Hence, this is best suited for estimating the RUL of bearings from their degradation data. The methodology proposed is evaluated using PRONOSTIA, a benchmarked dataset containing vibration readings from the degradation signals of bearings [21]. This mechanical big data harvested from the test rig is explored to reveal a lot of latent knowledge. The complete experimental setup is shown in Figure 4.6. This dataset is more realistic comprising data samples with inner race, outer race, cage, and ball failures of the bearings. The dataset characterizes the operational profile of the bearings till run-time-to-failure. The vibration signals are measured with 4kN radial force at a rotatory speed of 1800 rpm. Two types of sensors are deployed over the test bed for capturing vibration and temperature readings.

The vibration signals are measures using accelerometers which are placed orthogonally in vertical and horizontal axes at outer race of the bearings. RTD-Resistance Temperature Detector PT100 is the temperature sensor that is installed in a hole in proximity to the outer bearing's ring. The bearings are driven by an AC motor with a capacity of 250 W and the speed of rotation is 2830 rpm. The test bed is equipped with a shaft that drives the bearing's inner race. As the vibration sensors are mounted at right angles, the accelerometers can capture the signals from both horizontal and vertical axes. The sampling rate of 10 s at 0.1 s duration is maintained throughout the experiment. The size of each sample set is 2560 data points.

The amplitude of the vibration signals directly corresponds to the health condition of the bearing. The bearing is said to operate under normal working conditions if the amplitude is within 20 g (1 g = 9.8 m/s). The bearings are operated under normal working conditions to measure the natural degradation. There is no external fault induction. A picture of bearings in normal and degraded states is shown in Figure 4.7.

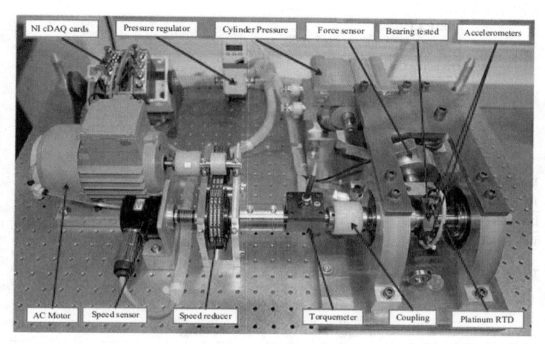

FIGURE 4.6
Experimental setup with accelerometers to measure the vibration signals of bearings.

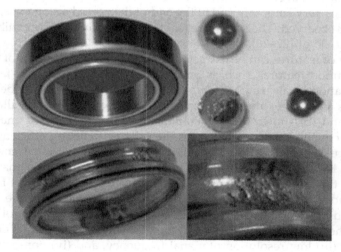

FIGURE 4.7
Bearings in normal and worn-out conditions due to wear and tear 17 ball bearings are experimented in the given three operating conditions (OC) as mentioned in Table 4.1. The test and training data details are given in Table 4.2. The vibration signals are measured till run-to-failure of bearings.

TABLE 4.1

Operating Conditions of Bearings

Operating Condition	Load (N)	Speed (rpm)
OC1	4000	1800
OC2	4200	1650
OC3	5000	1500

TABLE 4.2

Training and Test Dataset

Data Sets	OC1	OC2	OC3
Training set	Bearing1_1	Bearing2_1	Bearing3_1
	Bearing1_2	Bearing2_2	Bearing3_2
Test set	Bearing1_3	Bearing2_3	Bearing3_3
	Bearing1_4	Bearing2_4	
	Bearing1_5	Bearing2_5	
	Bearing1_6	Bearing2_6	
	Bearing1_7	Bearing2_7	

The raw vibration signals are an excellent source of useful features. The vibrational signal envelope of Bearing1_1 is shown in Figure 4.8. It is evident that the amplitude of the signal increases very smoothly and at the end of the period a step raise, indicating that the failure can be observed. The studies reveal that the faulty bearing exhibits a frequency range of {–30 g to 30 g} [22–26].

A wide variety of features can be extracted from the vibration signals of bearings. Some of the most common features such as amplitude, K factor, and crest factor with their signal representation of Bearing1_1 are shown in Figure 4.9. It can be observed that learning features from an exploratory analysis of PRONOSTIA is a challenging task.

Figure 4.9(a) and (b) shows the K factor measured by horizontal and vertical accelerometers, respectively. K factor represents the relative pelleting efficiency of a rotating object at a particular speed. It is evident that there is no monotonic trend in increase or decrease in the K factor of the bearings. The extremities in the signal peaks are represented using the crest factor. Figure 4.9(c) and (d) displays the crest factor measured by horizontal and vertical accelerometers, respectively. A steep increase in amplitude is observed toward the end of the signal spectrum. The exploration of these features highlights that the observed signals possess the following properties: (i) non-linearity, (ii) highly unstable, (iii) low resolution of signal frequency, and (iv) non-periodic.

Prominent degradation trend can be noticed in the signal spectrum as the faults evolve over its lifetime. Hence, precise and accurate feature selection is a pivotal factor in determination of RUL of bearings. The signal analysis shown in Figure 4.9 reveals that the statistical features could not describe the non-monotonic trends at its best. Hence, deep learning solutions can be explored to capture the natural trends and patterns from non-monotonic signals where manual feature extraction cannot effectively characterize the signals.

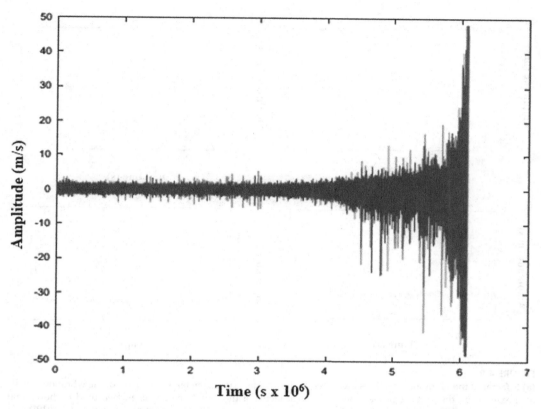

FIGURE 4.8
Amplitude envelope of vibration signals of Bearing1_1.

4.7 Exploration of the Experimental Results

The run-to-failure vibration data of the bearings have six datasets (Bearing1_1, Bearing2_1, Bearing3_1, Bearing1_2, Bearing2_2, and Bearing3_2) for training the model. Bearing1_3, Bearing1_4, Bearing1_5, Bearing1_6, Bearing1_7, Bearing2_3, Bearing2_4, Bearing2_5, Bearing2_6, Bearing2_7, and Bearing3_3 are the test datasets of vibration signals. The vibrational signals are recorded from origin till the total faulty condition. The degradation behavior of the bearings is non-monotonic without any uniformity in their distribution. The experimental results of the bearings in training phase do not adhere to any common pattern. So, the validation of the estimated RUL (RUL_E) by the proposed methodology is done by quantifying their accuracy score (A_C), Percent Error ($PerEr_i$), and final score (S_C) in accordance with IEEE PHM 2012 challenge as mentioned in Equations 4.11–4.13. All these equations are grounded on the deviation between the estimates RUL and actual RUL (RUL_{AT}):

$$PerEr_i = \frac{RUL_{AT} - RUL_E}{RUL_{AT}} \times 100 \qquad (4.11)$$

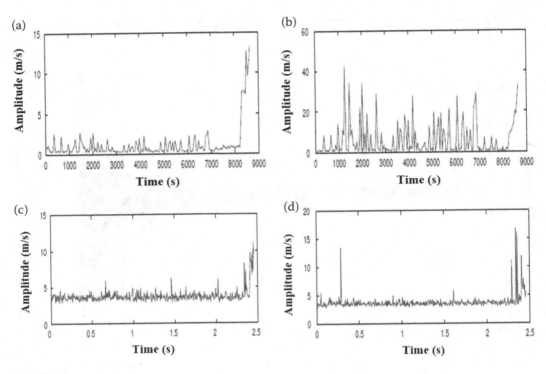

FIGURE 4.9
(a) K factor of the vibration signals as measured by horizontal accelerometer; (b) K factor of the vibration signals as measured by the vertical accelerometer; (c) crest factor of the vibration signals as measured by horizontal accelerometer ($\times 10^4$); (d) crest factor of the vibration signals as measured by vertical accelerometer ($\times 10^4$).

$$A_C = \begin{cases} \exp(-\ln(0.5)(PerEr_i/5) & \text{if} \quad PerEr_i \leq 0 \\ \exp(\ln(0.5)(PerEr_i/5) & \text{if} \quad PerEr_i > 0 \end{cases} \tag{4.12}$$

$$S_C = \frac{\sum_{i=1}^{N} A_{C_i}}{N} \tag{4.13}$$

The $PerEr_i$ and A_C are direct measures of the deviation between the actual and the predicted data. Some of the values move toward negative axes which indicate the overestimates of RUL_E. Bearing1_5, Bearing2_4, and Bearing2_7 exhibit overestimated RUL which means that the RUL_E is predicted very ahead of its RUL_{AT}.

Figure 4.10 shows the comparison of actual and predicted RUL of the bearings. These results confirm that the proposed methodology effectively predicts the RUL with much lesser deviation than the other state of art techniques, which is diagrammatically re-presented in Figure 4.11. The final Score function SC of the proposed methodology is 1.066050018, which is a low value. As the Score function is a measure of deviation of the actual and proposed RUL, a lower value indicates superior accuracy.

The comparative analysis with other techniques reveals that some methods predict the RUL_E much before actual failure time. This causes the bearing to be underutilized. On the other hand, some methodologies predict the RUL_E much later than its original RUL. This

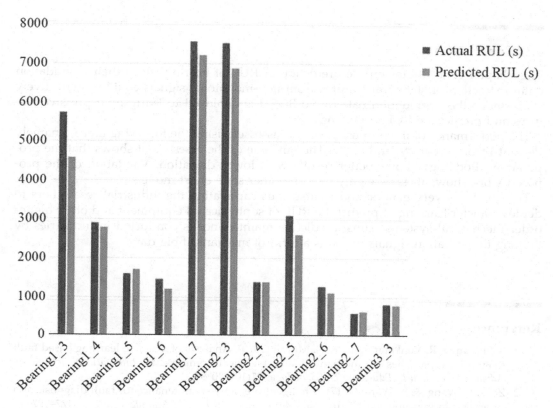

FIGURE 4.10
Comparison between actual vs. predicted RUL of bearings based on the predictions by proposed model.

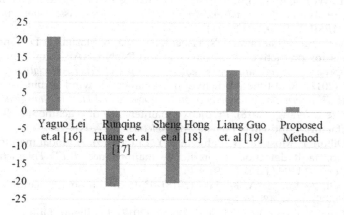

FIGURE 4.11
Comparison of average Percent Error of popular state of art techniques to predict RUL of bearings.

is an unfavorable condition that causes late scheduling of maintenance. However, the proposed prediction model has much low error estimates (PerEr$_i$), which gives a direct implication that the model learns better from the raw vibration signals, since there is no overlooking of noteworthy features.

4.8 Conclusion

This chapter concentrates on the prediction of RUL of bearings from their degradation data. Extraction of statistical features from non-monotonic signals could not effectively characterize the degradation pattern. So BGRU is deployed to learn the expressive features and predict the RUL of bearings.

The performance of the proposed work is assessed using the following metrics namely Percent Error, Accuracy, and Score. The outcome of the assessment shows that the proposed methodology shows better results with lower deviation. Validation of the proposed work shows its sovereignty over the other state of art models.

This model is very generic and robust, thus captivating the industrial researchers to deploy transfer learning to predict the RUL of sophisticated equipment and other higher order mechanical systems. Thus, predictive maintenance is conducted in industries by tapping the vibration signals which is a form of mechanical big data.

References

1. S. Sharanya, R. Venkataraman, & G. Murali (2020). Analysis of machine learning based fault diagnosis approaches in mechanical and electrical components. *International Journal of Advanced Research in Education & Technology, 11*(10), 80–94.
2. Z. Li, Y. Wang, & K. Wang (2017). Intelligent predictive maintenance for fault diagnosis and prognosis in machine centers: Industry 4.0 scenario. *Advanced Manufacturing, 5*, 377–387.
3. S. Selcuk. (2017). Predictive maintenance, its implementation, and latest trends. *Journal of Engineering Manufacturing, 231*(9):1–10.
4. P. Him, & L. W. Pheng. (2019). IoT-based predictive maintenance for smart manufacturing systems. *2019 Asia-Pacific Signal and Information Processing Association Annual Summit and Conference (APSIPA ASC)*, 1942–1944.
5. L. Decker de Sousa, L. Giommi, S. R. Tisbeni, F. Viola, B. Martelli & D. Bonacorsi. (2020). Big data analysis for predictive maintenance at the INFN-CNAF Data Center using machine learning approaches. *Proceeding of the 25th Conference of Fruct Association*.
6. M. Canizo. (2017). Real-time predictive maintenance for wind turbines using big data frameworks. *IEEE International Conference on Prognostics and Health Management*, 70–77.
7. B. Schmidt, & L. Wang. (2018). Predictive maintenance of machine tool linear axes: A case from manufacturing industry. *Procedia Manufacturing, 17*, 118–125.
8. W. Yu, T. Dillon, F. Mostafa, W. Rahayu, & Y. Liu. (2019). A global manufacturing big data ecosystem for fault detection in predictive maintenance. *IEEE Transactions on Industrial Informatics*. doi:10.1109/TII.2019.2915846.
9. F. Tao, Q. Qi, A. Liu, & A. Kusiak. (2018). Data-driven smart manufacturing. *Journal of Manufacturing Systems, 48*, 157–169.
10. H. Hu, B. Tang, X. Gong, W. Wei, & H. Wang. (2017). Intelligent fault diagnosis of the high-speed train with big data based on deep neural networks. *IEEE Transactions on Industrial Informatics, 13*(4), 2106–2116.
11. Y. Zhang, S. Ma, H. Yang, J. Lv, & Y. Liu. (2018). A big data driven analytical framework for energy-intensive manufacturing industries. *Journal of Cleaner Production, 197*(1), 57–72.
12. R. Y. Zhong, G. Q. Huang, S. Lan, Q. Y. Dai, X. Chen, & T. Zhang. (2015). A big data approach for logistics trajectory discovery from RFID-enabled production data. *International Journal of Production Economics, 165*, 260–272.

13. R. Y. Zhong, C. Xu, C. Chen, & G. Q. Huang. (2017). Big data analytics for physical Internet-based intelligent manufacturing shop floors. *International Journal of Production Research, 55*(9), 2610–2621.

14. C. Hu, X. Si, W. Wang, & D. Zhou. (2011). Remaining useful life estimation – A review on the statistical data driven approaches. *European Journal of Operational Research, 213*(1), 1–14.

15. P. Li. A. Luo, J. Li, Y. Wang, J. Zhu, Y. Deng, & J. Zhang. (2020). Bidirectional gated recurrent unit neural network for Chinese address element segmentation. *International Journal of Geo-information, 9*(11), 635. 10.3390/ijgi9110635.

16. H. M. Lynn, S. B. Pan, & P. Kim. (2019). A deep bidirectional GRU network model for biometric electrocardiogram classification based on recurrent neural networks. *IEEE Access, 1*, 99.

17. Mashhadi. (2018). Moving towards real-time data-driven quality monitoring: A case study of hard disk drives. *Procedia Manufacturing, 26*, 1107–1115.

18. S. Sharanya , & R. Venkataraman. (2020). An intelligent context based multi-layered Bayesian Inferential predictive analytic framework for classifying machine states. *Journal of Ambient Intelligence and Humanized Computing, 12*, 7353–7361.

19. U. R. Acharya, S. L. Oh, Y. Hagiwara, J. H. Tan, M. Adam, A. Gertych, & R. S. Tan. (2017). A deep convolutional neural network model to classify heartbeats. *Computational Biology Medicine, 89*, 389–396.

20. X. Zhang, Y. Zhang, L. Zhang, H. Wang, & J. Tang. (2018). Ballisto cardiogram-based person identification and authentication using recurrent neural networks. Proc. 11th Int. Congr. Image Signal Process., *BioMed. Eng. Inform. (CISP-BMEI)*, Beijing, China, Oct. pp. 1–5.

21. P. Nectoux, R. Gouriveau, K. Medjaher, E. Ramasso, & B. Chebel-Morello. (2012). PRONOSTIA: An experimental platform for bearings accelerated degradation tests. *IEEE International Conference on Prognostics and Health Management, PHM'12*, pp. 1–8.

22. Y. Yoo, & J.-G. Baek. (2018). A novel image feature for the remaining useful lifetime prediction of bearings based on continuous wavelet transform and convolutional neural network. *Applied Sciences, 8*(7), 1102. 10.3390/app8071102.

23. Y. Lei, N. Li, S. Gontarz, J. Lin, S. Radkowski, & J. Dybala. (2016). A model-based method for remaining useful life prediction of machinery. *IEEE Transactions on Reliability, 65*(3), 1314–1326.

24. R. Huang, L. Xi, X. Li, R. Liu, H. Qiu, & J. Lee. (2007). Residual life predictions for ball bearings based on self-organizing map and back propagation neural network methods. *Mechanical Systems and Signal Processing, 21*(1), 193–207.

25. S. Hong, Z. Zhou, E. Zio, & K. Hong. (2014). Condition assessment for the performance degradation of bearing based on a combinatorial feature extraction method. *Digital Signal Processing, 27*, 159–166.

26. L. Guo, N. Li, F. Jia, Y. Lei, & J. Lin. (2017). A recurrent neural network-based health indicator for remaining useful life prediction of bearings. *Neurocomputing, 240*, 98–109.

5

Integration of Industrial IoT and Big Data Analytics for Smart Manufacturing Industries: Perspectives and Challenges

K. Udayakumar and S. Ramamoorthy

Department of Computing Technologies, SRM Institute of Science and Technology, Kattankulathur, Tamil Nadu, India

R. Poorvadevi

Department of Computer Science and Engineering, Sri Chandrasekharendra Saraswathi Viswa Mahavidyalaya, Kancheepuram, Tamil Nadu, India

CONTENTS

DOI: 10.1201/9781003202776-5

5.1 Introduction

Industries play a drastic role in dropping the poverty margin of people across the country. The economic growth of any country relies on its industrial planning and development. According to a study from India's Ministry of Statistics and Programme Implementation, the industrial sector contributes 27.47% of the country's Gross Domestic Product (GDP). Specifically, the Micro, Small, and Medium Enterprises (MSME) sector has a high impact on economic growth and rural development [1]. In the last two decades, industries have been implementing an automated solution in different segments. Industrial automation increases production quality, reliability, labor safety, production quantity in less time, adaptability, and so on. In straight, cost engrosses in analysis, design, production, maintenance, and quality control are also declined. Such benefits of automation attract investors and entrepreneurs to adopt emerging technologies in business processes. Emerging technology comprises innovation, high performance, service-oriented, and integrated solutions to enhance the industrial environment [2].

First, the industrial automation process integrated machines and computation systems to carry out operational activities. Then, industries started exploring great possibilities for the invention of automated devices. As a result, Programmable Logic Controller (PLC), Supervisory Control and Data Acquisition (SCADA), Human Machine Interface (HMI), and robotics have been established. By means, industries harvested many rewards in terms of cost, customer satisfaction, and gap filling between demand and supply. Due to high initial cost and lack of infrastructure, large-scale industries have been liberated more in executing automation processes than medium- and small-scale industries. Later, an era started for all scalable industries to shift automation processes as revolutionary technologies reached the open market.

5.1.1 Industry Automation System

Regardless of industry size, automation has been deployed at several levels of industry. Most industry automation systems are described in the following four levels: field, control, supervision, and enterprise resource planning (ERP). Automation in the industry is a complex task as it involves a large number of devices. Synchronization and communication among the smart devices ensure the successful implementation of industry automation system. The smart devices used at different levels and their communication setup are illustrated in Figure 5.1.

Devices positioned in the field capture real-time data about processes and machines. Those data are transferred to control-level devices to regulate, monitor, and control devices. At the control level, real-time data analysis is performed to pass control signals. On receiving control signals, actuators instruct devices to take pre-defined action. Industrial PCs were installed with specialized software to facilitate visualization of processes in the production field as well as process adjustment through parameterization. Process planning, control, and quality management are defined as core functions at the supervisory level. Overall industry administration has been constituted at ERP level. Some of the major tasks defined in ERP include manufacturing execution system (MES), order management, production planning, supply chain management, and customer relationship management. The protocols configured to establish communication between levels are assorted according to the device requirement.

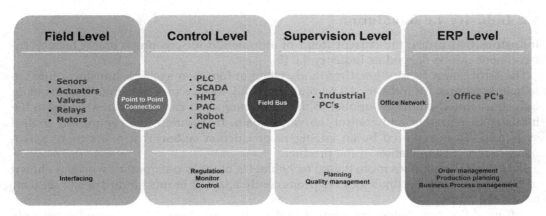

FIGURE 5.1
Industry automation system.

5.1.2 Industrial Automation Types

Once the industry had decided to install automated assembly machines in the production line, there would be choices for automation solutions based on design needs and cost. Customizable smart devices and robot systems are available to fulfill the needs of the industry. All such devices and systems should fall into one of the following categories.

5.1.2.1 Fixed Automation System

Equipment fixed in the production field to perform a sequence of operations continuously would fall under this category. Design changes in the automation system could not be done often as it is recommended for mass production systems.

5.1.2.2 Programmable Automation System

Programmed electronic control system positioned to operate a sequence of tasks mainly for a batch production system. Configuration change could be conceded in the program part for the production of a new product.

5.1.2.3 Soft Automation System

The machines of this kind usually controlled by computers also suit for implementing changes frequently. New code to the computer for a new product could be carried out after necessary changes in the physical setup.

5.1.2.4 Integrated Automation System

Independent machines are integrated and controlled by an electronic control system. The production process in the assembly line is usually implemented by this kind of automation system.

5.2 Industry 4.0 Revolution

Industries that utilize the current trend of automation for creating a smart factory environment can be flagged as Industry 4.0 [3].

The term smart factory greatly sounds when automation systems transform into intelligent systems. An Industry 4.0 revolution mainly focuses on all essential aspects of an industry value chain from supplier to the end customer. It can exhibit new stages in the industry to represent and control the value chain. In addition, the centralized control system has been replaced by an intelligent production system that offers more personalization or customization of the product.

Industry 4.0 comprises more digital technologies of the contemporary world as shown in Figure 5.2. Those technologies are prominently adapted in most industries to set their new stage.

Advanced Robotics: Advanced robotics in the industry is powered by complicated code and hardware to repeatedly do some action even without any supervision. Input data

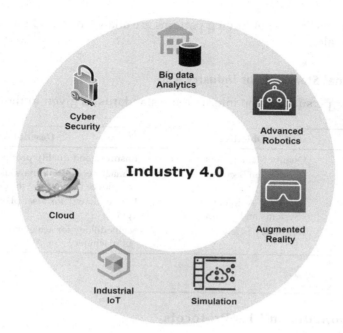

FIGURE 5.2
Converging technologies of Industry 4.0.

simulated by the sensor usually direct the code module to command the hardware. Recent advancement in both software and hardware technology has brought an ample range of sensors to capture data through touch, light, heat, and so on.

Augmented Reality: Through this technology, industries started focusing on digital planning. A visual representation of the existing digital data used for factory planning. This will reduce the time and cost significantly in the factory planning process.

Simulation: Most successful industries implemented manufacturing simulation to test various processes virtually. The information obtained from the virtual test could be used in enhancing the manufacturing system.

Cloud: Cloud technology is ideal for the large scale manufacturing industry to handle all manufacturing processes. Manufacturing resources such as ERP, SCM, and CRM are utilized in the manufacturing process through the cloud. Cloud provides flexible information access and appends at any time and from anywhere with seamless network connectivity.

Cyber Security: The product and process-related data and information should be shielded from hackers and counterfeiters. Security is the most important area to which the industry needs to pay extreme attention. Choosing the appropriate and best security model ensures data is unrevealed to business opponents.

Industrial IoT: The core Internet of Things (IoT) has a high impact on the digital transformation of an industry. Due to a lack of computing capability and physical hardware, IoT has been spotted below cyber-physical systems (CPS).

Big Data Analytics: The data from heterogeneous sources are gathered to discover insight information with the help of big data analytics. Industries seeking data-driven models to capture valuable data throughout the value chain. For instance, data about the material, product, and customer buying patterns are analyzed to find the association and trends related to sales.

5.2.1 International Standards of Industry 4.0

Industry 4.0 must persuade some international standards as given in the table below.

Standard	Objective	Description
ISO 9001	Quality Management	Ensures good quality products and services
ISO 27001	Information Security	Manage security of financial information, employee details, and third-party information
ISO 15926	Industrial Automation Systems and Integration	Data exchange for asset planning for process plants
ISO 12100	Machinery Safety	Methodology for achieving safety in the design of machinery

5.3 IoT Components and Its Protocols

An IoT system contains a range of components with unique functionalities. Most IoT system involves machine-to-machine (M2M) communication. In some environments, device-to-machine (D2M) communication and vice versa is also adapted with IoT protocols [4]. Major components of IoT and its protocols are discussed later.

5.3.1 Things

An object rooted with sensors that gather data and enriched with Internet technology for communication. Typically, rapid decisions are made at the upper layer based on data from things located across the industry. But, action is actuated and controlled by actuators. Case in point, robots placed in the industry need to slow down or speed up the process of receiving control responses based on generated data.

5.3.2 Gateways

A gateway plays a vital role in data transmission between two-end points. It provides functionalities such as data transfer, data preprocessing, data reduction, and control transmission.

5.3.3 Cloud Gateway

Cloud gateway smooths the progress of data compression in data centers. It addresses conflicts in field gateway protocols that ensure seamless communication. Moreover, device-to-device (D2D) communication requires some kind of protocols that are known as IoT protocols. Traditional protocols at the link layer, network layer, and transport layer are incorporated in IoT technology. But, need arises for more powerful protocols at the application layer in IoT technology and as a result following protocols have been defined.

HTTP – *Hyper Text Transfer Protocol*	Used for browser or application running on the client
MQTT – *Message Queue Telemetry Transport Protocol*	Can apply where memory and resource constraints exist.
DDS – *Data Distribution Service*	To provide D2D or M2M communication
Web Socket	Mainly for client-server communication
AMQP – *Advanced Message Queuing Protocol*	For business messaging
CoAP – *Constrained Application Protocol*	To provide M2M communication

5.3.4 Data Lake

Data Lake holds all IoT device-generated data in its original format. Usually, Data Lake is established in lower layers of IoT for holding data provisionally, later data are moved to the data center of the cloud layer for analysis and knowledge discovery.

5.3.5 Data Analytics

Trends and actionable insights have been gained from the big data warehouses by data analytics process. Insights discovered to aid in improving the performance and efficacy of an IoT system. Additionally, guides to enhance algorithms for control applications using correlations and patterns found.

5.3.6 Machine Learning

Machine learning algorithms build a precise model on observed data from IoT devices to control applications. An application deployed with such machine learning model delivers consistent performance in IoT systems by earlier predictions.

5.3.7 Control Applications

An application that issues automatic commands and alerts field devices for a specific action, for example:

- IoT devices with sensors used to supervise the industrial equipment, and auto-notification could be raised if the situation turns to cause the failure of the equipment.

Even though excellent automation is applied in an Industrial IoT system, an option for manual control is never refused.

5.3.8 User Applications

A software component at the user end to monitor and control an IoT system enabled by seamless network connectivity. Users of an application can supervise their IoT system and control applications by passing commands.

5.4 M2M Communication in Smart Manufacturing

It enables two machines to communicate by exchanging data. It requires seamless and secure connectivity in the Industrial IoT (IIoT). Recent advancement in wireless communication opens a path to connect more applications and enables seamless M2M communication.

Modern information technology society has named M2M communication as IoT. Fundamentally both deliver the same promising functionalities. Just like M2M, IoT uses sensors to capture data and communicate to computing systems via wired or wireless connectivity available. This way, monitoring or controlling end devices becomes possible. End devices will act according to the response from the processing node without any human intervention.

M2M is one of the fastest-growing forms of connected device technology on the market right now, according to Forbes, owing to its ability to link millions of devices within a single network. Manufacturing industries have started seeking feasible solutions through technology that are cost-effective to their level. The success of an industry depends on the adoption of technology at the right time. Automating the manufacturing processes will improve quality and overall performance. In the manufacturing world, automation is highly recommended to increase production efficiency with automated equipment maintenance notification and safety procedures. For instance, an application for M2M communication will alert the business owners or authorities regarding equipment servicing in advance. So authorities can plan and address the issue as quickly as possible.

According to a few primary experts, any object or computer would eventually be able to link to the cloud. This is a bold assertion, but it seems to be true. If more customers, users, and company owners expect greater accessibility, technology must evolve to address the demands and challenges of the future [5].

5.5 IoT in Smart Manufacturing

Smart manufacturing is defined by the National Institute of Standards and Technology (NIST) as systems that are "fully-integrated, collaborative manufacturing systems that respond in real-time to meet changing demands and conditions in the factory, in the supply network, and in customer needs."

The primary goal of smart manufacturing and smart factory is to optimize the manufacturing process. Manufacturing efficiency can be improved via computer controls, modeling, big data, and other automation technologies. The term smart in manufacturing or factory indicates that all the information about the manufacturing process needs to be utilized wisely [6]. For that, the availability of such information extended to entire manufacturing product life cycles.

Sensors in IoT devices are used in collecting precious data about entire manufacturing processes as well as business processes. The collected data can be used in finding industry development strategies and quality improvement policies. For instance, industrial robots in assembly lines perform an action based on the control response. But the decision on control response completely depends on data sent by an IoT device. Similarly, product design and production can be customized on predicting customer preferences. The traditional manufacturing process with humans has been completely transformed into numerous connected devices. The transformed new technology depicts the following benefits and makes the manufacturing process smart.

5.5.1 Advanced Analysis

With a variety of data from IoT devices, an industry can improve its efficiency by advanced analysis and facilitate caution measures in advance. Data from sensors help in advanced analysis and alert the authority to take the right decision at the right time.

5.5.2 Inventory Monitoring

An inventory tracking system connected with IoT devices gets onboard stock and supply data, which improves coordination between producers and suppliers.

5.5.3 Remote Process Monitoring

Employees may gather data on manufacturing procedures from a distance to verify if the processes or the results follow relevant regulations and specifications. They can also tune and customize machines remotely, which saves a lot of time and efforts.

5.5.4 Abnormality Reporting

A person participating in the evaluation is no longer expected to detect potential anomalies in equipment output or condition: IoT-connected computers notify responsible workers when infrastructure is deteriorating, leaving staff with only the task of remedial work.

The data flow between IoT devices and the cloud makes more sense in smart manufacturing. IoT technology, which employs both wired and wireless networking, enables this data flow. It enables remote process monitoring and administration, as well as the capacity to quickly alter development plans in real-time. It improves production results by reducing waste, boosting demand, and enhancing yield and product quality.

5.6 Big Data Analytics in Smart Manufacturing

Big data analytics is an exuberance technique to light out the significant information of an organization. It includes functions such as data capturing from multiple sources, high volume data storage, data sharing between computing devices, and querying large volumes of data. It can handle any data of an organization irrespective of its format but the quality of data matters a lot [7].

Some complex key areas such as manufacturing, operational and pricey equipment handling have emerged with IoT solutions to drive more sustainable, elastic, and well-organized processes. IoT devices installed at the operational site capture real-time data in different formats. In the automobile industry, sensors play an important role to make rapid decisions. Along with sensors, PLC, computer numerical control (CNC), robotics, and industry core-related equipment are engaged in real-time data collection. Those collected data are moved to the edge, and real-time processing and decisions are taken. Furthermore, initial

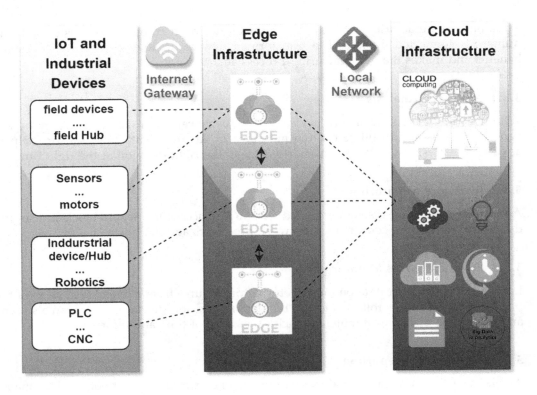

FIGURE 5.3
Industrial IoT architecture.

data processing can be performed at an edge server and complex tasks could be offloaded to a cloud server for advanced computation as shown in Figure 5.3. The edge nodes can avail of all services of cloud infrastructure through seamless connectivity [8]. While this may appear to be a simple process, it can be quite complex.

Big data at cloud infrastructure ensures large data storage for business analytics. Data gathered from multiple heterogeneous sources are made available for business analytics under a single roof called a data center. Datacenter usually contains a collection of structured, unstructured, and semi-structured data. Data present in big data has been processed in an early stage to ensure quality data. At preprocessing stage, cleansing and transforming operations are carried out on data extracted from multiple sources. High-quality data loaded in big data will be used for various business analytics. Significant as well as dynamic decisions on business processes can be made by referring to information discovered from big data analytics.

It is most important that an organization must sustain itself in a competitive market environment by introducing innovations in all key areas. For instance, customer retention is a challenging task in any enterprise in this contemporary world. So enterprises need to be aware of customer behavior in buying products, innovation, and quality expectations in products. Big data offers flexible solutions for all such business needs under a single umbrella.

IoT has been playing a vital role in achieving industry automation for the past more than one decade. In the same way, big data helps automation to smart manufacturing transformation. Intelligence in all stages becomes possible due to huge data collection from smart sensors and the computing infrastructure of big data analytics. Patterns or valuable information discovered from those data help to improve the efficiency of Supply Chain Management. It also helps in discovering hidden variables in production that lead to bottlenecks. Big data improves production efficiency by reducing breakdown.

5.6.1 Self-Service Systems

Big data analytics systems consolidate large amounts of real-time data from production plants through smart factory equipment. The self-service system finds patterns and insights in real-time data and creates a visualization for decision makers.

5.6.1.1 Elimination of bottlenecks

A manufacturer adopts big data to discover factors that affect performance. Identifying the problem in the early stages benefits in cost, time, and reduces wastage.

5.6.1.2 Predictive Maintenance

The outcome of big data analytics is used in the business decision-making process. Manufacturers can prioritize the actionable changes to avoid breakdown, unscheduled downtime, and equipment malfunction.

5.6.1.3 Automation Production Management

Using big data, particular production processes can be automated by analyzing historic data and integrating that with real-time. It reduces errors and human interventions. Actuators and advanced robots in the industry have inbuilt control software modules which take inference of big data analytics.

5.6.1.4 Predictive Demand

With accurate prediction, customer preferences and product trends are known to the manufacturers. Big data algorithms effectively analyze historic data and predict future trends in advance. With this prediction result, the industry does modifications to its product portfolio.

5.7 Convergence of IIoT and Big Data Analytics

The contribution of IoT in the global economy has been expected to increase by US$11 trillion by 2025. A number of sensors and devices connected to the Internet are growing exponentially and are expected to cross more than ten billion by 2021.

When an industry decides to collect data for analytics purposes, IIoT is the best option for collecting data from both internal and external environments. Once the source of data

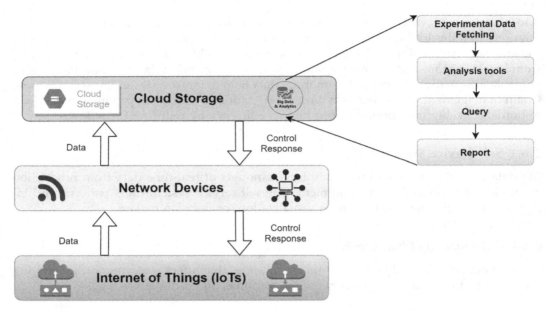

FIGURE 5.4
Convergence of IoT and big data.

is predetermined, focus on migrating to big data for analysis. IIoT devices generate real-time data through sensors at the operational level and big data performs analytics to control or monitor the production process. Also predicts many factors through externally collected data that influence efficient manufacturing. Based on predictions necessary decisions and design changes in product are carried out. Big data's purpose in IoT is to analyze a huge quantity of real-time data and store it using various storage solutions [9]. The association of IoT and big data is illustrated in Figure 5.4.

IoT devices create a significant volume of unstructured or structured data, which are gathered in a big data system. The features of big data are based on five Vs:

- Volume
- Velocity
- Variety
- Veracity
- Value.

Big data systems use MapReduce techniques to execute analytic tasks in distributed environments. All the required data have been replicated in a distributed database system. Analytical tools allowed accessing stored data for analyzing and discovering hidden variables and facts. The generated output visually presented to authorities for further decision-making.

In IoT, data is collected via the Internet and data is often in an unstructured format. Hence, requirements arise in big data for IIoT to perform fast analysis over unstructured data and gain facts to make rapid decisions. Since big data can handle all types of data it is irreplaceable with other contemporary technologies. The comparison between deploying standalone IIoT and big data-enabled IIoT is illustrated in Table 5.1. The Benefits

TABLE 5.1

Functionality/Process Comparison

Functionality/Process	Standalone IIoT	IIoT with Big Data Analytics
Monitoring	Moderate	High
Status alerts and alarm	Moderate	High
Predictive maintenance	Low	High
Control operations	High	–
Uncover new business opportunities	Low	High
Improves customer experience	Moderate	High
Increases productivity	High	High

of implementing big data enabled IIoT placed high with respect to various business processes.

IIoT and big data are balanced technologies. So evolution in IIoT has a potential impact on big data and vice versa. For example, when more IIoT devices are deployed for various business requirements, advanced storage and computing technologies in big data become a core part of the growth [10].

Industrial devices connected to generate data which are used in big data analytics to:

- Examine hidden variables that cause problems in production
- Reveal trends in supply and customer preference
- Find unseen patterns in machinery fault detection
- Find hidden correlations in price optimization
- Reveal new information that gives direction for updating business strategy.

When an industrial device is equipped with sensor, the following benefits are observed:

- Monitoring – The behavior of industrial devices can be monitored using IoT sensors.
- Collecting – Real-time operational data can be collected via an IoT sensor.
- Exchanging – Enables data exchange between IoT devices and computing systems.
- Analyzing – Collected data in a big data system used for analysis.
- Instantly acting on information – Industrial devices will act according to decisions taken on big data output.

5.8 Smart Manufacturing in Industries

Smart manufacturing is a convergence of current technologies and communication solutions that put together in a manufacturing environment. The incorporation of these innovations and solutions by the company aids in the optimization of the whole production process, thus the net revenues [11].

Implementation of smart manufacturing in the industry involves three key areas. First, identify the product and control solution required for the industry. Some companies such as Honeywell, Schneider, and Siemens are well known for their automation products. Software development companies such as HP, Intel, Microsoft, Google, SAS, and many others provide software infrastructure to control, monitor, and analyze manufacturing process. Modern technologies like Artificial Intelligence, cloud, big data, IoT, and cyber security are deployed in the industry for smart manufacturing. As modern technologies need communication platform to exchange data, connectivity solution becomes mandatory. Finally, the telecom service provider ensures the smooth flow of data between different layers of the smart industry. Companies such as Cisco, Huawei, and AT&T provide the best connectivity solutions.

5.8.1 Building Blocks of Smart Manufacturing

Smart manufacturing comprises many aspects as given in Figure 5.5. Some of the important things that influence smart manufacturing are discussed later.

5.8.1.1 Flat

In the smart manufacturing process, traditional hierarchies of business data access have been relaxed to more people. This flattening method helps in quick decision-making rather than waiting for a decision from the top.

5.8.1.2 Data-Driven

Big data, machine learning, CPS, and the IoT are data-driven paradigms that contribute to the basic aspect of smart manufacturing [12]. Smart manufacturing attributes such as self-monitoring, self-controlling, self-analyzing, and self-organizing had been conferred using a successful implementation of data-driven paradigms.

5.8.1.3 Sustainable

The term sustainable has a close association with smart manufacturing since all feasible solutions are known in advance with respect to economic, social, and environmental. Data analytics as a core part plays a vital role in industry sustainability.

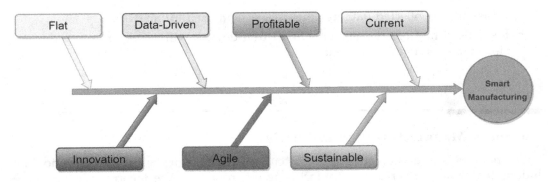

FIGURE 5.5
Building blocks of smart manufacturing.

5.8.1.4 Agile

Smart manufacturing allows for faster data collection, analysis, and collaboration, which leads to faster decision-making. Advanced discovery and resolution of prospects or problems aid policymakers in adapting to global and local economic changes and moving activity to the most active locations.

5.8.1.5 Innovative

Innovation is the most prominent key to grasping development in any process. It provides smart solutions for continuously improving work practices to save time and cost.

5.8.1.6 Current

An industry adapts smart manufacturing techniques for their development than they are said to be current. This involves the implementation of agile, data-driven, innovation, and smart production.

5.8.1.7 Profitable

The ultimate objective of implementing smart manufacturing is to make a profit easily and effectively.

5.8.2 IIoT Implementation

Field devices collect real-time data through connected sensors about processes and industrial machines. To regulate, track, and govern automatic systems, those data are passed to control-level devices. To transfer control signals, real-time data processing is done at the control stage. Actuators receive control signals and order automated systems to perform a predetermined operation. Smart production is not commonly used, although it does exist in some organizations in bits and parts. To integrate any of those sensors and other similar technologies, it is difficult to change the basic configuration of industrial machines [13]. This makes integrating IoT into traditional industrial practices challenging.

5.9 Smart Manufacturing in MSMEs

Most of the developing countries are taking serious efforts to implement Industry 4.0 in all industries. The main focus of such initiatives turns on MSMEs. The latest Industry 4.0 compliance includes IoT, CPS, cloud, and big data that necessitate a significant investment in terms of money, time, and other resources. Due to realistic constraints (cost, space, etc.) on their IT adoption, the capabilities of MSMEs in relation to manufacturing information are underdeveloped compared to large-scale industries. As a result, MSMEs need new techniques for constructing appropriate smart factories [14]. SMEs are now integrating contemporary smart manufacturing-related information and digital technologies (SMIDT) such as Artificial Intelligence and the IoT into their company processes to allow smart manufacturing. Ongoing studies and initiatives on CPS for MSMEs and the creation of domain experts on the latest technology, resources, and equipment will create a flexible platform for the successful implementation of smart manufacturing in MSMEs.

5.9.1 Smart Manufacturing in Large-Scale Industry

The concept of "smart manufacturing" refers to that data from around the factory being transmitted and analyzed in real-time, resulting in manufacturing information that can be used to improve all facets of operations. Big data, machine learning, simulation, IoT, and CPS are examples of data-driven technologies that help factories run more efficiently. Transmission and exchange of actual data over ubiquitous networks with the goal of generating manufacturing insight across all aspects of the plant [15].

Large-scale industries invest more in smart manufacturing to fulfill demand-based production, product design change, and high quality. Due to domain expert availability, the latest technology, resources, and equipment are utilized effectively for smart manufacturing. With intelligence in the manufacturing process, large-scale industries can tackle competently in the market and sustain success for a longer period of time [16].

5.9.2 Intelligent Robots for Smart Manufacturing

An industrial robot contributes a crucial part to implementing a smart manufacturing facility. Industrial robotics has been in use for more than three decades. The only difference between industrial robotics and previous generations is that they are now intelligent because they are embedded with modern technologies [17]. Previously, robots were only designed to do one task at a time. If you try to do something else, you have to update the design.

5.9.2.1 Industrial Robots

Generally, industrial robots are placed where repeated heavier jobs need to be carried out and sometimes where human resources cannot be deployed as more risk is involved in the environment [18]. Robots are now well connected with sensors to receive real-time and change their behavior accordingly. Robotics systems are steadily adopting Artificial Intelligence and machine learning, allowing them to become self-sufficient. Based on the input from the sensors, robotic systems may alter their behavior in real time. In the automobile sector, industrial robots play a critical role. One of the most essential elements to the development and expansion of robots is government initiative. According to a study, the industrial robotics industry would be valued US$71.72 billion by 2023.

5.9.2.2 Collaborative Robots

These machines work by imitating human activity as they repeatedly observe the same activity. Artificial Intelligence, cloud, and machine learning algorithms jointly train the machine for certain scenarios [19]. The machine learns the different environments and builds models appropriate for the scenario where used. A subset of machine learning called reinforcement learning pays a potential impact on the development of collaborative robots. Reward-based learning method directs the collaborative robots to perform very effectively. Furthermore, collaborative robots have progressed to the point that it is impossible to distinguish them from factory robots in terms of application. According to a study, the collaborative robot industry would be valued US$4.28 billion by 2023.

5.10 Challenges in Integrating Industrial IoT and Big Data Analytics

In recent times, industries are turning to digital platforms by deploying advanced IIoT and big data analytics. The benefits of such IoT deployment in the industry have been discussed by Morgan Stanley in the world industrial automation survey. Highlights of his survey are presented in Figure 5.6. Another survey from SANS Institute on Industrial IoT security claims that the highest use case of IIoT data at present is monitoring and status alerts. Still, the greatest opportunities are unrevealed with the available data. Advancement in big data analytics utilizing IIoT data to explore various aspects of business development beyond predictive maintenance and control operation as mentioned in Figure 5.7. In this continuation, the challenges in Industrial IoT that implement big data are explored and discussed in this section.

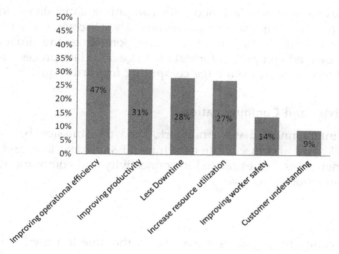

FIGURE 5.6
Benefits of deploying industrial IoT.

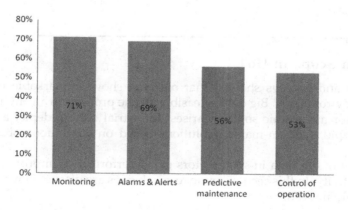

FIGURE 5.7
Comparison of industrial IoT data under different use cases.

5.10.1 Privacy

Industry big data holds sensitive data from different ends. For example, IoT generated operational data, business process data, product production data, and customer data. Preserving the data from personal data theft and business data leakage is the most important challenge involved in big data.

5.10.2 Cyber Security

Due to system openness and security vulnerability threats arise in the form of internal and external attacks. Protecting data from suspicious access and attacks in communication systems are major challenges in big data systems.

5.10.3 Scalability

Generally, IoT devices are not designed with computing capabilities. IoT devices seek computing resources to complete data processing. The Discovery of such resources and their computing capability is difficult in real-time. Sometimes the situation turns to off-loading data to powered computing for data storage and data processing. For example, data is offloaded to the cloud from edge computing for further processing.

5.10.4 Connectivity and Communication

IoT devices are interconnected via a network. Data transmission between devices encounters issues like bad and inaccurate data transmission, data loss, and high latency in communication networks. Issues related to connectivity and communications are crucial and need more attention to resolve.

5.10.5 Efficiency

IoT devices and computing systems are active all the time to provide seamless service. This leads to high energy utilization and resource constraints. Improving IIoT efficiency is a complex task with respect to energy consumption.

5.11 Research Scope in IIoT

Recent research and surveys showed that big data shows remarkable performance in industrial IoT environments. Big data is feasible for the problem in an environment where a requirement for a dynamic solution arises. Industrial sectors depict a high need for dynamic and rapid decision-making solutions based on continuous observation of an environment.

The placement of big data in such sectors gains performance improvement as well as efficient productivity. In this section, some research gaps are discussed where the scope of big data is highly noticed.

5.11.1 Energy Management

Due to a massive number of IoT devices and their concurrent access nature, enforcement of energy management schemes becomes imperative. Energy consumption of IIoT devices sometimes exceeds the predetermined energy budget due to delays in resource allocation and channel allocation. Big data-based energy management schemes could be the better choice to adapt dynamic network topology and resource allocation.

5.11.2 Heterogeneous QoS

An industrial IoT device exhibits heterogeneity in different aspects. The capabilities and functionalities of the IIoT device are unique in nature (e.g., trip sensor, temperature sensor). Next, the communication requirement of IIoT devices depends on the volume of data generated. It varies for sensors, RFID tags, Industrial hubs, and robots. So the requirement of a model arises to handle the heterogeneous quality of service with a dynamic programming approach.

5.11.3 Resource Management

Resource allocation takes place in different infrastructures of industrial IoT. The traditional resource management scheme follows a static prefixed cost mapping table strategy for resource allocation. Prediction-based technique could dynamically update the cost mapping table to provide flexibility in resource allocation. More research investigations are expected on this to obtain industry acceptable results.

5.11.4 Data Offloading Decision

Computational capabilities of edge and fog infrastructure are limited comparing cloud infrastructure. Due to restrictions on hardware resources and access policy, some data processing tasks allowed local execution whereas others need to be offloaded to the upper layer. Decisions on task offloading and local execution are crucial in real-time IIoT. An efficient strategy needs to be deployed in IIoT to carry out dynamic decisions on task offloading for execution and data offloading for storage.

5.12 Conclusion

Having a proper strategy to handle both operational and business data confers an efficient manufacturing process. A huge volume of data from IIoT devices has abundant information inside it. Taking up the right technology delivers valuable insights out of stored data. The convergence of IIoT and big data has paved industry 4.0 significantly. Big data in industry makes more sense and transforms the automation industry into the smart industry. Self-service systems in the manufacturing industry are potentially promoted by big data. IIoT and big data together turn industry smart from supplier to the customer level. A massive number of connected industrial devices help in monitoring, controlling, and analyzing various manufacturing processes. At the back, big data analytics performs data preprocessing, data management, storage, and analysis and creates report visualization. Authorities make decisions based on the facts delivered by big data analytics. Sometimes an intelligent system decides what to do and when to do with delivered facts of big data. Analytical techniques used in big data technology are capable of handling large amounts of standalone data as well as streaming data. So human intervention in the manufacturing process has been reduced to a great extent. Integration of IIoT and big data analytics achieves smart manufacturing and ensures sustainable, consistent, and scalable production in all industries.

References

1. Nursini, N. (2020). Micro, small, and medium enterprises (MSMEs) and poverty reduction: Empirical evidence from Indonesia. *Development Studies Research, 7*(1), 153–166.
2. Boyes, H., Hallaq, B., Cunningham, J., & Watson, T. (2018). The industrial internet of things (IIoT): An analysis framework. *Computers in Industry, 101*, 1–12.
3. Georgios, L., Kerstin, S., & Theofylaktos, A. (2019). Internet of things in the context of industry 4.0: an overview. *International Journal of Entrepreneurial Knowledge, 7*(1), 4–19.
4. Kim, B. H., Ahn, H. J., Kim, J. O., Yoo, M., Cho, K., & Choi, D. (2010, November). Application of M2M technology to manufacturing systems. In *2010 International Conference on Information and Communication Technology Convergence (ICTC)* (pp. 519–520). IEEE.
5. Qu, Y. J., Ming, X. G., Liu, Z. W., Zhang, X. Y., & Hou, Z. T. (2019). Smart manufacturing systems: State of the art and future trends. *The International Journal of Advanced Manufacturing Technology, 103*(9), 3751–3768.
6. Yang, H., Kumara, S., Bukkapatnam, S. T., & Tsung, F. (2019). The internet of things for smart manufacturing: A review. *IISE Transactions, 51*(11), 1190–1216.
7. Moyne, J., & Iskandar, J. (2017). Big data analytics for smart manufacturing: Case studies in semiconductor manufacturing. *Processes, 5*(3), 39.
8. Gai, K., & Qiu, M. (2018). Optimal resource allocation using reinforcement learning for IoT content-centric services. *Applied Soft Computing, 70*, 12–21.
9. Ahmed, E., Yaqoob, I., Hashem, I. A. T., Khan, I., Ahmed, A. I. A., Imran, M., & Vasilakos, A. V. (2017). The role of big data analytics in internet of things. *Computer Networks, 129*, 459–471.
10. ur Rehman, M. H., Ahmed, E., Yaqoob, I., Hashem, I. A. T., Imran, M., & Ahmad, S. (2018). Big data analytics in industrial IoT using a concentric computing model. *IEEE Communications Magazine, 56*(2), 37–43.
11. Xu, X., Han, M., Nagarajan, S. M., & Anandhan, P. (2020). Industrial internet of things for smart manufacturing applications using hierarchical trustful resource assignment. *Computer Communications, 160*, 423–430.
12. Tao, F., Qi, Q., Liu, A., & Kusiak, A. (2018). Data-driven smart manufacturing. *Journal of Manufacturing Systems, 48*, 157–169.
13. Cheng, J., Chen, W., Tao, F., & Lin, C. L. (2018). Industrial IoT in 5G environment towards smart manufacturing. *Journal of Industrial Information Integration, 10*, 10–19.
14. Ghobakhloo, M., & Ching, N. T. (2019). Adoption of digital technologies of smart manufacturing in SMEs. *Journal of Industrial Information Integration, 16*, 100107.
15. Liao, X., Faisal, M., QingChang, Q., & Ali, A. (2020). Evaluating the role of big data in IIOT-industrial internet of things for executing ranks using the analytic network process approach. *Scientific Programming.*
16. Ohlhorst, F. J. (2012). *Big Data Analytics: Turning Big Data into Big Money* (Vol. 65). John Wiley & Sons.

17. Yao, X., Zhou, J., Zhang, J., & Boër, C. R. (2017, September). From intelligent manufacturing to smart manufacturing for industry 4.0 driven by next generation artificial intelligence and further on. In *2017 5th International Conference on Enterprise Systems (ES)* (pp. 311–318). IEEE.
18. Evjemo, L. D., Gjerstad, T., Grøtli, E. I., & Sziebig, G. (2020). Trends in smart manufacturing: Role of humans and industrial robots in smart factories. *Current Robotics Reports,* *1*(2), 35–41.
19. Yan, H., Hua, Q., Wang, Y., Wei, W., & Imran, M. (2017). Cloud robotics in smart manufacturing environments: Challenges and countermeasures. *Computers & Electrical Engineering,* *63*, 56–65.

6

Multimodal Architecture for Emotion Prediction in Videos Using Ensemble Learning

Santhi Venkatraman and Puja Saha

Department of CSE, PSG College of Technology, Anna University, Coimbatore, Tamil Nadu, India

CONTENTS

6.1 Introduction

For many smart industry applications, automated methods of understanding the emotions in various web videos created by users are helpful. A smart industry, for example, can use the emotions in clips about a new technological device to enhance the product

DOI: 10.1201/9781003202776-6

and undertake targeted sales. Emotion detection software is being used in the smart automobile industry to increase vehicle safety depending on driver emotions. Specifically, emotion detection software will aid in the production of new goods, the reduction of potentially hazardous situations on the manufacturing floor, and the promotion of technical innovation in design jobs for smart industries. Governments also use this feature to better analyze how people react to recent events or new legislation, as well as video surveillance, automation, and other technologies. The current emotion reaction systems [1] are incompatible with customer and company requirements. This progress gap is very noteworthy once the pleasant quality leaps recorded for the emotion recognition task are taken into account. Current emotion recognition systems have either been based on rules or have been specifically programmed. Deep learning is based on extracting and modeling hierarchical data representations in order to improve prediction accuracy.

To the extent, no work has been performed on this issue in conjunction with user-generated movies and audios, which have more diverse content and no quality control and post-editing. Ensemble learning was created to incorporate relevant information about emotions in individual frames over a variable length sequence with voice input to give a useful prediction. We propose a hybrid CNN-SVM-MLP architecture to predict the emotion in video and audio. As a result, the problem of predicting instantaneous emotion reactions from videos and audios is addressed.

6.2 Related Work

The establishment of the International Affective Picture System (IAPS) [2] standard in 2008 sparked a lot of interest in computer inference of emotions in images [3]. For emotion prediction, Machajdik and Hanbury used more prominent processes influenced by psychology and art theory [4], extracting color, texture, composition, and faces. Lu et al. looked at the link between form attributes and visual emotions in more depth [5]. The authors proposed a method for calculating features that can be used to simulate a variety of shape qualities such as roundness and angularity. It is also worth noting that several ways to modeling the aesthetics and meaningfulness characteristics of images or videos have been offered [6].

Existing research on identification of video emotions focused mainly on the movie domain. Kan et al. explored using a Hidden Markov Model to analyze movies based on low-level properties like color and motion [7]. Rasheed and Sheikh [8] employed an average shift-based classification framework to discover a link between a variety of visual characteristics and six different movie genres. Combining numerous visual aspects is effective in these works, according to a similar view. Jiang et al. focused on user-generated videos [1], these differ from movies in several ways. First, user-produced videos are typically short (e.g., just few minutes), resulting in a singular emotion in each video. In contrast, in movies, where multiple emotions coexist and expression detection must be done section by segment. Second, assessing the videos is more challenging due to the wide variety of content and the lack of quality control. Unlike movies, they are frequently created by novice users who do not adhere to the norms or styles of way to enhance.

Limitation of the above-mentioned model [1] is that the audio characteristics in the proposed approach are constrained, which yields to less accuracy (20%) and performance of the model. Using more significant ones will help you get better outcomes. To recognize emotions in video and voice, Nimish et al. [9] suggested an emotion response predicting system which uses a CNN and an SVM. The Hopfield RNN analyzes the gathered emotion and generates 4-bit digital encodings of emotion labels as a reaction to the previously identified emotion. Limitation of this model is that the prediction accuracy gained by SVM is less. Hence, multiple models can be built and performed analysis of those models. For increasing the accuracy and performance, we have implemented hybrid CNN-SVM-MLP architecture for real-time emotion prediction from both video and audio.

6.3 Dataset Acquisition

Emotion Reaction Prediction is a very difficult task. The lack of well-defined datasets with explicit annotations is a key concern. It has impeded the necessary evolution of emotion analysis in user-generated videos and audios. To stimulate research into this fascinating and significant problem, we used "FER2013" [10] and "JAFFE" [11] dataset for emotion prediction in videos and extracted audio signal from a benchmarked dataset "AAAI" [12] combined with "RAVADES" audio dataset [13] to predict emotion from the audio. The datasets used for emotion prediction from videos are true, authentic, and standard.

6.3.1 Dataset

The following are the datasets used for training and testing:

- FER2013 – The data consists of grayscale images of automatically captured faces at a level of 48 × 48 pixels. The goal should be to sort every face into each of seven categories depending on the emotion expressed throughout the expressions (0 = Angry, 1 = Disgust, 2 = Fear, 3 = Happiness, 4 = Depression, 5 = Surprise, 6 = Neutral). There are 28,709 entries in Train.csv, having two sections: "emotion" and "pixels." The "emotion" section provides a code number ranging from 0 to 6 that indicates the emotion present in the image. For each image, the "pixels" section comprises a string enclosed in quotes. In row major order, the string comprises pixel values separated by spaces. In test.csv, just the "pixels" section and 3589 rows are present. The goal is to anticipate the emotion section properly.
- JAFFE – The Japanese Female Facial Expression (JAFFE) Database is abbreviated as JAFFE. The database comprises 213 pictures of 10 Japanese female models posing for 7 face expressions (6 fundamental facial expressions + 1 neutral). Six emotion adjectives were assigned to each picture by 60 Japanese individuals.
- AAAI – AAAI is a video dataset, from where image frames and audio have been extracted.
- RAVADESS – Approximately 1500 audio files from 24 different performers are included in this collection. Twelve men and women performers record short audio clips representing the following emotions: 1 = neutral, 2 = calm, 3 = joyful, 4 = sad, 5 = angry, 6 = afraid, 7 = disgusted, and 8 = surprised. Every audio file has a seventh character that corresponds to the different emotions spoken.

6.3.2 Data Pre-Processing

The datasets must be pre-processed in order to fit the data for further classification. "FER2013" and "JAFFE" datasets are collected and combined together. The data is cleaned, filtered, resized, and normalized using "MINMAX NORMALIZER." The data is separated into training and testing datasets into 7:3 ratio. Now the pre-processed data is stored in numpy array. The audio dataset is extracted from the "AAAI" video dataset and short-term features are extracted from the audio dataset. The features are retrieved from the "RAVADES" audio dataset and the features extracted from both of the datasets are combined together. The data is separated into training and testing datasets into 8:2 ratio. Now the pre-processed audio data is stored in numpy array.

6.4 System Design

The proposed method explains the importance of predicting automatic emotion reactions from videos. The model defines a CNN architecture that predicts appropriate emotion responses by modeling the spatiotemporal and spectral aspects of emotions across a configurable length of time. Both of the models are going to predict emotion among the standard seven emotions such as Happy, Surprise, Sad, Anger, Disgust, Fear, and Neutral.

6.4.1 System Pipeline

The system pipeline is shown in Figure 6.1. Image frames and audio are extracted from input video. The frames are fed into convolution neural network (CNN). Audio sampling has been done with the extracted audio signal and the features are fed to Support Vector Machine (SVM) as well as Multi-Layer Perceptron (MLP). As SVM prediction accuracy is more than MLP, we have combined emotion output from CNN and SVM and the result has been given by Ensemble Learning Techniques.

6.4.2 Convolutional Neural Network

When evaluating images, convolutional neural network (CNN) is well-known to simulate how well the human mind operates. The usual architecture of a CNN normally includes an input layer, several convolutional layers, several dense layers, as well as an output layer. These are stacked layers that are organized in a linear fashion. The system is developed as Sequential () in Keras, as well as further layers are incorporated to form the architecture. Figure 6.2 shows CNN prediction.

6.4.2.1 Input Layer

Because the input layer's dimensions are set and fixed, the image should be processed before being fed into it. Face detection and cropping in the image are done using OpenCV [14], a computer vision library. The clipped face is then scaled to 192 by 192 pixels and turned to grayscale. When evaluated to the traditional RGB format of color dimensions, this step considerably decreases the dimensions (3, 192, 192). This process guarantees that all images can be transferred to the input nodes as a (1, 192, 192) numpy array.

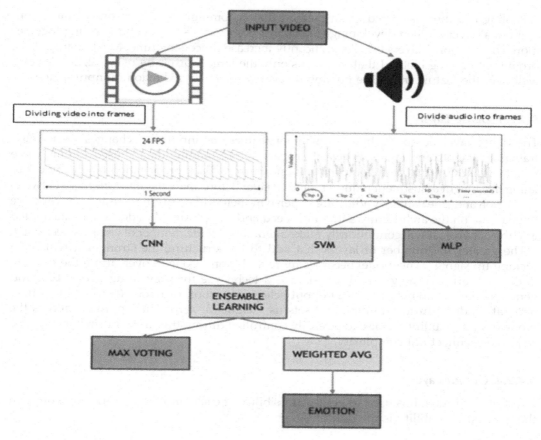

FIGURE 6.1
System pipeline.

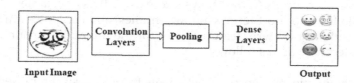

Input Image   **Output**

FIGURE 6.2
Convolutional neural network.

6.4.2.2 Convolutional Layer

The Convolution2D layer is handed the numpy array, and one of the hyper-parameters is the number of filters. The collection of filters is the one, with weights that are produced at random. Every filter (3, 3) or (5, 5) receptive field passes all over the source image having shared weights to create a feature map. Edge and pattern recognition, for example, are represented by feature maps, which show how pixel values are increased. A feature map is built by using filter 1 to the whole image. To produce a series of feature maps, various filters are applied one by one.

Pooling is a dimension reduction method that is commonly used on one or more convolutional layers. When developing CNNs, this is a crucial stage because adding together more convolutional layers could significantly increase processing time. MaxPooling2D is a prominent pooling method that maintains only the largest pixels by using (2, 2) windows well over the feature map. The pooling pixels result in a 4x reduction in input image.

6.4.2.3 Dense Layer

The dense layer accepts a huge number of features as input also changes them using trainable weights and layers. Forward propagation of training data is used to train these weights, followed by backward propagation of errors. Back propagation begins by calculating the weight adjustment required for each layer before analyzing the difference between prediction and true value. By adjusting hyper-parameters like learning rate and network size to take care on the architecture's training speed and complexity. As additional data are fed into the network, it will continuously make alterations till the number of errors is decreased.

The greater the number of layers that add to the structure, the stronger it will be in picking up signals. The model becomes more and more prone to over-fitting the training data, as smart as it may sound. Dropout is a technique for preventing over-fitting and generalizing on unknown data. Dropout selects a portion of nodes (typically less than 50%) at random during training and sets its weights at zero. This approach allows the model's susceptibility to noise to be easily controlled during training while preserving the required architectural complexity.

6.4.2.4 Output Layer

The softmax function is used to get the possibility of each emotion and the emotion with the greatest probability is the output.

6.4.3 Audio Feature Extraction

The tool pyAudioAnalysis is used to extract attributes from the audio. Short-term attribute extraction is used by pyAudioAnalysis to extract these attributes in two steps. It divides the audio file into short-term windows (frames) and computes attributes for each of them. As a result, a short-term feature vector for the full audio stream is formed. The attributes extracted here are as follows:

- MFCCs: Mel Frequency Cepstral Coefficients from a cepstral representation with non-linear frequency bands dispersed as per the mel-scale.
- Chroma vector: The bins represent the 12 Western-type pitch groups in this 12-element spectral energy representation (semitone spacing).
- Spectral contrast: Contrast of the normalized spectral energies for an audio frame.
- Mel-Spectrogram: Acoustic time-frequency representation of a sound.
- Tonnetz: Tonal centroid features for each audio frame.

6.4.4 Support Vector Machine

For classification and regression issues, the SVM is a supervised machine learning methodology. Each function's value is the value of a certain coordinate in this algorithm, and the data object is depicted as just a point within n-dimensional geometry (because n represents the total of features). Then we locate the hyper-plane that clearly separates two classes to complete classification. After the audio features are extracted, the whole dataset is divided into training and testing datasets. This model is trained using the training dataset, then tested using the testing dataset, with accuracy determined and compared to other created models.

6.4.5 Multi-Layer Perceptron

A feed-forward artificial neural network called Multi-Layer Perceptron (MLP) generates a collection of outputs from a number of inputs. Between both the input and output layers of an MLP, a directed graph is formed by many layers of input nodes. MLP uses back-propagation to train the network. The MLP model we created had two layers, softmax function at the output, drop-out of 40%, "relu" activation function at the input and the hidden layers, batch size of 64 and 1000 epochs. Thus, MLP model is built by training with the training dataset. The testing dataset is used to evaluate the model, and finally accuracy is calculated.

6.4.6 Ensemble Learning

Ensemble learning has the potential for improving a model's performance. It is the process of integrating a variety of separate models in order to improve the model's stability and prediction capacity. The models, which are used as inputs of ensemble methods, are called "base models."
There are two ensemble techniques used here:

Max Voting – For each test instance each model makes a decision (votes) and the final performance prediction is the one that receives most of the votes. In this method, the emotion with greater probability between audio and video outputs is selected as final output of the particular frame.

Weighted Averaging – Weighted average is a slightly modified version of simple average, in which the weight multiplies the estimate of each variable and then their average is determined. In this method, some weights are assigned to video and audio probabilities and weighted probability is calculated for each frame. The emotion with probability (video or audio) nearest to the weighted probability is taken as final output. In both the ensemble methods, accuracy is calculated.

6.5 System Implementation

The models described in the previous section are implemented as follows.

6.5.1 Emotion Prediction from Videos: CNN Model Training

The model is built with the following specifications.
Three types of convolutional layers are used.

- 2×32 filters – (5×5) relu max pooling layer – (2×2)
- 2×64 filters – (3×3) relu max pooling layer – (2×2)
- 3×128 filters – (3×3) relu max pooling layer – (2×2)

Three Flatten layers are used.

- Dense layer – 128 relu dropout (0.5)
- Dense layer – 64 relu dropout (0.5)
- Dense layer – 6 softmax

Categorical cross-entropy is utilized as loss function and Adam optimizer is employed to optimize the weights of the model. The model is then trained with the training dataset for 15 iterations. The model is stored in ".json" format and weights are stored in ".h5" format.

6.5.2 Emotion Prediction from Audio: SVM-MLP Training

Both SVM and MLP models are built by training with the training dataset. Simulation is performed to choose the best parameters for the neural network. Test runs are carried out, and the model with the highest accuracy is chosen for implementation. The following are the various parameters of the best model so far:

- Initial weights: Weights are initialized randomly
- Learning rate: 0.01
- Total layers: 2 + 1 input layer
- Input neurons: Number of features (4)
- Hidden Layer Neurons: 50
- Output neurons: 7 (Since there are total seven emotions)
- Limit of epochs: 1000
- Batch size: 64
- Activation function: input and hidden layers: ReLu
- Activation function: output layer: Softmax
- Categorical cross-entropy is utilized as loss function and Adam optimizer is employed to optimize the weights of the model.

SVM model is built using the following parameters:

- C – Regularization parameter
- Kernel function – It takes the input and transforms it into the required form. By default, SVC uses RBF kernel function.
- Gamma – Kernel co-efficient.

The model is stored as a ".json" file, while the weights are recorded as a ".h5" file.

6.5.3 Combining the Video and Audio Using Ensemble Learning

Input: A video (.mp4 file)
Output: Emotion in each second.

The steps involved here are as follows:

1. Audio is extracted from an input video using "ffmpeg" command and is saved as an audio in.wav format.

2. Image frames are extracted from the .mp4 file and audio frames are extracted from the .wav file in each second interval.

3. Faces are detected, cropped from each image frame, resized to (1, 192, 192) feature vector, and normalized.

4. The normalized feature vector is fed into built CNN model. Emotion is predicted and probability of that emotion is calculated in each second.

5. The audio features such as mel spectrogram, spectral contrast, MFCC, and tonnetz are extracted from the .wav file and saved as an audio feature vector.

6. The audio feature vector is fed in SVM model. Emotion is predicted and probability of that emotion is calculated in each second.

7. The predictions from both the video and audio models are compared and analysis has been performed.

8. The video and audio output is combined together using Max Voting and Weighted Averaging ensemble methods. In both ensemble methods, accuracy is calculated.

6.6 Result and Analysis

After building and training all the models, these models are evaluated using the test dataset.

6.6.1 Testing the CNN Model

The test data (20% of the whole video pre-processed dataset) are fed into the CNN model and accuracy is calculated using "RMSE." The accuracy found is 52.27%.

6.6.2 Testing the SVM and MLP Model

The test data (20% of "AAAI" and "RAVADESS" datasets) are fed into both SVM and MLP models and comparative analysis is carried out. SVM yields 50% accuracy and MLP yields 27% of accuracy. As SVM gives better accuracy than MLP, SVM is decided to be used in the ensemble technique.

6.6.3 Testing the Ensemble Model

The output emotions from video and audio frames of each second are predicted and compared with each other. Table 6.1 shows the comparison between audio and video frame probabilities. Two ensemble methods (Max Voting and Weighted Averaging) are used to combine the video and audio outputs and the accuracy of prediction is calculated for both of the methods. The Max Voting accuracy and Weighted Averaging accuracy are 79% and 82%, respectively. Tables 6.2 and 6.3 show Max Voting, Weighted Averaging output and accuracy, respectively.

TABLE 6.1

Comparison Between Audio and Video Frames Probability

Frame Number	Audio		Video	
	Emotion	Probability	Emotion	Probability
1	1	0.583847	−1	−1.000000
2	1	0.542842	2	0.791736
3	3	0.910647	2	0.994095
4	3	0.911516	−1	−1.000000
5	1	0.994455	0	0.426958
6	1	0.766339	−1	−1.000000
7	3	0.534193	−1	−1.000000
8	1	0.560153	0	0.296403
9	1	0.666164	−1	−1.000000
10	1	0.969070	2	0.741648
11	1	0.969780	−1	−1.000000
12	3	0.912335	0	0.379741
13	1	0.996322	2	0.743001
14	1	0.880168	−1	−1.000000
15	1	0.951605	−1	−1.000000
16	3	0.758294	2	0.837102
17	1	0.638027	−1	−1.000000
18	1	0.877427	0	0.615004
19	3	0.562782	2	0.721807
20	1	0.589261	0	0.385886

TABLE 6.2

Max Voting Emotion Output and Accuracy

Frame Number	Emotion	Probability
1	1	0.583847
2	2	0.791736
3	2	0.994095
4	3	0.911516
5	1	0.994455
	Max Voting accuracy: 79.52380952380952	

TABLE 6.3

Weighted Average Emotion Output and Accuracy

Frame Number	Emotion	Probability
1	1	0.108693
2	1	0.617510
3	3	0.935682
4	3	0.338062
5	1	0.824602
	Accuracy: 82.3809523809523	

6.7 Conclusion

Our method generates emotion reaction predictions focusing on the complete spatial-temporal and spectral aspects with emotion transition. We evaluated the CNN model for predicting emotion in the test video dataset and the accuracy found is 52%, which is better than the existing work. The multimodal comparative analysis has been done to predict the emotion in audio. The SVM and MLP yield 70.00% and 49.75% accuracy, respectively. Hence, SVM is decided to be used finally. Both the video output from CNN model and audio output from SVM model are ensembled together and the final output has increased the accuracy (82.38%). So, an ensemble method is thus used for improving the efficiency of both the CNN and SVM models.

The model can be enhanced by including attribute features like sentiment-level semantic meaning in each dimension, such as "birthday celebration" and "skiing." However, little effort has been made to comprehend the emotions sent by the videos, which are quite powerful. The audio characteristics in the proposed framework use more advanced features, which could improve the results greatly. For emotion reaction prediction, we can use a Hopfield RNN as fusion network to improve the accuracy. Emotional analysis in user-generated videos must be progressed as well-defined datasets including manual annotations. This information can provide a basis for the real-time adaption of the new methodology for the development of some applications in smart manufacturing industry, such as robotics behavior to optimize the patient's emotional experiences in medical treatments.

References

1. Yu-Gang Jiang, Baohan Xu and Xiangyang Xue (2014). Predicting emotions in user-generated videos. *Proceedings of the Twenty-Eighth AAAI Conference on Artificial Intelligence*, 73–79.
2. Zhicha Xu, Rongsheng Zhu, Chanchan Shen, Bingren Zhang, Qianqian Gao, You Xu and Wei Wang (2017). Selecting pure-emotion materials from the International Affective Picture System (IAPS). doi:10.1016/j.heliyon.2017.e00389.
3. Yoann Baveye, Jean-Noël Bettinelli, Emmanuel Dellandrea, Liming Chen and Christel Chamaret (2013). A large video data base for computational models of induced emotion. *Proceeding of Humaine Association Conference on Affective Computing and Intelligent Interaction*, 1–6.
4. Jana Machajdik and Allan Hanbury (2010). Affective image classification using features inspired by psychology and art theory. *Proceedings of the 18th ACM International Conference on Multimedia*, 83–92.
5. Xin Lu, Poonam Suryanarayan, Reginald B. Adams, Jr., Jia Li, Michelle G. Newman and James Z. Wang (2012). On shape and the computability of emotions. *Proceedings of the ACM International Conference on Multimedia*, 229–238.
6. Naila Murray, Luca Marchesotti and Florent Perronnin (2012). AVA: a large-scale database for aesthetic visual analysis. *IEEE Computer Society Conference on Computer Vision and Pattern Recognition*.
7. Wonjoon Kan, Dongkyoo Shine and Doingil Shin (2010). Prediction of state of user's behavior using Hidden Markov Model in ubiquitous home network. *IEEE International Conference on Industrial Engineering and Engineering Management*, 1752–1756.

8. Zeeshan Rasheed and Yaser Sheikh (2005). On the use of computable features for film classification. *IEEE Transactions on Circuits and Systems for Video Technology*, 15, 52–64.

9. Nimish Ronghe, Sayali Nakashe, Ashish Pawar and Sarika Bobde (2017). Emotion recognition and reaction prediction in videos. *Proceedings of the Third International Conference on Research in Computational Intelligence and Communication Networks (ICRCICN)*, 26–32.

10. FER2013 Dataset, https://www.kaggle.com/deadskull7/fer2013

11. JAFFE Dataset, http://www.kasrl.org/jaffe.html

12. AAAI Dataset, http://www.yugangjiang.info/research/VideoEmotions/index.html

13. RAVDESS Dataset, https://zenodo.org/record/1188976/XLIOszbRY.html

14. P. Van Gent (2016). Emotion recognition using facial landmarks python dlib and opencv, 2016, [online] Available: http://www.paulvangent.com/2016/08/05/emotion-recognition-using-facial-landmarks/

7

Deep PHM: IoT-Based Deep Learning Approach on Prediction of Prognostics and Health Management of an Aircraft Engine

R. Mohammed Harun Babu

iNurture Education Solutions, Bangalore, India

P. Sivaprakash

Rathinam College of Arts and Science, Bharathiyar University, Coimbatore, Tamil Nadu, India

K. Arun Kumar

Rathinam College of Arts and Science, Bharathiyar University, Coimbatore, Tamil Nadu, India

M. Shebana and S. Gnana Sowndharya

Rathinam College of Arts and Science, Bharathiyar University, Coimbatore, Tamil Nadu, India

CONTENTS

DOI: 10.1201/9781003202776-7

7.1 Introduction

The ability of an asset to function as planned is referred to as reliability performance standards in field use situations for a certain period of time. Customers are anticipating their goods to be trustworthy, and trustworthiness determines their readiness to manufacturers must strike a balance between client expectations and profitability, by planning for dependability and quality, as well as profit expectations goals. Operators of infrastructure (for example, roads and ports) and utilities (for example, water, power, and gas) that offer services to their communities must strike a balance between costs, risks, and asset performance [1]. In terms of direct expenses and reputational damage, asset reliability can have a significant impact on an organization's success. As a result, it's critical to be able to foresee an asset's dependability. Appropriate prognostics and systems health management (PHM) approaches are castoff to allow this organizational expertise [2]. According to PHM, the machine or engine's "health" may be determined as well as its reliability (and remaining useful performance during the asset's life) (or degeneration). As a result, it's critical to be able to foresee an asset's dependability. Appropriate prognostics and health management (PHM) approaches are castoff to allow this organizational expertise [2,3]. According to PHM, the machine or engine's reliability (and remaining useful performance during the asset's life) as well as the asset's "health" can be established (or degeneration). Technicians may take readings from a machine to analyze its functioning before discarding the data. Sensor data are wirelessly exchanged from "things," which can be systems, subsystems, or assets, to remote cloud servers, thanks to the Internet of Things (IoT). This method can be used to approximate any health-related data. It is available for health monitoring and prognostic reasons (for example, ambient factors, maintenance, and operating data) [4]. This data sharing across resources and platforms allows for the creation of a restructured picture as well as the ability to analyze and respond to new and previously unexpected threats. The term "Internet of Things" was coined in 1997 [5], so it isn't a completely new concept. The Internet of Things is "a network of products, each integrated with sensors, and connected to the Internet" (IoT). This network allows geographically distant people and assets to be linked together [6]. The Internet of Things is quickly expanding nowadays as a result of a mix of technical, cost, and standards-related advances [7–18]. As microelectronic-mechanical systems (MEMS) technology advances, sensors are becoming smaller and cheaper. For the first time in history, the number of linked devices (things) on the planet outweighed people in 2016. According to Gartner, Inc., 6.4 billion networked gadgets will be in use globally in 2016, up to 30% from 2015, and 20.8 billion in 2020. Every day in 2016, 5.5 million fresh things are expected to be coupled. Real-time data access is being improved by wireless technologies such as RFID tags and embedded sensors, as well as the proliferation of sensor nodes and addressing schemes that assign each "thing" a unique address. As more spectrum becomes accessible, the cost of connectivity decreases, and the ability to communicate with a wider range of sensors improves. Customer confidence in cloud computing and its utilization has grown as the cost of data storage has decreased, allowing for the storage of big datasets and offering a platform for data analytics and machine learning techniques used by prognostics and system wearable health models.

7.2 Overview of Prognostics and Health Management

Prognostics and Health Management (PHM) is a technique that has developed in popularity as a clever way for organizations to boost claim availability. Techniques such as health monitoring, feature extraction, fault diagnosis, and fault prognosis are used to guess the equipment's remaining useful life (RUL). It not only helps RUL prediction but also optimizes maintenance and logistic decisions by taking into account available resources, operating circumstances, and the economic ramifications of various defects. One of the ideal processes of a PHM is System Health Management, which can take periodic maintenance based on a sequence of outputs from diagnostics and prognostic work done on resources available and operational demand. The primary purpose of the PHM is to reduce the operational effect of equipment failure as well as the financial investments required to maintain the assets.

A high number of sensors are often used to monitor the condition and operation of complicated systems. We could detect changes in signals such as temperature, pressure, flow, vibration, pictures, and even video streams based on a continuous timeframe using these sensors. The measurement and transmission noise can impact the retrieved signals from many types of sensors. Because numerous sensors are monitoring the same system characteristic, the sensors are frequently discharged. Every signal generated by the sensors does not contain information on a single problem, but rather a collection of faults that are related to each other in a one-to-one relationship.

To detect faults or potential breakdowns, using raw condition sensor stations in machine learning algorithms is insufficient. As a result, to acquire a more meaningful representation of signals in the data, manual pre-processing will be required. The Feature Engineering process is required for effective PHM applications. Manually or automatically modifying uncooked data using statistical indicators or else other signal processing methodologies, such as time–frequency analysis, as well as procedures to reduce the data's dimensionality, if applicable, are all part of feature engineering (filter, wrapper, or embedded approaches).

Contacts created during the detection process are subjected to feature extraction. It is dependent on previous observations or understanding of the various types of signal deterioration and their effects.

If you choose too few or too many features, you risk missing alarms, especially for problem types you've never encountered before. In order to attain the greatest results, the number of false alarms must be reduced as this will have an undesirable impact on the developed model's credibility. In a supervised fault classification task, feature selection must help reduce the rate of false alarms (false positives) while boosting the rate of detection (true positives).

For the first time, condition indicators, which are similar to feature extraction, were also included. The status indicator is one of the most important aspects of conditioning tracking system data when the system degrades or operates in numerous operating modes. The system's behavior changes would be predictable as it deteriorated or operated in different operational modes. As a result, the condition indicator is a criterion for distinguishing between normal and abnormal system conditions. It can also be used to calculate how long something has left in its useful life (RUL). When many condition indicators are utilized for a single system, monitoring its health becomes more appealing by merging those multiple impairments into a single health indicator, a rate that communicates with component's health state to end user. The required properties of monotonicity, resilience, and flexibility must be followed by the health indicators. Recently, a method for knowledge the healthy system state and by means of the distance measure to apply the educated healthy condition as a boundless health indicator was developed.

Due to the existence of various problem types, employing the feature engineering approach to show distinctions between all conceivable fault types is difficult. As a result, handcrafted features aren't always necessary providing the ability to generalize and transfer from one system to another, as well as for additional fault kinds. Due to the expert-driven manual technique, they may have restricted scalability. The capacity of the domain specialists doing the task to do feature engineering is greatly contingent on their knowledge and skills. The quality of extracted features has a significant impact on the effectiveness of machine learning algorithms that employ them. The effort of feature extraction for diagnostics engineers grows as the number of observed parameters grows, forcing the automation of these techniques or the entire elimination of feature engineering. From start to finish, deep learning (DL) can include feature engineering, or at the smallest parts of it, into the knowledge process. Fault detection and diagnosis has been recently regarded as significant approaches by DL principles. DL has struggled to navigate the prognostics technique since then. Prognostics is a discipline of engineering concerned with predicting when a system or component may cease to function as intended. This loss of performance is typically caused by a failure beyond which the system can no longer be used to achieve the planned goals.

The estimated duration is then converted to the remaining usefullife (RUL), an important notion in contingency planning.

In order to anticipate future performance of a component, prognostics examines the degree of a system's divergence or degradation from its predicted normal operating conditions. Model-based approaches employ multi-physics models to mimic asset normal operation and physical degradation laws, data-driven approaches rely on state monitoring data. "Hybrid methods" are approaches that combine these three methodologies.

Although any combination of data-driven strategies and physics-based procedures is feasible, "hybrid techniques" refers to methods that combine the two. By means of DL approaches in PHM, we can solve complex PHM problems that traditional approaches are unable to solve, as well as improve the presentation of traditional approaches by powering the growth of applied models and building their use more healthy and actual cost in industrial contexts (PHM). The presentation of DL in PHM is now being determined by discoveries in other DL application fields, known as computer vision and natural language processing (NLP). Although the transfer of current improvements in DL to industrial applications has been restricted, DL applications in PHM are rapidly mirroring recent advances in DL.

7.3 Steps Involved in PHM

7.3.1 Data Acquisition

This process of gathering and storing data since a physical component or system that is being monitored for diagnostic and prognostic reasons is defined as the first and most critical phase in PHM. Data will be collected in two ways: sensory data and event data (ED). Physical component care and repair activities, as well as care technician tasks known as corrective maintenance, assert maintenance, installation, breakdown, scrubbing, and oiling, are all covered by ED. Sensory data consists of acoustic emission data, vibration data, temperature, pressure, humidity, resistance, voltage, and other sensory data.

7.3.2 Data Pre-processing

Data purification and data analysis are the two processes of data pre-processing. Cleaning mistakes or noise from uncooked data improves likelihood of acquiring error-free data for later investigation. Feature extraction, feature evaluation, and feature selection are all part of the data analyzing step. Sensory time series data should be cleaned before feature extraction, which is useful for extracting critical features that represent the health state of the system being monitored on its own. These retrieved features should be able to predict how frequently the system would fail. There are three types of feature extraction methodologies: time-based, frequency-based, and time-frequency-based approaches. Time-domain-based feature extraction techniques are used to assess data's global features (e.g., root mean square, kurtosis, and so on).

Frequency domain-based feature extraction methods convert data into the frequency domain and castoff to determine and diagnose faults that are missed by time domain-based procedures. In both time and frequency domains, time-frequency domain techniques are utilized to study the data feature evaluation and selection technique follows data extraction as the next crucial stage in data analysis. A feature assessment is a way for determining the quality of a feature in feature selection. Many approaches, such as monotonicity, organizability, and transability, castoff to evaluate feature goodness. Following examination, the best features with a clear deprivation trend are further picked using a feature selection technique.

7.3.3 Detection

Many factors lead to system components degrading and losing their initial performance over time, all of which must be considered when developing detection models. The technique of sensing and recognizing emerging failures and/or anomalies using CM data is known as health state detection. Quantifying discrepancies between the actual and projected behavior of a system under minimal conditions is a common way to find faults.

7.3.4 Diagnostics

Diagnostics is a crucial data analysis phase in condition monitoring that comprises operations such as fault detection (determining which component in the system has failed), failure mode identification (determining the reason of that failure), and degradation level evaluation (i.e. determining the severity of the failure). Diagnostics are essential for successful prognostics since the uncertainty of the assessed system status influences every future prediction. Both reactive and proactive decision-making can benefit from diagnostic data.

7.3.5 Prognostics

Prognostics is the practice of evaluating how long a product will be used once it has deviated or degraded from its predicted state of health under its expected usage settings (RUL).

Diagnostics is focused with isolating and classifying issues, whereas prognostics is concerned with preventing system failures by anticipating future states. The study of failure processes, the early identification of wear and ageing, and the determination of fault conditions are all part of prognostics.

7.3.6 Decision-Making

Making a decision is a procedure that leads to the assortment of the most logical and/or appropriate care action from a set of options. Based on the diagnostics or prognostics results, the maintenance technician must weigh the advantages and disadvantages of each activity. In order to make informed selections, the technician must be able to predict the outcomes of each option. Making decisions may be found in decisions that can have operational or design-based outcomes. Maintenance, hardware/software reconfigurations, and fault tolerance control are examples of operational decisions (FTC). Adding and/or replacing sensors, as well as changing and/or positioning components, are examples of design-based outcomes.

7.3.7 Human-Machine Interface

The Graphical User Interface stands for a human machine edge for envisaging component health, performing tasks, analyzing data, and controlling maintenance activities. This chapter can teach us about the steps involved in PHM. In the following research, the importance and application of PHM in the aerospace industry is studied.

7.4 PHM in Aerospace Industry

PHM systems are widely used in the aerospace sector, where they first appeared. For aviation engines, PHM can offer early caution of failure and guess the outstanding usable life. Modeling the complex deterioration process is difficult, but because aircraft engine systems are multifaceted, with both insubstantial and unknown components, we can utilize the prognostic technique to address this important and difficult problem. The industry must ensure that its asset utilization is optimal, and as a result, the present aircraft maintenance management system must be exact in order to ensure that the aircraft spend the maximum amount of time in the fleet, making the best use of its machinery. This is because maintenance is prohibitively expensive, owing to the high cost of individual components and spare parts. As a result, one wishes to maximize the usage and exploit the remaining life of the installed parts by maintaining and repairing them until their life limit is reached and they need to be replaced. PHM's job is to make sure that this happens and that no parts are replaced prematurely. Thus, by monitoring equipment failures, adequate lead time may be provided for the appropriate personnel, equipment, and replacement parts to be planned and deployed, reducing both equipment downtime and repair costs while also optimizing maintenance. Furthermore, because current PHM systems are application or equipment specific, a systematic strategy for building and deploying one has yet to be devised. This integrated health management system assesses the aircraft's safety and enables for state management and component maintenance assurance.

7.4.1 Sensors Used in the Gas Turbofan Engine

A propulsion system generates thrust to propel an aeroplane through the air. Most modern aircraft employ turbofan engines because of their high thrust and fuel efficiency. The thrust of a turbofan engine, also known as a fanjet or bypass engine, is generated by combining jet core efflux with bypass air enhanced by a ducted fan determined by the jet core. This research focuses on the sensors that are used to monitor the operation of components of the turbofan engine in aircraft. It is the aircraft's most expensive asset and the heart of the plane. The sensors based on the parameters are described further down.

7.4.1.1 Temperature Sensors

Thermometric Oil Temperature Sensor (OTS) measures and displays the temperature of the engine oil in a vehicle. The engine of a car might be damaged if it runs at too high temperature. The OTS prevents this by allowing the driver to come to a complete stop and turn off the engine if the oil temperature rises too high due to an overheated engine.

7.4.1.2 Total Air Gas Temperature Sensor

A thermistor is used as an air temperature sensor, which means it responds to temperature changes by changing electrical resistance. It functions similarly to a coolant sensor. The PCM applies a reference voltage to the sensor and then computes air temperature using the voltage signal. As the air temperature fluctuates, the return voltage signal will alter as well. Automatic climate control systems also use air temperature sensors.

The temperature of the air inside the passenger compartment, as well as the temperature of the outside air, is measured using one or more air temperature sensors. The temperature control system is not impacted by engine heat because it is generally located outside the engine compartment. The outside air temperature sensor is normally located behind the grille or around the base of the windshield in the cowl region. A sensor and an indicator with a resistance balancing circuit are included in simple TAT systems.

The airflow across the sensor is designed to contact a platinum alloy resistance element with the exact temperature. The sensor is designed to catch temperature differences by altering the element's resistance. When utilized in a bridge circuit, the indicator pointer moves in response to the variable resistor's imbalance.

7.4.1.3 Exhaust Gas Temperature Sensor

The temperature of the exhaust gas is restrained by the use gas temperature sensor. The engine control unit, or ECU, receives this information and performs the required action. In Turbofan engines, its primary function is to shield key components from the higher temperatures associated with smaller engines. If the ECU detects high temperatures, it will lower them, for example, by lowering turbocharger boost pressure or increasing the amount of gasoline delivered into the catalytic converter.

7.4.1.4 Vibration Sensors

Engine vibration is one of the most critical issues in ensuring flight safety for airplanes. High Cycle Fatigue, which is produced by alternating stress induced by excessive vibration or resonance, accelerates part degradation, leads to structural failure, and ultimately reduces engine life. A vibration sensor is also identified as a piezoelectric sensor. These sensors are multifunctional devices that can track a variety of operations.

By switching to an electrical charge, this sensor uses piezoelectric phenomena to measure changes in acceleration, pressure, temperature, force, and strain. The signal from accelerometers installed on or in the engines is acquired and processed by engine vibration monitoring (EVM) units. The use of rotational speed inputs and tracking filters allows the vibration spectrum to be focused on specific frequencies. Transducers on the engines produce hundreds of separate vibration signals, which must all be monitored to guarantee they are not changing.

Alarm levels are utilized to help analysts identify potential issue areas, and these alarms must be set every time the engine is fixed. These sensors are used to monitor core vibrations, fan vibrations, and other system vibrations.

7.4.1.5 Speed Sensors

An important component of the engine control system that allows planes to take off and land on a daily basis. The speed, direction, and position of the rotating engine shaft are all measured using speed sensors. A speed-changing mechanism is included in a gas turbofan engine. The speed-changing mechanism is mounted to a radially extending surface on a fan drive shaft. Next to the radially extending surface is a speed sensor. These sensors are used to monitor an aircraft engine's core speed (N1) and fan speed (N2) and (N3).

7.4.1.6 Fuel Sensors for Flow

Flow sensors are devices that monitor the pace or volume of a liquid or gas as it moves (22). New materials have been added to flow sensors to improve their performance. A calibrated platinum resistance sensor was inserted into the turbofan engine flow meter's body to assure accurate temperature measurement. A flow meter (sometimes called a flow sensor) is a device that measures the lined, nonlinear, build, volumetric flow rate of liquids or gases. A simple multiplication of the fuel to air ratio yields the fuel mass flow rate. Conditions in the nozzle usually determine the engine air flow rate. The value of the fuel-to-air ratio can be used to calculate the engine's particular fuel consumption.

7.4.1.7 Altimeter Sensors

The altimeter is a device that measures an aircraft's height above a fixed level. The sensor detects this by reading the static port's ambient air pressure. The air is pumped into the altimeter's back casing through the back of the panel. An aneroid, or bellows, is a sealed disc inside the altimeter. Based on these reference assessments, a thorough description of the implementation and application of PHM in the aerospace sector has been established.

7.5 Dataset Description

The National Aeronautics and Space Administration [19–26] provided the Turbofan Engine Degradation Simulation Data Set for this effort.

The dataset was stimulated by means of the Commercial Modular Aero Propulsion System Simulation (C-MAPSS) technique toward detecting engine damage. Four different sets of operational conditions and fault modes were simulated using four different techniques. To characterize fault progression, record a large number of sensor channels. The purpose of this dataset is to figure out how long each engine in the test dataset has left to live. After the last data point in the test dataset, RUL equals the number of flights left for the engine.

The dataset, which is based on a multivariate time series, is separated into exercise and testing subsets. The data can be assumed to be from a fleet of comparable engines because each time series is from a separate engine. Each engine has various degrees of initial wear and industrial change, which the user is ignorant of. This wear and variation are normal and do not indicate a defect. The engine's routine is influenced by three operational situations. The data also include this information. The data have been corrupted by sensor noise. Each time series begins with the engine functioning normally, but at some point, during the series, it develops a malfunction. In the exercise set, error changes in size until the system flops. Before the system breaks, the time sequence in the test set reaches a conclusion. The competition's purpose is to estimate how many operational cycles remain in the test set before it fails, or how many operational cycles the engine will run after the previous cycle. For the test data, a vector of genuine RUL values was also supplied. The data are organized into 26 integer columns separated by spaces in a text file. Each column takes a unique variable, and each existing system a snapshot of data gathered during a single operational cycle. The following topics are covered in the columns: (1) number of units; (2) the passage of time can be broken down into cycles; (3) operational setting-1; (4) operational setting-2; (5) operational setting-3; (6) sensor measurement-1.

Displayed below, the dataset has been divided into four categories based on simulations of various turbofan engines throughout time.

TABLE 7.1

Simulations of Various Turbofan Engines Throughout Time

Dataset	Operating Conditions	Fault Modes	Train Size (No. of Engine)	Test Size (No. of Engine)
ED001	1	1	100	100
ED002	6	1	260	259
ED003	1	2	100	100
ED004	6	2	248	249

In this work, we used the ED004 dataset for analysis, which contains six operating condition engines with two fault modes: HPC deterioration and Fan degradation. There are 248 total training trajectories and 249 total testing trajectories.

7.5.1 Long Short-Term Memory

LSTMs were intended to solve the problem of vanishing gradients, which regular RNNs have difficulties with. The architecture of an LSTM is identical to that of an RNN, with the distinction that recurrent cells are replaced by LSTM cells, which are designed to store knowledge for long periods of time. This LSTM cell recurs previous output, just like conventional RNN cells, but it additionally keeps track of an internal cell state Ct, which is a vector that serves as long-term memory. As a result, the LSTMs can access both short- and long-term memory. The cell's condition can be compared to that of a conveyor belt that transports data down the line for further calculations. Gates carefully change the contents of this cell state vector within the LSTM cell, yet vital information and gradients pass unhindered. The LSTM cell's major goal is to keep long-term memory (cell state) updates under control so that data and gradients (for training) can flow freely between rounds. Take, for example, an LSTM tasked with predicting the next scene in a film starring Sam and Jeni. The main goal would be to preserve any Jeni-related content in the movie sequences that do not feature Sam. We were able to show a half-hour of sequences without interfering with Jeni's cell state weights using Sam, saving both time and data. The three gates are used by the LSTM to manage the cell state correctly.

The forget gate prevents earlier knowledge from being forgotten. When a scenario is over, we want to forget about the scene's complexities and concentrate on Sam and Jeni.

The input gate is in charge of determining the relevance and saving of new information. The input gate "writes" the key information about the scene to memory when a new scene is given.

Output gate combines long- and short-term data to create a more precise forecast of the next hidden unit/output.

To fully know how LSTMs work, we must first comprehend the components of the LSTM cell. The cell's internal gates are forget gate, input gate, and the output gate. The internal cell state Cs and the hidden state Hs are controlled by these gates. Four separate matrices, Wm [k, k + 1], and four different biases, bj[k, 1], are used to multiply and add the input vector, Xs [1 − 1], and the prior hidden state, Hs − 1[k, 1].

The outputs of these gates are then used to compute the new hidden state hs[k, 1] and the cell state is updated to Cs[k − 1]. The matrices' dimensions, provided by the expression within the parenthesis, are [k, 1] and [k, k + 1]. Both the "cross-sign" and the "plus-sign" modifications in the gates are unit vectors.

Inside the cell, a one-layer neural network is represented by the four permutations of a matrix W, a bias b, and an activation function (sigmoid or tanh). Each of these extra neural networks is defined as a functional unit using the generic formula.

Forget about the gate: The forget about the gate determines which materials and how much memory should be erased from the cell state. As indicated in Equation 7.3 and the knowledge in the cell state Cs − 1 is modified by multiplying the forget gate's output fs2 elementwise. The forget gate's Gaussian neural network ensures that the control output of the gate is always between 1 and 0 (stay) (erase).

The forget gate is indicated by the prefix "f" on the vector and the skew in Equation 7.1.

$$fs = \sigma(Wf. \, [hs − 1, \, Xs] + bf) \, Cf = Cs − 1 \times fs \qquad (7.1)$$

Input gate: The input gate is the following crucial gate. This gate is made up of two different parts that work together. The first functional unit uses a tanh activation to identify the change in cell state Cs, which produces values ranging from −1 to 1. The input gate combines the results of these two processing units together once they've been integrated.

The cell state is modified as a result of equation 7.3 and the cell state Cs is modified.

$$Cs = \tanh(Wc \cdot [hs − 1, \, xs] + bc) \, ks = \sigma(Wk \cdot [hs − i, \, xs] + bk) \qquad (7.2)$$

$$Cs = Cf + Cs * KS \tag{7.3}$$

Output gate: The output gate collects crucial data about the current input and prior output using a taught vector Wout with bias bout, as shown in Equation 7.3. To forecast the next production, ht, Equation 7.4, this knowledge is paired with the freshly updated cell state ct. This is a recursive output, which means it can be used again in the next iteration. If there are multiple layers, this output is also utilized as an input in the next layer; if there aren't, this result is used as the forecast.

$$outs = \sigma(Wout\,[hs-1,\ xs] + out)\,hs = outs * \tanh(Cs) \tag{7.4}$$

7.5.2 Experimental Analysis on C-MAPPS

7.5.2.1 Performance Metric Selection

For the ED004 dataset, temporal input data from 21 sensor values is used throughout the studies. It states explicitly that sensor data produce consistent readings and have low predictive power RUL values. The data are then scaled with RUL values that are respected to normalize it. Using each feature one at a time till it reaches the (0–1) range, the min-max normalization strategy is used to standardize data.

$$x_{i,j}t = x_{i,j}t - \min(x\,j)\max(x\,j) - \min(x\,j) \tag{7.5}$$

The unique ith data point of the jth input article at time t is noticeable by x_{ij}, t and the vector of all inputs of the jth feature is indicated by x_j.

RUL goals are only accessible in the final time stage's test datasets aimed at a piece engine. When the engines are running regularly, the RUL can be assumed to have a constant value (Heimes, 2008). Like Listou Ellefsen et al. (2019) and Lei et al. (2019), recommend using a piece-wise linear deprivation model to determine the correct RUL values in the exercise datasets. Expect RUL targets to fall linearly as the number of experimental cycles rises following a period of stable RUL levels. We propose utilizing a piece-wise linear deterioration model to calculate the right RUL values in the training datasets, similar to Listou Ellefsen et al. (2019) and Lei et al. (2019). After a dated of constant RUL levels, predict RUL targets to drop linearly as the number of experimental cycles grows.

We utilize two metrics to assess the performance of the suggested target datasets strategy, which are related to previous prognostic studies that employed the similar datasets. We advocate using the Root Mean Squared Error because it is strongly related to data quality (RMSE).

$s = (P_n\,i = 1\,e\,c_i\,a_{11}$, if $c_i\,0\,Pn\,i = 1\,e\,c_i\,a_{21}$, if $c_i\,0$ where $a_1 = 13$ and $a_2 = 10$ and $c_i = RUL$ iRUL$_i$ where $a_1 = 13$ and $a_2 = 10$ and $c_i = RUL$ iRULi, where $a_1 = 13$ and $a_2 = 10$ (Saxena et al., 2008). The discrepancy between expected and observed RUL values is denoted by ci. Because positive errors have an influence on RUL prognostics tasks, they are penalized more than negative ones.

7.5.2.2 Result Analysis

Deep layer algorithms used include Bi-gram, LSTM, CNN, GRU, and a hybrid network CNN-LSTM. The constant network parameter is set at 0.1 for learning rate, 32 for batch size, and 0.2 for dropout to test the performance of all algorithms. In recurrent algorithms, RNN, LSTM, GRU, and Bigram approaches are used, and SoftMax is used as an activation function with embedding vector. The length is set to 128 in LSTM and GRU memory cells, while the maximum feature is set to 40. A 1D convolution architecture with 64 filters of length 3 is employed for analysis. In a hybrid neural network, the weight produced from the fully connected last layer is fed into the LSTM layer as an input. According to the results of trial 1 testing, all networks have a greater root mean square error (RMSE) rate, with bigram not performing well compared to other algorithms and LSTM outperforming with an RMSE of 28.043, displayed below.

TABLE 7.2

Comparison with Other Algorithms

Method	RMSE
Bigram	42.01
CNN	32.12
LSTM	28.043
CNN-LSTM	36.127
Bi-LSTM	39.231

Based on LSTM performance in trial 1, hyper-parameter tuning is employed using numerous tuning parameters in the LSTM architecture. The length of the trail 2 embedding vector is kept constant at 50, and various LSTM memory sizes, such as 256, 128, 64, and 32, are used to identify the true parameter for study. It is claimed unequivocally that as the number of input neurons decreases, accuracy improves. As a result, input neurons with 64 and 32 have RMSE values of 23.051 and 21.127, respectively, whereas other parameters such as 256, 128, and 64 do not perform as well. From the network, it is clear that as the quantity of neurons in the network grows, here is a substantial amount of overfitting, resulting in increasing error values displayed below.

TABLE 7.3

Compare the Results

Method	Embedding	LSTM	RMSE
LSTM	50	256	31.231
LSTM	50	128	27.031
LSTM	50	64	23.051
LSTM	50	32	21.127

In the literature piece, we describe and compare the results obtained with the suggested architecture to those obtained with alternative techniques.

The RMSE and scoring mechanism are castoff to demonstrate the routine of our architecture. We also show the attention activations at each time step so that time-related features employed in RUL prediction may be seen.

7.6 Conclusion

This paper provides a clear overview of PHM, including the steps involved in acquiring data for PHM analysis using IoT, as well as a clear overview of Predictive Maintenance (PdM) techniques used in industries to find failure analysis using various DL methods. The C-MAPPS datasets are used to evaluate hyper-tuned LSTM architecture parameters aimed at RUL prediction of turbofan deprivation engines. We demonstrated a well-tailored architecture with a technique for viewing RUL findings. When compared to other proposed approaches, our data imply that the proposed methodology is competitive in RUL predictions. The model outperforms additional DL methods that have been planned previously for similar data. The LSTM network focuses on distinct parts of the sequential input though producing a forecast based happening whichever phase of the deterioration cycle is analyzed, as indicated by our provided parameters. The outcomes of the LSTM hyper tuned appliance can be used to improve the interpretability of DL algorithms. The proposed method has the disadvantage of not providing temporal attention correlations for each input variable independently. This method could be used to detect damaged components visually before they fail. To validate the methodology for multiple use cases, additional empirical results from distinct PHM datasets are required.

References

1. K. C. Kapor and M. Pecht. 2014. *Reliability Engineering*, Wiley, Hoboken, NJ.
2. M. G. Pecht. 2008. *Electronics Prognostics and Health Management*, Wiley, Hoboken, NJ.
3. Standard ISO 55000. 2014. *Asset Management—Overview, Principles, and Terminology*.
4. L. Winig. 2016. GE's Big Bet on Data and Analytics. *Proceedings of the MIT Sloan Management Review*, 57, 1–16.
5. R. Minerva, A. Biru, and D. Rotondi. 2015. Towards a Definition of the Internet of Things (IoT) [Online]. http://iot.ieee.org/images/files/pdf/IEEE_IoT_Towards_Definition_Internet_of_Things_Revision1_27MAY15.pdf
6. IEEE. 2014. Special Report: The Internet of Things [Online]. http://theinstitute.ieee.org/static/special-report-the-internet-of-things
7. M. Alam, R. H. Nielsen, and N. R. Prasad. 2013. The Evolution of M2M into IoT. In *Proceedings of the First International Black Sea Conference on Communications and Networking (BlackSeaCom)*, pp. 112–115.
8. J. Gubbi, R. Buyya, S. Marusic, and M. Palaniswami. 2013. Internet of Things (IoT): A Vision, Architectural Elements, and Future Directions. *Future Generation Computer Systems*, 29, 1645–1660.
9. P. J. Werbos. 2005. Applications of Advances in Nonlinear Sensitivity Analysis. In *System Modeling and Optimization*, Springer, pp. 762–770. doi:10.1007/bfb0006203
10. Y. LeCun, B. Boser, J. S. Denker, D. Henderson, R. E. Howard, W. Hubbard, and L. D. Jackel. 1989. Backpropagation Applied to Handwritten Zip Code Recognition. *Neural Computation*, 1, 4, 541–551. doi:10.1162/neco.1989.1.4.541
11. Y. Li, T. R. Kurfess, and S. Y. Liang. 2000. Stochastic Prognostics for Rolling Element Bearings. *Mechanical Systems and Signal Processing*, 14, 5, 747–762. doi:10.1006/mssp.2000.1301
12. A. J. Robinson and F. Fallside. 1987. *The Utility Driven Dynamic Error Propagation Network*. University of Cambridge, Department of Engineering Cambridge.

13. P. J. Werbos. 1988. Generalization of Backpropagation with Application to a Recurrent Gas Market Model. *Neural Networks*, 1, 4, 339–356. doi:10.1016/0893-6080(88)90007-X

14. C. Scholar and P. Smolensky. 1986. Parallel Distributed Processing: Explorations in the Microstructure of Cognition. In *Information Processing in Dynamical Systems: Foundations of Harmony Theory*, Vol. 1(667), MIT Press, Cambridge, MA, pp. 194–281. https://pdfs.semanticscholar.org/3ceb/e856001031cfd22438b9f0c2cd6a29136b27.pdf?{_}ga=1.15022902.1038306691.1479690262

15. X. Li, Q. Ding, and J. Q. Sun. 2018. Remaining Useful Life Estimation in Prognostics Using Deep Convolution Neural Networks. *Reliability Engineering and System Safety*, 172, 1–11. doi:10.1016/j.ress.2017.11.021

16. L. Li, M. Liu, W. Shen, and G. Cheng. 2017. An Expert Knowledge-Based Dynamic Maintenance Task Assignment Model Using Discrete Stress-Strength Interference Theory. *Knowledge-Based Systems*, 131, 135–148. doi:10.1016/j.knosys.2017.06.008

17. C. Zhang, D. Song, Y. Chen, X. Feng, C. Lumezanu, W. Cheng, J. Ni, B. Zong, H. Chen, and N. V. Chawla. 2019. A Deep Neural Network for Unsupervised Anomaly Detection and Diagnosis in Multivariate Time Series Data. In *Proceedings of the AAAI Conference on Artificial Intelligence*, Vol. 33. 1409–1416. doi:10.1609/aaai.v33i01.33011409

18. P. Li, X. Jia, J. Feng, F. Zhu, M. Miller, L. Y. Chen, and J. Lee. 2020. A Novel Scalable Method for Machine Degradation Assessment Using Deep Convolutional Neural Network. *Measurement: Journal of the International Measurement Confederation*, 151, 107106. doi:10.1016/j.measurement.2019.107106

19. A. Saxena, K. Goebel, C. C. Larrosa, and F. K. Chang. 2015. CFRP Composites Dataset, NASA Ames Prognostics Data Repository.

20. L. Liao and F. Köttig. 2016. A Hybrid Framework Combining Data-Driven and Model-Based Methods for System Remaining Useful Life Prediction. *Applied Soft Computing Journal*, 44, 191–199. doi:10.1016/j.asoc.2016.03.013

21. H. Wang, M. J. Bah, and M. Hammad. 2019. Progress in Outlier Detection Techniques: A Survey. *IEEE Access*, 7, 107964–108000. doi:10.1109/ACCESS.2019.2932769

22. C. Colemen, S. Damodaran, M. Chandramoulin, and E. Deuel. 2017. *Making Maintenance Smarter*, Deloitte University Press, pp. 1–21.

23. Y. Lavi. 2018. The Rewards and Challenges of Predictive Maintenance. *InfoQ*. https://www.infoq.com/articles/predictive-maintenanceindustrial-iot/

24. J. Deutsch and D. He. 2017. Using Deep Learning-Based Approach to Predict Remaining Useful Life of Rotating Components. *IEEE Transactions on Systems, Man, and Cybernetics: Systems*, 48, 1, 11–20. doi:10.1109/TSMC.2017.2697842

25. Z. Zhang and P. Zhang. 2015. Seeing Around the Corner: An Analytic Approach for Predictive Maintenance Using Sensor Data. *Journal of Management Analytics*, 2, 4, 333–350. doi:10.1080/23270012.2015.1086704

26. F. Zhao, Z. Tian, and Y. Zeng. 2013. Uncertainty Quantification in Gear Remaining Useful Life Prediction Through an Integrated Prognostics Method. *IEEE Transactions on Reliability*, 62, 1, 146–159. doi:10.1109/TR.2013.2241216

8

A Comprehensive Study on Accelerating Smart Manufacturers Using Ubiquitous Robotic Technology

Divyansh Singhal and Roohi Sille

School of Computer Science, University of Petroleum & Energy Studies, Dehradun, Uttarakhand, India

CONTENTS

8.1 Introduction

As we are in the fourth revolution of the industry, we are now shaking hands with heavy machineries including robots [1–3]. Mechanical robots are presently not the prearranged robots setting independently doing their rehashing occupations. As the assembling undertakings become more individualized and more adaptable, it shows extraordinary possibility to foster keen assembling frameworks, where machines are not liable to be preconfigured by conventional showing techniques, however doing variable errands and adapting to a wide assortment of surprising normal and utilitarian alterations. According to the obligations and errands of the future assembling industry, the structure could effectively design the endeavors for these machines. The universal mechanical innovation is attained by implementing various errands using coordinated effort with various errands of circulated gadgets that is mostly applied in the assistance robot's space [4].

A reasonable pattern is arising in the field of independent advanced mechanics, toward the combination of advanced mechanics with surrounding knowledge and universal

DOI: 10.1201/9781003202776-8

figuring. This chapter presents an idea for ubiquitous modern mechanical technology just as future examination needs and how does the robotic technology will play its role in accomplishing it.

In a common ubiquitous automated framework, mechanical gadgets are formed into modules [5–7]. These modules are associated with an organization, empowering information sharing and usefulness calls. This modularized system, which brings easy alteration, extension, and cancellation, could likewise be applied to the keen assembling area. The need of recoding the robots for improving arranging module and assignment level learning such that different undertakings and powerful climate can be handled, which is still a major challenge in universal robotized systems [8,9]. This is essential for keen production lines, where there might be an assortment of orders and various circumstances for each request. For instance, in a future cell phone get-together processing plant, clients could make profoundly modified requests, like button shape, individualized shading, and cover material. Based on the different input requests, the assembling system is modified. Some factors such as preparing disappointments, individual obstructions, request changes, and different vulnerabilities still be considered. Subsequently, the assignment arranging module for enormous scope issues with vulnerability shows incredible significance.

Contrasted with the ubiquitous automated frameworks, task arranging in the modern area is considerably more testing because of its bigger arranging space. For instance, even in a little and medium industrial facility, there could be many hardware measures and the arranging space develops dramatically.

Subsequently, the huge assignment can be partitioned into an undertaking tree comprising little subtasks, which can be tackled all the more proficiently. To improve arranging productivity, a multi-leveled work arranging method is presented in this chapter. A review instance of the shrewd mechanical production system is carried out as a show stage for our strategies [1].

The NIST workshops characterize the Preliminary Smart Assembly guide [10] that defines the importance of the personality of an individual (engaged, a multi-restrained, learned individuals, profoundly gifted labor) working cooperatively with robotization in protected and shared climate for all assignments. The Manufuture Vital Exploration Plan 2006 [11] and the Innovation Stage on Advanced Mechanics, EUROP Key Exploration Plan 2006 [12] both distinguish versatile assembling as encompassing the fields of mechanization and mechanical technology, as well as robots as human collaborators, half-breed assembly, and administration robots. Versatile assembling incorporates new robotization arrangements through the reconciliation of new techniques for intellectual data preparing, signal handling, and creation control by fast data and correspondence frameworks. In cooperative human-focused computerization, the fundamental goal is to help human specialists with qualified apparatuses to build efficiency. The methodology joins human inventiveness, insight, information, adaptability, and abilities too as the upsides of modern specialized frameworks and devices, modern intellectual advanced mechanics, and productive utilization of ICT. One important issue is defining the degree of automation, which is discussed elsewhere [13,14].

This chapter presents an idea for pervasive modern advanced mechanics just as future exploration needs. The idea joins an independent brilliant robot, arranged creation hardware, sensor organizations, and human coordinated effort in the shrewd get-together space [14].

8.2 Related Works

Recent research on smart plants accelerates the implementation of embedding RFID into the production for acquiring additional data [15–17]. The production process is improved by managing data. It will attain more adaptability and knowledge by integrating the creation with all of the hardware processes. So unique mechanical gadgets could team up into various gatherings as indicated by various undertakings. The ubiquitous mechanical innovation is broadly concentrated in these years. Various structures have been proposed [18–20]. Recently, there has been a greater focus on task-level planning and learning improvements. Concentrated arranging and decentralized arranging are two types of project arranging techniques for multiagent frameworks. Decentralized planning approaches are mostly used to address challenges that are closely related, such as multi-UAV ecological observation [21] and helpful planning and limitation [22]. As the person hardware processes are exceptionally coupled in manufacturing assignments, we lean toward the unified arranging technique. The most usually utilized concentrated methods depend on mechanized arranging in man-made brainpower. Ha et al. utilized SHOP2 organizer to break down administrations dependent on semantic information [18]. Answer set programming was first introduced to housekeeping advanced mechanics by Erdem et al. [23]. Niemueller et al. moved toward the assignment arranging issue by conveying a standard motor [24]. These arranging techniques can't manage dynamic circumstances with vulnerabilities just like the case in reality. As a result, some analysts have used algorithms to solve task-planning problems. Barbosa et al. researched on visualizing the errands using Partially Observable Markov Decision Processes (POMDP) [25]. Cirillo et al. implemented an RTL design for deterministic spaces [26]. Nondeterministic difficulties can be dealt with using high cost stochastic model-based approaches such as the POMDP model and Markov Decision Interaction (MDP) model. The state guess and varied levels arranging are the two types of MDP arranging approaches for large challenges that have been investigated. The previous has significant trouble in applying to broadly useful organizer talked about in this review. This chapter focussed around the various leveled arranging techniques.

The endeavors of accomplishing the progressive arranging of MDP issues are isolated into two sections: first, how to consequently produce the various leveled structures [27,28]; second, how to foster arranging calculations to settle subproblems presented by the progressive construction [29,30]. Sutton et al. [31] utilized choices to transiently digest information dependent on Semi-Markov Decision Interaction (SMDP) hypothesis. Parr [32] fostered a way to deal with progressively organizing MDP approaches called chains of the importance of Dynamic Machines. Dietterich [29] fostered another methodology called the MAXQ Worth Capacity Deterioration. These techniques assume that the chain of command has been predestined by experts. Hengst [33] suggested the HEXQ technique to address the issue of planned job degradation for developing an order of deliberations based on altered recurrence of state variables. For degrading regarded MDPs that are dependent on causal relationships between variables, Jonsson [34] suggested the VISA method. Kheradmandian and Rahmati [27] collaborated on a paper that looked at the ability of information mining techniques to identify structures and instances in a predetermined order. The majority of these techniques focus on factual tactics to become familiar with the basic phases as smaller tasks.

8.3 Smart Manufacturing Systems

Smart manufacturing (SM) is an innovation-driven methodology that uses web-associated hardware to screen the creation cycle. The objective of SM is to distinguish openings for computerizing activities and use information investigation to further develop manufacturing execution. Smart manufacturing is a fully integrated, community producing frameworks, which adapt changing demands and conditions in the smart production line, stock organization, and client needs on a continual basis.

The terms "smart industry" and "smart manufacturing" are sometimes used interchangeably. Producing is the process of creating products that can be sold. The term "business" has a broader definition, encompassing product development, associated biological systems, and related administrations within both an economy and a specific location; products, the connected biological systems, and related administrations inside both an economy and a particular area.

Via a model, the auto business incorporates vehicle producers yet the vehicle fabricating industry doesn't approach the car business. The same can be said for the majority of the various ventures we address here, which primarily involve essential and optional enterprises (the latter being producing), with our focus on fabricating, mining, coordination, and also the production network, as well as power businesses such as oil and gas, development, and so on.

At the end of the day, normally businesses are customarily in direct or indirect contact with a person based on his own capability as a buyer, resident, patient, etc. This indicates that financial administrations such as retail or medical care industries are not looked, despite the fact that the issues they confront, the changes they go through, and the innovations they utilize are all similar [35].

Commonly, creation is a high blend and low volume of modified customized items. Creation frameworks are additionally getting more mind-boggling because of cutting-edge fabricating advances. Little parcel estimations, item variety flexibility, and shorter life spans all have their own list of requirements. The creation equipment should be simple to install and reconfigure, and the time it takes to set up the equipment should be minimal. Individual specialists, using their critical thinking and intellectual capabilities, are still the most perfect approach for providing the required adaptability, flexibility, and unwavering quality in the adaptable manufacture of little parcel sizes. The trend toward computerization is being driven by cost competition and the need for utility. Another factor driving computerization is the possibility of a shortage of skilled personnel in the future. The complexity of the items imposes additional constraints and limitations on both computerization and individual administrators' talents and capacities. Particularly item scaling down has accuracy prerequisites that imply that a few errands are past the span of the human specialist [14].

In the severe sense, producing is the creation of products to be sold and purchased, utilizing fabricating hardware and apparatuses, human work, and a blend of assembling measures.

Although this type of expertise survives recently fabricating predominantly implies mechanical creation, and modern assembling occurs in computerized ways with a great deal of advances utilized at scale and inside an associated supply and worth chain [35].

8.3.1 Why Do We Need Ubiquitous Robotics?

A manufacturing climate where labor forces are encircled by an assortment of re-configurable creation parts (actual specialists) that incorporate control, mechatronics, and insight (keen sensors and information handling units, independent, self-fix and self-tuning machines, instinctive multi-modular human-machine interfaces, and so on) is a shrewd gathering space. In these conditions, the test is to foster the creation of mechanization and control frameworks with independence also, knowledge or cognitive capacities for co-employable/collective work, lithe also, quick transformation to ecological changes, power against the event of aggravations, and the simpler reconciliation of manufacturing assets and heritage frameworks [1].

8.4 Ubiquitous Robotics

Recently, a novel category of organized robots named ubiquitous robots has been implemented because of rise of universal figuring innovation [14]. Ubiquitous advanced mechanics is a term utilized in a practically equivalent way to universal registered programming valuable for incorporating automated innovations. This research advances from the fields of universal and inescapable figuring sensor organizations. This encompassing knowledge such as cell phones, wearable PCs, and pervasive processing makes it likely that individuals will live in the ubiquitous world. This world refers to where all gadgets have completely arranged the presence of universal space coming about because of improvements in PC and organization innovation will give inspirations to offer wanted administrations by any IT gadgets whatsoever spot and time through client associations and consistent applications. This shift has rushed the insurgency, which has additionally showed itself in the new multi-disciplinary examination region. Universal advanced mechanics starts the third era of advanced mechanics following the original of the modern robot and the second era of the individual robot. Pervasive robot UB Bot is a robot fusing three parts including a virtual programming robot or symbol. Genuine portable robot and implanted sensor frameworks and environmental elements programming robot inside a virtual world can handle a true robot as a cerebrum and co-operate with individuals' analysts of taste Korea depicted these three parts as a prospectus programming robot, versatile robot and welcome installed robot. The organized mechanical gadgets in keen conditions, universal advanced mechanics, give a drastically better approach to assemble robot frameworks in the help of individuals. Ubiquitous robotics is the plan and sending of robots in shrewd organization conditions in which everything is interconnected.

Ubiquitous robotics is considered the mechatronic partner of ubiquitous processing, the developing pattern toward installing microchips in regular items so that they can impart data. Ubiquitous robotics has arisen as an assembly with systems administration, robotics, and computer-based intelligence (man-made consciousness).

8.4.1 System Design

In contrast to traditional manufacturing methods, brilliant producing benefits from appropriately arranged machines that work together to complete diverse tasks. The framework established by these mechanical components is quite diverse with respect to stages such as working frameworks, software design languages, and communication modes. Middleware is used to consolidate the components into such a unified reflection that system, requirements correspondence, and synchronization between any two components [36]. This implies for both the recent innovations and modifying the previously developed models. Various capabilities, such as the individual framework interface, stacking the board, task arranging, simulated production, and huge data assortment, are generated at the center level in the inner cloud. A human-framework interface is used by the customer to place orders. The request includes rebuilt requests based on the preferred shade, condition of the components, and cleaned or uncleaned fragments. The assignment planning module delivers products that utilizes data from the board module's capacity. The organizer is the vital piece of the framework's spryness and insight. It transforms clients' orders into subtask groupings, which is completed by relating automated parts. Manufacturing execution frameworks, dealing the executive frameworks, and configuration emotionally supporting networks are all found at the top level. These are largely basic pieces of the modern creation measure.

8.4.2 Part-Based Hardware Measure

Connectors are used by parts to communicate with one another and with major-level regulators. Information ports and administrative interfaces are the two types of terminals [37]. An information channel serves as a subject to continuous data stream. In this technology, a large number of gate-in and gate-out channels are there for receiving various signals. An information out-gateway delivers the data to a comparing in-gateway, which receives it. The aid port allows for system communication. The component with an aid connection helps in receiving signal requests and replying to those requests.

Every part might have quite a few information ports for constant information trade between parts. For example, the confinement data are moved from the information out-port of the laser part to the information in-port of the way arranging part. When two information ports are associated, those two parts can perform continuous correspondence to achieve the undertaking cooperatively.

The individual automated capacities are likewise basic to the framework's insight. The customary modern robots resemble visually impaired and hard-of-hearing muscles re-hashing some predefined movements. In the savvy plant, automated parts are fit for detecting the climate and settling on choices in the advancement of assets and time.

Customarily, the cleaning way is instructed by master engineers. This showing system could be mind-boggling and drawn-out. In our keen plant, the cleaning way is consequently produced from the computer-aided design information. Then, at that point, the robot follows this way by a movement arranging calculation with crash aversion. Additionally, the cleaning region is not difficult to indicate with an easy-to-understand GUI.

The transportation duty, which moves parts and workpieces between workstations and capacity, is handled by AIMM. Such transit projects have a physical barrier that is larger than the robot controller's work area. This will need a significant amount of progress, for example, object acknowledgment, handling point-producing, movement arranging, restriction, and way arranging. It utilizes an RGB-D camera to do the article acknowledgment and obstruction aversion furthermore, which utilizes a laser sensor to do the limitation.

The collecting robot additionally needs to detect capability. It gets a handle on the functioning parts by web-based distinguishing the area and direction. The visual discovery depends on the layout coordinating with strategy and can perceive complex shapes with limitation mistakes under 1 mm. We likewise utilize a movement arranging and movement controlling module for collecting and impediment staying away from [1].

8.4.3 Concept for Ubiquitous Industrial Robot Work Cell

Our calculated picture of pervasive administrative robots that provide the sorts of support clients require on the industrial facility floor is the Ubiquitous Industrial Robot Work cell. Instead of being statically prepared for its current situation, this robotic framework with its current assistance circumstances ought to be naturally interoperable with sensors, sensor organizations, and gadgets. To overcome the situation, artificial intelligence algorithms play a major role [38]. The robot framework should be self-contained and can easily collaborate with an individual administrator in the same smart or wise space. Because the industrial climate is somewhat defined, fixed, and understood, the robot work cell may include a considerable level of independence, regardless of whether there are many climates, procedures and job mistakes, or dubious limits (Figure 8.1) [14].

Ordinarily, clients' fundamental assignments in mechanized, for example, manufacturing using robots frameworks are designing and showing the framework, observing and calibrating the framework, charging and dumping, managing impromptu occasions, and speaking with another group faculty. The human administrator's role becomes more basic as the framework becomes more sophisticated, complicated, and intelligent, according to prior experience [39–41]. Brilliant frameworks are helpless against disappointment and, along these lines, they are significantly more subject to human mediation than less shrewd ones. Brilliant apparatuses and antiquities ought to support clients' ordinary conduct, yet more significant is likewise dealing with a capricious circumstance; for instance, on account of human blunder, the devices ought to be sufficiently powerful while being keen. They should assist individuals with overseeing complex circumstances, use sound judgment, and act in a sensible manner.

A critical component in adaptable coordinated manufacturing is the capacity to effortlessly arrange also, program the frameworks simultaneously, considering the pertinent human factors and thinking about the difference in frameworks and human exercises to give adequate affordance. To teach robots to do complicated tasks, a few techniques have been developed. Some promising new methods rely on the ideal models that gain knowledge from the previously learned and trained models, in which customers

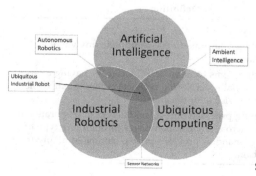

FIGURE 8.1
Smart manufacturing environment.

initially represent the target output or approach to be attained [42–45]. Significant issues in this methodology are as follows:

1. Recognizing the plan as well as the human expectation
2. Gaining knowledge about and tackling the methods
3. Using the framework to design and execute the approach [45]. The development of these frameworks relies heavily on data on human-robot interaction [14].

8.5 Ubiquitous Computing

Ubiquitous depicts a registering climate wherein clients can convey data utilizing any gadget on any organization and data are sent in the ideal technique as the setting of clients' prerequisites is independently perceived while the clients don't know about it. In the ubiquitous climate, data administration is profoundly versatile and inserted that data clients become dynamic and PC gadgets become broadened [46].

Besides, unique in relation to existing data administration that just gives data needed by clients, in ubiquitous climate, the PC serves data as well as performs fundamental activities as it insightfully perceives the concerning circumstance. The ubiquitous computing climate developed in recent research implement dispersed admittance control along with the recognizable proof of every part must have the following qualities like heterogeneity, receptiveness, versatility, and dynamicity.

There are numerous normal components about the meaning of ubiquitous computing; these changes are somewhat unique as indicated by the researcher, time, and association. Table 8.1 organizes the meanings of ubiquitous computing [47–50].

Ubiquitous computing can be redefined as the inventive computing in which pre-trained models can also be used maintaining high accuracy and precision. With respect to these attributes of ubiquitous computing, some countries like Japan and Europe pick their own methodologies of ubiquitous computing, and attempt to continuously profit from

TABLE 8.1

Idea Correlation of Pervasive Figuring

Researchers and Exploration Establishments	Definition
Friedemann Mattern (2001)	Tomorrow ordinary
Sakamura (1987)	Pervasive computing allows us to use computers anywhere and whenever we choose.
Mark Weiser (1993)	Pervasive computing aims to increase PC usage by having a large number of PCs available across the physical environment while remaining almost invisible to the client.
IBM (2004)	Pervasive computing provides unrestricted access to corporate data from any device, across any company, and through any type of connection. On-demand, it provides people command at any time and in any location.

FIGURE 8.2
Applications of ubiquitous computing globally.

the profoundly engaged research and development. Figure 8.2 shows the ideas of ubiquitous computing of every nation [51].

All designs of core pervasive computing share the notion of minor, low-cost, well-organized prepared devices that are transported at all sizes for such time of ordinary lifespan. For example, in a domestic pervasive computing environment, multiple bio-sensors are implemented for multiple functions such as lighting, environmental controls, and displays woven into clothing, allowing for continuous and vague management of lighting and warming settings in a space.

Ubiquitous computing poses challenges throughout the software engineering spectrum, including framework planning and design, framework demonstration, and user interface planning. Cell phones, sophisticated music players, radio-recurrence ID labels, GPS, and intelligent whiteboards are some of the modern devices that can aid with this final concept [52].

Weiser proposed three vital configurations, that is, tabs, pads, and boards for ubiquitous framework gadgets. The major properties represented by these configurations are full-scale measurable, having a planar arrangement, and fusing graphic yield shows. Consequently, three improved architectures such as dust, skin, and clay for ubiquitous frameworks have been proposed [53].

The Ascent of the Organization Society is a continuous transition from currently decentralized, independent microcomputers and centralized servers toward completely unavoidable computing. In his model of an unavoidable computing framework, the case of the web as the beginning of an inescapable computing framework is introduced. The legitimate movement from that worldview is a framework where that systems administration rationale becomes pertinent in each domain of day-by-day action, in each area, and in each specific circumstance [52,54].

8.5.1 Advantages of Ubiquitous Computing

The advantages of ubiquitous computing can be summed up as empowering us to use data in more than one way. The reason for the programming framework for ubiquitous computing is to recover data from our certifiable that couldn't be made accessible previously and to control different ordinary articles that couldn't be controlled before by installed computers [55]. Numerous specialists are chipping away at comparable points, for example, conscious computing [56], inescapable computing [46], unmistakable pieces [57–59], emotional computing, troupe computing, and preemptive computing. The vital aspect of ubiquitous computing for understanding its vision is to explore more about the product foundation. The groundwork makes it plausible to share different gadgets and sensors and to fabricate ubiquitous computing applications without any problem.

8.6 Conclusion

This chapter concludes the basic difference between a smart manufacturing system and smart factory. This chapter discusses about the need for this product in the market. Further, the chapter discusses about the meaning of ubiquitous robotics and stuff related to it. It also discusses about the architect design of the product which created the awareness regarding the requirements of parts and the strategy to how to overcome the challenges while accomplishing it. This chapter discussed the difference between traditional and smart manufacturing methods. From where the in-depth knowledge regarding how the parts are connected to each other and what are the terminals which are connected, the types of connectors, by taking the example of AIMM. Through the same example, this chapter looked at the interconnectivity of the machines with each other with the help of this technology and how the work is been transmitted manually to automation. It also discussed the core concept of industrial robotic work cell where it discussed about the type of robots required. This part discusses the major points regarding the use of robots and how they can assist human beings and lessen the probability of errors. This chapter discusses not only about the perspective of robotics but also covers the general discussion of pervasive computing. This chapter also mentions the benefits of ubiquitous computing. World being in the fourth revolution of the industry has a lot to discover in ubiquitous computing. Many research and fresh ideas are yet to be received and accomplished.

8.7 Future Scope

Just like the evolution of human beings, we started experiencing change. Robotic technology is now strengthening its root deep. Still, we see that this is the early phase of robotics. There is a lot to explore in it. This chapter made it very clear how much ubiquitous computing and robotics are important. A lot of research is still going on related to it. It is highly unpredictable what new segment in it may originate or maybe another technology which can ease the work more. If we stick to the current scenario, we can see that there is an ascent of AI/ML, IoT, and many more, which relates to the topic of this chapter. There are various ideas in the form of seeds that only need nourishment and they will give sweet fruits in future. The other technologies which are continuously building up are data science, Cloud computing, Cyber Security (as the tech industry will grow new methods will be formed and discovered to keep the data safe), Blockchain Technology, Drones, Augmented and Virtual Reality, Nano Technology (an interesting topic which can decrease the production cost and increase the efficiency), 3D spectral visions, and many more. The robotic industry is expected to cross 175+% of its growth in the near future.

References

1. W. Wang, X. Zhu, L. Wang, Q. Qiu, and Q. Cao, "Ubiquitous robotic technology for smart manufacturing system," *Computational Intelligence and Neuroscience*, vol. 2016, p. 14, 2016. doi:10.1155/2016/6018686

2. J. Lee, H.-A. Kao, and S. Yang, "Service innovation and smart analytics for industry 4.0 and big data environment," *Procedia CIRP*, vol. 16, pp. 3–8, 2014.

3. J. Davis, T. Edgar, J. Porter, J. Bernaden, and M. Sarli, "Smart manufacturing, manufacturing intelligence and demand dynamic performance," *Computers & Chemical Engineering*, vol. 47, pp. 145–156, 2012.

4. A. Chibani, Y. Amirat, S. Mohammed, E. Matson, N. Hagita, and M. Barreto, "Ubiquitous robotics: recent challenges and future trends," *Robotics and Autonomous Systems*, vol. 61, no. 11, pp. 1162–1172, 2013.

5. J. Rashid, M. Broxvall, and A. Saffiotti, "A middleware to integrate robots, simple devices and everyday objects into an ambient ecology," *Pervasive and Mobile Computing*, vol. 8, no. 4, pp. 522–541, 2012.

6. R. B. Rusu, B. Gerkey, and M. Beetz, "Robots in the kitchen: exploiting ubiquitous sensing and actuation," *Robotics and Autonomous Systems*, vol. 56, no. 10, pp. 844–856, 2008.

7. W. Wang, Q. Cao, X. Zhu, and S. Liang, "A framework for intelligent service environments based on middleware and general purpose task planner," in *Proceedings of the11th International Conference on Intelligent Environments (IE'15)*, pp. 184–187, Prague, Czech Republic, July 2015.

8. R. Lundh, L. Karlsson, and A. Saffiotti, "Autonomous functional configuration of a network robot system," *Robotics and Autonomous Systems*, vol. 56, no. 10, pp. 819–830, 2008.

9. G. Amato, M. Broxvall, S. Chessa et al., "Robotic ubiquitous cognitive network," in *Ambient Intelligence—Software and Applications*, pp. 191–195, Springer, Berlin, Germany, 2012.

10. J. Caie, ARC Strategies. NIST Workshop Defines Preliminary Roadmaps for Smart Assembly. ARC Advisory Group, p. 16, February 2007.

11. MANUFUTURE – Strategic Research Agenda, Manufuture Technology Platform, September 2006. http://www.manufiature.org/strategic.html, accessed 13 July 2007.

12. EUROP – Strategic Research Agenda, Technology Platform on Robotics, May 2006. http://www.robotics-platform.eu.com/documents.htm, accessed 13 July 2007.

13. K. Dencker, J. Stahre, P. Grondahl, L. Martensson, T. Lundholm, and C. Johansson, "An approach to proactive assembly systems: towards competitive assembly systems," *IEEE International Symposium on Assembly and Manufacturing, ISAM '07*, Ann Arbor, MI, 22–25 July 2007, pp. 294–299.

14. J. Heilala and M. Sallinen, "Concept for an industrial ubiquitous assembly robot," in Ratchev S., Koelemeijer S. (eds) *Micro-Assembly Technologies and Applications. IPAS 2008. IFIP—International Federation for Information Processing*, vol. 260, Springer, Boston, MA, 2008. doi:10.1007/978-0-387-77405-3_40

15. G. Q. Huang, Y. F. Zhang, and P. Y. Jiang, "RFID-based wireless manufacturing for real-time management of job shop WIP inventories," *International Journal of Advanced Manufacturing Technology*, vol. 36, no. 7–8, pp. 752–764, 2008.

16. E. W. T. Ngai, D. C. K. Chau, J. K. L. Poon, A. Y. M. Chan, B. C. M. Chan, and W. W. S. Wu, "Implementing an RFID-based manufacturing process management system: lessons learned and success factors," *Journal of Engineering and Technology Management*, vol. 29, no. 1, pp. 112–130, 2012.

17. R. Y. Zhong, Q. Y. Dai, T. Qu, G. J. Hu, and G. Q. Huang, "RFID enabled real-time manufacturing execution system for masscustomization production," *Robotics and Computer-Integrated Manufacturing*, vol. 29, no. 2, pp. 283–292, 2013.

18. Y.-G. Ha, J.-C. Sohn, Y.-J. Cho, and H. Yoon, "A robotic service framework supporting automated integration of ubiquitous sensors and devices," *Information Sciences*, vol. 177, no. 3, pp. 657–679, 2007.

19. A. Sanfeliu and J. Andrade-Cetto, "Ubiquitous networking robotics in urban settings," in *Proceedings of the Workshop on Network Robot Systems. Toward Intelligent Robotic Systems Integrated with Environments*, pp. 10–13, 2006.

20. A. Saffiotti and M. Broxvall, "PEIS ecologies: ambient intelligence meets autonomous robotics," in *Proceedings of the Joint Conference on Smart Objects and Ambient Intelligence: Innovative Context-Aware Services: Usages and Technologies (sOcEUSAI '05)*, pp. 277–281, October 2005.

21. J. Capitan, M. T. J. Spaan, L. Merino, and A. Ollero, "Decentralized multi-robot cooperation with auctioned POMDPs," *The International Journal of Robotics Research*, vol. 32, no. 6, pp. 650–671, 2013.

22. B. K. Kim, N. Tomokuni, K. Ohara, T. Tanikawa, K. Ohba, and S. Hirai, "Ubiquitous localization and mapping for robots with ambient intelligence," in *Proceedings of the IEEE/RSJ International Conference on Intelligent Robots and Systems (IROS '06)*, pp. 4809–4814, IEEE, Beijing, China, October 2006.

23. E. Erdem, E. Aker, and V. Patoglu, "Answer set programming for collaborative housekeeping robotics: representation, reasoning, and execution," *Intelligent Service Robotics*, vol. 5, no. 4, pp. 275–291, 2012.

24. T. Niemueller, G. Lakemeyer, and A. Ferrein, "Incremental task level reasoning in a competitive factory automation scenario," in *Proceedings of the AAAI Spring Symposium: Designing Intelligent Robots*, pp. 43–48, March 2013.

25. M. Barbosa, A. Bernardino, and D. Figueira et al., "ISROBOTNET: a testbed for sensor and robot network systems," in *Proceedings of the IEEE/RSJ International Conference on Intelligent Robots and Systems (IROS '09)*, IEEE, St. Louis, MO, pp. 2827–2833, October 2009.

26. M. Cirillo, L. Karlsson, and A. Saffiotti, "A human-aware robot task planner," in *Proceedings of the 19th International Conference on Automated Planning and Scheduling*, AAAI Press, Thessaloniki, Greece, pp. 58–65, September 2009.

27. G. Kheradmandian and M. Rahmati, "Automatic abstraction in reinforcement learning using data mining techniques," *Robotics and Autonomous Systems*, vol. 57, no. 11, pp. 1119–1128, 2009.

28. D. Xiao, Y.-T. Li, and C. Shi, "Autonomic discovery of subgoals in hierarchical reinforcement learning," *The Journal of China Universities of Posts and Telecommunications*, vol. 21, no. 5, pp. 94–104, 2014.

29. T. G. Dietterich, "An overview of MAXQ hierarchical reinforcement learning," in T. Walsh and B. Y. Choueiry (eds) *Abstraction, Reformulation, and Approximation*, vol. 1864 of Lecture Notes in Computer Science, pp. 26–44, Springer, New York, NY, 2000.

30. T. G. Dietterich, "Hierarchical reinforcement learning with the MAXQ value function decomposition," *Journal of Artificial Intelligence Research*, vol. 13, pp. 227–303, 2000.

31. R. S. Sutton, D. Precup, and S. Singh, "Between MDPs and semiMDPs: a framework for temporal abstraction in reinforcement learning," *Artificial Intelligence*, vol. 112, no. 1–2, pp. 181–211, 1999.

32. R. Parr, Hierarchical Control and Learning for Markov Decision Processes [Ph.D. thesis], University of California, Berkeley, CA, 1998.

33. B. Hengst, *Discovering Hierarchy in Reinforcement Learning with HEXQ*, vol. 2, ICML, 2002. Sydney.

34. A. Jonsson, A Causal Approach to Hierarchical Decomposition in Reinforcement Learning, University of Massachusetts Amherst, 2006.

35. https://www.i-scoop.eu/industry-4-0/manufacturing-industry/

36. N. Ando, T. Suehiro, K. Kitagaki, T. Kotoku, and W.-K. Yoon, "RT-middleware: distributed component middleware for RT (robot technology)," in Proceedings of the IEEE/RSJ International Conference on Intelligent Robots and Systems, Edmonton, Canada, pp. 3933–3938, August 2005.

37. W. Wang, Q. Cao, X. Zhu, and M. Adachi, "An automatic switching approach of robotic components for improving robot localization reliability in complicated environment," *Industrial Robot*, vol. 41, no. 2, pp. 135–144, 2014.

38. A. Saffiotti and M. Broxvall, "PEIS ecologies: ambient intelligence meets autonomous robotics," in Proceedings of the International Conference on Smart Objects and Ambient Intelligence (sOcEUSAI), Grenoble, France, pp. 275–280, 2005.
39. L. Bainbridge, "Ironies of automation," *Automatica*, vol. 19, pp. 775–779, 1983.
40. J. Rasmussen, *Information Processing and Human-Machine Interaction: An Approach to Cognitive Engineering*, New York: North-Holland, p. 215, 1986.
41. K. J. Vicente and J. Rasmussen, "Ecological interface design: theoretical foundations," *IEEE Transactions on Systems, Man, and Cybernetics*, vol. 22, no. 4, pp. 589–606, 1992.
42. R. D. Schraft and C. Meyer, "The need for an intuitive teaching method for small and medium enterprises," in *VDI-Wissensforum et al.: ISR 2006 - ROBOTIK 2006: Proceedings of the Joint Conference on Robotics*, May 15–17, 2006, Munich: Visions are Reality. Dtisseldorf, 2006, 10 p. (CD-ROM), Abstract p. 95 (VDI-Berichte 1956). www.smerobot.org-sientific publications
43. B. Resko, A. Gaudia, P. Baranyi, and T. Thomessen, "Ubiquitous sensory intelligence in industrial robot programming," *5th International Symposium of Hungarian Researchers on Computational Intelligence*, Budapest, November 11–12, 2004.
44. A. Billard and R. Siegwart, "Robot learning from demonstration," *Robotics and Autonomous Systems*, vol. 47, pp. 65–67, 2004.
45. R. Dillman, "Teaching and learning of robot tasks via observation of human performance," *Robotics and Autonomous Systems Al*, vol. 47, pp. 109–116, 2004.
46. C. S. Leem, N. J. Jeon, J. H. Choi, and H. G. Shin, "A business model (BM) development methodology in ubiquitous computing environments", *ICCSA 2005*, LNCS 3483, pp. 86–95, 2005.
47. Friedemann Mattern: The Vision and Technical Foundations of Ubiquitous Computing. UPGRADE, vol. II, pp. 3–6, 2001.
48. K. Sakamura, "The TRON Project," *IEEE Micro*, vol. 7, no. 2, pp. 8–14, 1987.
49. Mark Weiser: Ubiquitous Computing. IEEE Computer, 1993.
50. http://www-306.ibm.com/software/pervasive/module/index.shtml
51. W. S. Kim, J. K. Kim, H. K. Kim, C. S. Kim, H. S. Koo, S. B. Lee, T. W. Park, and S. K. Kim, "The technology, infrastructure and trend of ubiquitous computing," *Korea Information Processing Society Review*, vol. 10, no. 4, 2003.
52. Wikipedia.orgs
53. S. Poslad, "Ubiquitous computing smart devices," *Smart Environments and Smart Interaction*, Wiley, 2009. http://www.elec.qmul.ac.uk/people/stefan/ubicom/index.html
54. B. Kang, "Ubiquitous computing environment threats and defensive measures," *International Journal of Multimedia and Ubiquitous Engineering*, vol. 2, pp. 47–60, 2011.
55. W. Buxton, "Less is more (more or less)," in P. J. Denning (ed) *Invisible Computing*, 2002.
56. A. Harter, A. Hopper, P. Steggles, A. Ward, and P. Webster, "The anatomy of a context-aware application," in *Proceedings 5th Annual ACM/IEEE International Conference on Mobile Computing and Networking*, 1999.
57. R. Picard, *Affective Computing*, MIT Press, 1997.
58. M. F. Zah, C. Lau, M. Wiesbeck, M. Ostgathe, and W. Vogl, "Towards the cognitive factory," in *Proceedings of the 2nd International Conference on Changeable, Agile, Reconfigurable and Virtual Production (CARV 2007)*, 2007.
59. https://blog.robotiq.com/a-glimpse-into-the-future-of-industrial-robotics

9

Machine Learning Techniques and Big Data Tools in Design and Manufacturing

Vishwanadham Mandala

Enterprise Architect, Greenwood, Indiana, USA

C.D. Premkumar

Department of IT, Hindusthan College of Engineering and Technology, Coimbatore, Tamil Nadu, India

K. Nivitha

Department of IT, Rajalakshmi Engineering College, Chennai, Tamil Nadu, India

R. Satheesh Kumar

Department of CSE, Sahrdaya College of Engineering and Technology, Thrissur, Kerala, India

CONTENTS

DOI: 10.1201/9781003202776-9

9.1 Introduction

The cloud computing, big data, and Artificial Intelligence have all had a major impact on manufacturing as a result of technical progressions. In manufacturing, the amount of data collected is increasing [1–3]. When it comes to transforming the current industrial paradigm into smart manufacturing, big data presents an enormous opportunity and it is shown in Figure 9.1. Big data gives firms the ability to become more competitive by using data-driven initiatives. As a result, traditional manufacturing systems are being replaced by heterogeneous cyber-physical systems that communicate through event-based communiqué and collaborate in unified networks. A collective view of these new ecosystems produces new technology options that are possibly adequate for satisfying high-end client demands. In other words, new KPIs [4] are needed. Production flexibility and product and production visibility are also important.

During the product lifetime, manufacturing generates a lot of structured, semi-structured, and unstructured data. As production becomes increasingly digitalized, new possibilities for smart manufacturing are emerging. Smart manufacturing systems' complexity creates new R&D, innovation, and development problems. To deal with these new systems effectively and efficiently, new methodologies, even for classic applications such as control, monitoring, observation, or optimization, are required [5]. Analysis of Big Data created by such technologies will be the focus of this endeavor.

The concepts mostly created in computing have influenced smart manufacturing. It is true that manufacturing will reap the benefits of these and other innovations that arise in the future, but it has its own distinct identity, as shown in Figure 9.2.

Smart manufacturing systems generate a wide range of data, which can be combined with data from other networked systems [6–8]. Big Data investigation in smart industry has as one of its primary goals the discovery of novel relationships, influencing variables, and designs in these data, and the observation of such discoveries via Big Data stream statement (including in real time). As a basis for choice support. With the development and implementation of machine learning techniques, it is necessary to have access to large amounts of data. This is because extracting knowledge is the most significant activity that leads to the realization of error-free processes. It is also crucial to keep improving machine learning applications since this allows the learning process to include more artificial/computational

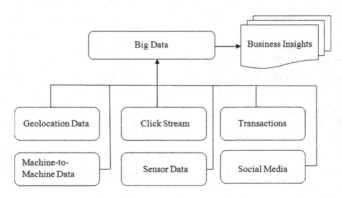

FIGURE 9.1
Sources of big data.

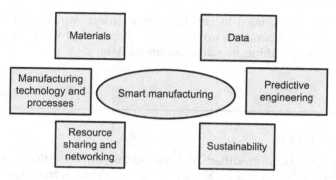

FIGURE 9.2
Smart manufacturing.

intelligence [9,10]. A wide range of manufacturing applications use machine learning algorithms such as optimization, control, and debugging. This increases transparency in the entire manufacturing environment, which reduces costs without compromising quality. The results of the experiment suggest that using ML algorithms improves process quality in semiconductor and LEAN manufacturing environments [11].

When these cases are exploited, they have the potential to innovate business fields by providing better maintenance services stretched industrial system reports, improved KPIs/monitoring, customer demand documentation based on Big Data simulation. Although this is only a tiny sample, it should give you a good idea of the potentials for utilizing Big Data exploration in the field of smart industry [12]. Figure 9.3 shows the role of Big Data in smart manufacturing.

Overall, Big Data is closely linked to traditional data analysis and mining methods, which are also used on enormous datasets. A range of processes, such as sampling and

FIGURE 9.3
Big Data in smart manufacturing.

querying [13], are typically used to get data from various sources. In relation to smart manufacturing, additional concerns are required, such as vast volumes of multi- specific data, constructions, and mining in active streamed data.

9.2 Literature Survey

Firefly heuristics have been modified by Valarmathi [14] for efficient feature selection. Using FireFly Algorithm (FA) for local search is a great idea. It may, however, be pushed into a local optima and hence be unable to do effective global searches. During cycles, FA variables don't alter over time. FA is based on how fireflies attract one another by flashing their lights. Light intensity aids firefly swarms in their quest for better solutions in search space by moving them to brighter regions. In order to classify the features, we use neural networks such as NB, KNN, and Multilayer Perceptron Neural Networks (MLPNN). In order to better classify twitter data, a firefly-based Feature Selection is shown here. An FS of this type minimizes both the dimensionality and the time complexity of the feature set. Studies have shown that using an FA-based feature selection strategy improves the performance of classifiers by a significant margin. A 1.5–2.32% increase in categorization accuracy has been reported.

Using MR models, Grolinger et al. [15] developed a method for classifying large amounts of Big Data. MR implementation hurdles for huge data are examined, and an MR-based categorization model is developed to address these issues. The method increases computer parallelism and establishes computing classes. Quantum Support Vector Machines (QSVMs) were proposed by Rebentrost et al. [16] for the efficient classification of large amounts of data. To assess the logarithmic in the extent of the courses and in the sum of instances of training, the approach kinds use of SVM in the quantum processer. Triguero et al. [17] developed effective evolutionary under-sampling approaches that hold more potential for massive data categorization. The issue of having fewer instances is addressed by introducing the MR model, which divides the operation of evolutionary under-sampling methods among a collection of computational components.

Machine learning algorithms such as SVM and DT are analyzed for supporting Big Data classification [18]. The analysis of ML algorithms provides a clear idea about the requirements for classifying a huge volume of data efficiently. A node selection in predictive models [19] was proposed to find the optimal quantity of hidden nodes in Extreme Learning Machine (ELM) with the help of SVM to improve the performance of classification. In this approach, a median and mean of ELM is used as the threshold value to remove the inactive hidden nodes in ELM.

Predictive maintenance was applied to a genuine machining process in a case study conducted by Jimenez-Cortadi et al. [20]. The study's goal is to extend machine tool life through the use of ML algorithms for RUL forecasting. Estimate of data conducted in the analysis using real-time data retrieved from the processer. Their research used linear and quadratic regression replicas to develop a design application for estimating RUL values. Finally, they were able to obtain precise predictions of RUL in their research for the purposes of making a comparison.

To avoid failures and causalities, Luo et al. [21] used a predictive keep strategy for a machine tool powered by a digital twin. The researchers used a hybrid method to compute RUL results, which represent the prediction error ratio as a percentage.

9.2.1 Analytics in Climate Big Data

Climate change has a significant impact on the lives of citizens on a daily basis. Spatio-temporal mixing of 26 weather characteristics has been created by Schnase and colleagues using the huge data-based spatial indexing approach termed MERRA. It is commonly used by researchers in the fields of global climate change studies and health decision-making systems. High-performance processing, data proximate analytics, scalable storage, and virtualization of a software program are just some of the features of the suggested method. Big Data spatial indexing has been maintained by a NASA Global Modeling and Assimilation team to translate the satellite observations into a weather perspective, as shown in this illustration.

It is compared to other climate processing frameworks, such as the ECMWF ReAnalysis, to see if the MERRA technique is superior. Experiments were carried out to examine the effects of surface fluxes and precipitation on experimental outcomes. MERRA platform's surface fluxes and precipitation are superior to CFSR and ECMWF ReAnalysis frameworks in terms of accuracy. Reanalysis is also used to track seasonal variations in the climate using the MERRA platform. Visualization of the MERRA platform's simulation findings is assisted by NASA's service center.

Climate change is also highlighted as a concern by data scientists. Researchers from a wide range of fields are needed to understand the effects of global warming. Those in the fields of climate modeling, data analytics, and management system are particularly needed to deal with the enormous number of large data and assess the worldwide global climate change (Faghmous and Kumar, 2014). Recent years have seen an increase in the number of researchers and practitioners from several disciplines who specialize on global climate change scenarios.

The duty of uploading, storing, analyzing, and preparing a report based on massive data is carried out by the sites. In addition to SQL servers, there are various ways to process the huge amounts of data that populate websites. It is a significant use of IoT for creating reports and forecasts for future use. The Classification Tree Model is one of the approaches used in the large processing, which helps to separate the various types of data and documents in the SQL servers and also handles the maintenance of user profiles in social media and a few Internet sites. Additionally, the classification tree architecture aids in the grouping of payloads of a similar nature for simple processing without defragmentation. Classification Tree Model isolates and categorizes the numerous payloads contained in the SQL Server throughout this implementation of the payloads and documents.

Analytical methods such as clustering, frequent pattern recognition (pattern recognition), classification, uncommon item set searching, and many more have been developed using various data processing approaches. It is possible to extract models to explain the class labels of knowledge, which are necessary for classification, or these models can also be used to predict long-term data patterns using classification approaches. These methods of data analysis can help us gain a better understanding of the enormous data sets. If a training dataset is analyzed and each instance of it is assigned to a certain class, the classification error is going to be the lowest possible. Models that accurately describe the most significant data classes in a dataset are often extracted. Classification may need two steps. A classification technique is applied to a training data set, and then the extracted model is tested against a preset test data set to live the model trained performance and accuracy. So classification is the process of assigning a class label to a dataset whose class label is unknown.

Choice tree models are constructed using the training data set. Decision tree models built at each site are not sufficient to provide a global view for prediction since the local training data sets are not in co-relation with other data sets at other geographically distributed sites either all of the data sets must be gathered at one location and then processed, or the entire decision tree must be generated. Intermediary message passing among training sites is the antithesis of this strategy.

Analysis tools are used in data processing to discover new patterns, the links between those patterns, and the longer-term patterns/classes that may be predicted by training a model on the available data set. For this, the data mining tools used machine learning techniques, statistical models appropriate to the problem, or algorithms based on mathematical models. It also consists of gathering information from numerous sources, pre-processing and organizing it so that it can be used correctly. Clustering, categorization, regression, and the creation of new patterns are all tools used in data processing.

As a result, classification techniques are frequently used to handle a broader variety of data than regression or correlation. As a result, classification is gaining popularity amongst people everywhere.

9.2.2 Problem and Challenges

In order to construct ML algorithms that can learn automatically from patterns and previous behavior, the most difficult task is to collect huge data from manufacturing environments. This is also where the biggest trend is coming from. Sometimes Big Data can be irrelevant, fuzzy, noisy and redundant which additionally complicates the learning process. Also, because of the fact that the extremely large amount of data is collected, the storage space represents the other challenging issue which leads to privacy, security, and economic questions. However, still the biggest challenge and future trend that manufacturing is facing today is reflected in the further development and application of ML algorithms. Today, manufacturing is facing a raise of challenges related to complexity and dynamic behaviors while adding the fact that the manufacturing is affected by uncertainty. In other words, because the knowledge cannot be retrieved, the constant expansion of Big Data and its availability, high-dimensionality, variety, as well as homogeneity constitute the key obstacles in the production environment.

9.3 Contribution

Most of the manufacturing issues appertain under classification problems, where the experts of industrial field have to determine a label of the class to specific object or a situation based on the Big Data set.

- In order to overcome these challenges and problems, the machine learning techniques as Naive Bayes (NB), Logistic Regression, and XGBoost algorithms are used to predict the data. The data, which gather by using Big Data technology.
- However, the gathered Big Data has tendency to contain irrelevant, missing and redundant information which can lead to the impact on the performance of the ML learning abilities so we pre-process the data to avoid the misclassification.

- Industrial analytics requests in large-scale manufacturing necessitate information and data engineering requirements.
- This research identifies these requirements and designs a Big Data pipeline to meet them, demonstrating the full data lifecycle for these applications in large-scale manufacturing situations.

9.4 Proposed Method

In this section, we discuss the proposed practice flow, which is represented in Figure 9.4. In primary, the smart industry data is collected, then we pre-process the data by removing unwanted data. Then the pre-processed data is given to Big Data analysis, then the data is given to the feature selection scheme of FA, here important and relevant features are designated, the selected features are given to the classifier models as NB, Logistic Regression, and XGBoost. These classifier models take the data to train and test the model to predict the data efficiently.

9.5 Big Data Analysis

Heuristics are used in Big Data analysis. Analyzing Big Data necessitates taking into account vast amounts of data that can't be processed using traditional data mining methods. Big Data analysis necessitates algorithms, as well as storage techniques, in order

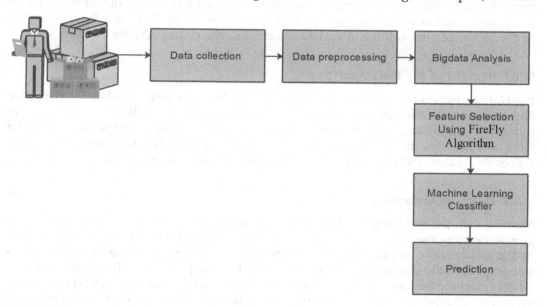

FIGURE 9.4
Proposed methodology flow diagram.

to access and handle such large amounts of data quickly. Several methods that meet these requirements for quick processing of Big Data are included in simple Big Data investigation. Simple Big Data examines often yield interim results that serve as a springboard for further in-depth data mining aimed at simplifying the data while preserving useful information. Simple Big Data examination outcomes include, but are not limited to, averages, distribution histogram forms (normal, exponential, Poisson), sums, minimums and maximums, among other descriptive statistical methods. Such a simple Big Data study can yield final or intermediate results that can be used in more advanced data mining, Artificial Intelligence, or machine learning techniques. No one can deny the growing importance of Big Data. However, there is still no consensus on what Big Data is.

Large quantities of organized, semi-structured, and unstructured data generated by data sources are referred to as "Big Data," because storing and analyzing them would require an enormous amount of time and money in order to extract significant value. Large amounts of information cannot be gathered and stored using traditional technologies in a reasonable amount of time. This is what is meant by the term Big Data when applied to the data itself. The value of data is more important to data users than the sheer volume. Large amounts of data can be regarded as having hidden value and information, which is what Big Data refers to. It goes above and beyond what the average user is capable of processing. The attributes Volume, Variety, Velocity, and Value, i.e., the 4Vs, of Big Data can also be used to characterize it. PB (1000 TB) to ZB (zettabytes) is the data volume scale that is being discussed, (a billion TB). Variety refers to the fact that the data's size, substance, format, and intended use are all different. As an example of organized and semi-structured data types, there are digits, symbols, tables, and XML documents as well as unstructured data types like logs, audio, and video files. Velocity mentions to the speed at which data is made and the timeliness required for data processing. The lifeblood of businesses is velocity in the face of huge totals of data. Big Data's importance is not based on sheer volume, but rather on the data's enormous worth. The key to improving competitiveness is to figure out how to get the most value out of Big Data by using sophisticated algorithms. Besides that, the features of Big Data have been expanded to the 10 Vs, i.e., the volume of variety of velocity, value, and veracity.

9.5.1 Benefits of Big Data Analytics

Big Data collection and storage alone do not yield business benefits. Only by analyzing and acting on the data can value be produced. The advantages of Big Data analytics are numerous, significant, and serve as the foundation for gaining a competitive edge. Big Data now has a fourth "V": high Value. This is due to the prospective benefits. Only after thorough consideration and execution does this value become apparent.

9.5.2 Data Understanding

Starting with the collecting of basic data, this section continues with activities aimed at comprehending the data. For example, these actions might involve getting an initial look at the information, identifying data for analysis, identifying problems with the data's integrity, or finding intriguing patterns in smaller groups of data. It is Dolle's role to deliver machine data and data from the ERP system. Binary values (0s and 1s) are used to represent the machine data. The number of qualities a machine can have varies from one manufacturer to the next. There are 85 attributes in the product dataset, 69 properties in the job execution dataset, and 10 attributes in the work calendar dataset. Each job is a unique business action that is completed over a specified period of time in order to produce a specific sort of product. The data's structure doesn't follow any standard, and there's no way to know for sure that two identical devices will have the same structure. It is evident from Dolle's case study just how difficult it may be to analyze data in the smart manufacturing business. Machine data must be logged in this case study in order to keep track of machine statuses. Initially, the logged data is stored in a thorough fashion across various database tables. Each machine has its own unique set of sensors and features, which is why only one of them is used in the presentation. The following characteristics describe the machine you've chosen: MachineOn, DateTime, PaceOut, FaultyString, PaceIn, ScrewError, and Alarm). The DateTime contains a 1-second granular recording of a date and time occurrence. The MachineOn sensor detects whether or not a machine is actively working on a particular job. PaceIn indicates an incoming string or beam in a string/beam sensor. A ladder sensor's PaceOut corresponds to the pace of a departing ladder. To identify faulty strings, look for bent or twisted strands on your cable using the FaultyString sensor. To put it another way, the ScrewError sensor is a screw machine sensor. Finally, the Alarm is a metaphor for anything going wrong with the equipment. Dolle's real-world machine dataset is utilized to provide a quick look at the current state of the data. The snapshot includes seven job no. 307810 attributes for creating a Click 6-type ladder. Table 9.1 shows complete data down to the second by job and machine level. For example, the text in row 1 is as follows: (represents: second granularity) DateTime = 1902–2019 09:53:07. Please keep in mind that in cases where subsequent rows have exactly matching data, they will not be logged to the database, and as a result there are noticeable holes at granularity two.) PaceIn = 0 (signifies: no string enters the machine), PaceOut = 1 (signifies: the ladder exits), FaultyString = 0 (signifies: the quality is OK), ScrewError = 0 (signifies: no error), and Alarm = 0 (signifies: the machine is functioning) (signifies: no abnormality). Unlike Id, which can be used for everything besides row identification, id is reserved just for that. Another noteworthy feature revealed by an initial examination at the data in Table 9.1 is that the ladder (row 5) is created in 57 seconds, whereas the next ladder (row 10) is created in 09:56:29 – 09:54:04 = 145 seconds. A screw machine problem has created a delay in the construction of the next ladder, which is why it is taking longer than expected (row 8).

TABLE 9.1

Analysis of Sensor and Alarm Data

ID	Date and Time	Machine On	Pace IN	Pace Out	Faulty String	Screw Error	Alarm
1	23-05-2021 09:53:17	1	1	1	0	0	0
2	23-05-2021 09:53:19	1	0	0	0	0	0
3	23-05-2021 09:53:30	1	1	0	0	0	0
4	23-05-2021 09:55:07	1	0	1	0	1	0
5	23-05-2021 09:56:07	1	0	1	0	0	0
6	23-05-2021 09:53:33	1	1	1	0	1	0
7	23-05-2021 09:54:43	1	1	0	0	0	0
8	23-05-2021 09:56:23	1	1	1	0	0	0
9	23-05-2021 09:57:75	1	0	0	0	0	0
10	23-05-2021 09:58:04	1	1	1	0	0	0
11	23-05-2021 09:59:02	1	0	1	0	0	0
12	23-05-2021 09:59:67	1	1	0	0	0	0

After getting a glimpse of the data, it becomes clear that it needs to be thoroughly cleaned. When looking at the data there are a lot of things to be concerned about including the occurrence of partial duplicates as well as duplicates that are incorrect, incomplete, or missing data. Multiple rows are linked to a single observation because of partial duplication, but the row values are not identical. In addition, a number of intriguing subsets are found to form hypotheses about the initial patterns of data. For instance, if screw machine faults are more likely to cause machine shutdowns than defective strings.

9.5.3 Data Preparation

In this section, the business concerns are explained in detail before data modeling is started. When it comes to getting ready for analysis, there are a number of activities that need to be completed. It is possible to do data preparation procedures more than once, and not necessarily in any particular order. These steps include identifying the relevant data, cleaning it up, tossing out irrelevant information, and considering how the ERP scheme's data can be merged into the final data sets. A cleaning methods could be used in this situation as well. Data validation relies heavily on metadata derived from interactions among data scientists and domain experts. Some Meta concerns cannot be deduced from sensor data but necessitate domain expertise, for example: Is the machine output dependable, especially while the alarm is ON, can this be confirmed? Is the sensor data reliable? The answer is logically YES, as the alert is ignored throughout the manufacture of some types of ladders. Another strange thing about the results was that they indicated twice as many ladders being produced than were actually being produced. The pace out sensor was activated twice during the folding phase of the ladder, and this was fixed during the recording process as a result. Adequacy is a measure of data validity; does the amount of data exist to generate accurate predictions? The question "why" is raised by looking at data from a ladder machine that produced no output. Because the ladder machine couldn't deliver its output because it was jammed, it stood still. If there had been one more sensor, the system could have predicted why there was no output. The format and granularity of the final data sets are also decided at this stage. Even though the highest sample rate for data granularity is "1 second one sensor status," the changed inside the limited time frame when looking at the data itself (see rows 11 and 12 in Table 9.1). Because the sensors' status hasn't changed over time, no row has been recorded in row 11, which shows that both the PaceIn and PaceOut sensors have "1" as their value. When both the PaceIn and PaceOut sensors indicate "0" in time, it is worth that multiple sensors' status modifications in 1 second, as shown in row 12. It is crucial to know if A follows B or not while trying to form a relationship, so recording sensor status every 1 second may not be the best solution; instead, it should be done every 500 milliseconds or better. The construction of data pipelines and the execution of EDA are both aspects of the data preparation phase.

9.6 Feature Selection

Feature selection is a primary stage in knowledge exploration of data and the resultant of the feature selection is the subset of the original features that produces more extraordinary information of the data. The feature selection is one of the important stages as it assists in deducing the dimensionality of the data features. The dimensionality of the datasets is diminished by eliminating the irrelevant and noisy data. The feature selection is also referred as subset selection, which makes use of the ML systems to select the ideal data applicable for learning algorithm.

9.6.1 FA-Based Feature Selection

Algorithms that are developed by the motivation of nature are powerful for the optimization problems especially for NP-hard issues. In this, a novel technique is developed toward dimensionality reduction on the basis of FireFlyFilter algorithm. The inspiration of FF algorithm is by the social behavior of the original fireflies. A short and rhythmic light is emitted by the fireflies in order to provide a warning as well as to attract the partners. On the basis of this behavior, FF algorithm is used to solve the optimization problems. The FF algorithm's basic formulation is given by the proceeding rules

The pseudo code of the conventional FA is illustrated below.

PSEUDO CODE OF FIREFLY ALGORITHM

Objective function $f[z]$, $z = (z_1, z_d)T$
Produce fireflies primary population),. $z_1 (i = 1,2,\ldots n)$
Light intensity iI at iz is executed by $f(z_1)$
Explain the light absorption coefficient γ
While $t <$ genMaxt.
for $i = 1: n$ entire nfireflies
  for $j = 1: n$ entire nfireflies
  if $I_j > I_i$
    Using Levy flights, move ith firefly towards j in d – dimension
    End if
    Attractiveness changes with distance r through $exp[-\gamma r^2]$
    Compute new solution and update the light intensity
    End for j
End for i
Determine the present best and rank the fireflies
End while
Post process visualization and result

- Fireflies attract their partners irrespective of sex, because of its unisexual property.
- The firefly with less brightness moves toward the brighter one, since because of the decrease in brightness as there is an increase in the distance among both flies.
- The fireflies move randomly on account of incapability of detecting the brighter one.
- The landscape of the objective function is used for determining the brightness of a firefly.

9.7 Exploratory Analysis

To begin understanding the data, exploratory data analysis (EDA) uses a visual method. No formal rules exist for EDA, but common approaches include summary statistics, correlation, and aggregation (visualization and aggregation). The first step in understanding data is summarizing it or performing a univariate analysis. The simplest type of data analysis is known as a univariate analysis because it involves only one variable. Multivariate analysis, often known as data correlation, aids in the discovery of connections between two or more variables. Predictive model selection and construction are greatly aided by discovering relationships between variables. Data visualization aids in finding anomalies and outliers by giving us a broader view of the data. Last but not least, data aggregation aids in better understanding by allowing us to put data of various granularities together. Skewness and kurtosis are the most intriguing results from the univariate EDA. In terms of symmetry, skewness indicates symmetry, while kurtosis indicates how long the tails are. MachineOn (–6.59) has a very pronounced rightward bias (98% of the rows show that machine is on). There is a significant leftward skewness in the FaultyString (6.18) and Screw-Error (3.08) variables. MachineOn (41.50) and FaultyString (36.24) both have very high positive Kurtosis values, indicating that MachineOn has a substantial peak near 1 and FaultyString has a peak toward 0. In other words, the kurtosis is 3 for completely symmetrical data, which means that at least half of the machine data variables are heavily skewed toward either 1 or 0. To perform multivariate EDA, correlation matrices are built. The second-granularity correlation matrix demonstrates no interdependence between the sensor and the alert variables. As a result, data is gathered on a daily basis, broken down by job.

An interesting positive and negative association is shown in Figure 9.5. In particular, it is interesting to look at the connections between speed (in and out), screw error (faulty string), machine off, and downtime (number of unscheduled stops). Given that one of the primary objectives of this research is to identify the elements that inhibit productivity and ultimately cause the machine to malfunction. With respect to pace in/out duration, there are mild negative correlations (–0.35 between the two) as well as positive correlations (+0.37) between the two coefficient values. Screw error and defective string duration and machine stops have weak positive relationships, as indicated by coefficient values (+0.37 and +0.38) of screw error and faulty string period and stops. Furthermore, moderate to strong positive relationships exist between downtime and job duration/machine off duration, as indicated by coefficient values (+0.54 and +0.96). Screw fault and faulty string have a modest to reasonable effect on the number of unscheduled machine stops, but the duration of these stops has a high positive link with down time, so it can be concluded.

According to Figures 9.6 and 9.7, which show the results of a daily granularity analysis, more jobs can be taken on as well as the "machine on" duration can be increased. Downtime and "machine off" duration are equally important. Defects in screw machines are more common than in faulty strings, and warning duration is also rather high.

A breakdown of product frequencies, screw machine problems, incorrect strings, alarms, and stops can be found in Figure 9.6. There is a considerable increase in the number of screw machine problems, alarms, and machine stops. It is also possible to calculate the average speed of arriving and exiting ladders. Though the ideal incoming and exiting paces are both about 9.5 seconds, the actual incoming and outgoing paces are 93.5 seconds.

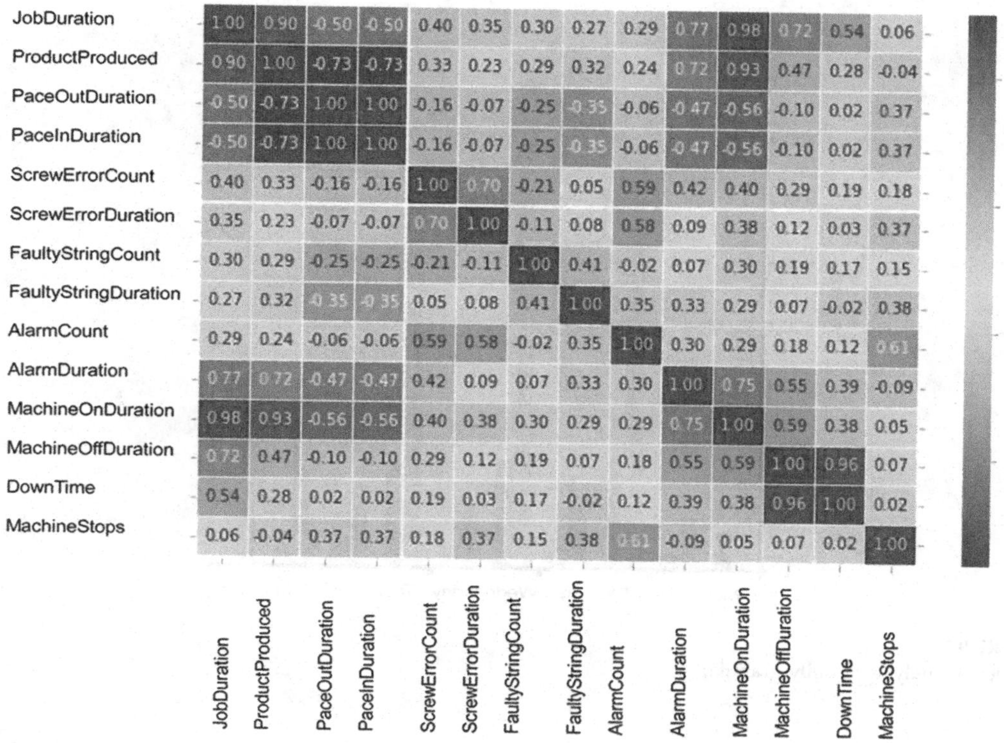

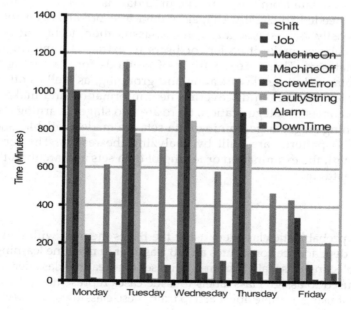

FIGURE 9.5
Sensor and alarm correlation heat map.

FIGURE 9.6
Time data analysis at daily granularity.

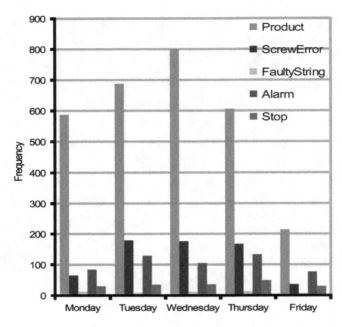

FIGURE 9.7
Frequency analysis at daily granularity.

9.8 Classification

To identify accurate data from huge unstructured data is a tedious job for users. Hence, a mechanism is needed to classify shapeless data into pre-arranged form and also to help users to easily access essential data. Classification techniques used in large transactional databases make it easier for users to extract the information they need from massive datasets. There are a variety of methods for classifying and grouping unstructured data, including classification and grouping, as well as other data mining approaches. It aids the user in discovering new information and makes educated decisions. When it comes to categorization, there are two stages: learning and application. During the learning stage, large training data sets are made available, and applications such as rules and patterns are built by analyzing the results. The second phase execution begins with the examination or testing of data sets and archives the precision of categorization patterns.

9.8.1 NB

A set of simple probabilistic classifiers using the Bayes theorem with naive assumptions about feature independence constitutes an NB classifier in machine learning. The primary technique for selecting class labels from a finite set for creating classifier models is to use NB, which are used to assign class labels to issue cases represented as vectors of feature values. Instead of using a single approach to train these classifiers, a collection of methods based on a common principle must be used. Because of this, the value of each NB classifier's class variable is assumed to be completely independent of all other features.

The NB classifiers can be learned very quickly in a supervised learning environment for certain types of probability models.

9.8.2 Multiple Regression–Logistic Regression

Multivariate linear combination of regression coefficients is referred to as Linear Regression. The generalized least square method is used to compute the coefficients. Because Linear Regression is deterministic and has a small parameter, nothing besides the data break needs to be changed for model training and validation. Multiple Regression defines the relationship among a single response variable Y and a number of predictor variables X. There are n predictors (X1–Xn) and one response (Y) in this Multiple Regression model.

$$y = b0 + b1\,x1 + b2\,x2 + \ldots + bn\,xn + e \tag{9.1}$$

With respect to e, those are the model's residual terms, and we base our distribution assumption on those terms. There will be an inference on the remainder of the model parameters if we use this term (e). B0, B1, B2, B3, …, Bn are the coefficients for the Linear Regression. Linear Regression uses an extended linear model, whereas Logistic Regression uses a slightly different technique.

$$y = 1 \tag{9.2}$$

if b0 + b1 x1 + e > 0

Else

$$y = 0 \tag{9.3}$$

Linear Regression can estimate continuously dependent changes based on a set of liberated variables. However, Logistic Regression is used to approximation definite contingent variations utilizing a given set of independent variables. Figure 9.7 depicts the Linear Regression and Logistic Regression graphs.

9.8.3 XGBoost Classifier

Data scientists rely on XGBoost, a scalable tree boosting scheme that delivers cutting-edge outcomes on a wide range of issues. For the implementation of the XGBoost algorithm, open source C++ was used. This algorithm uses real-time predictions of impending failures to forecast the downtime of a printing machine and uses unstructured historical machine data to train the ML algorithms. The models' goodness of fit was assessed using a variety of indicators. According to the findings, all algorithms outperformed each other in terms of ROC, with results that were nearly identical. However, XGBoost and RF outperform LR when it comes to decision thresholds. The final class is defined by XGBoost algorithm tree using the majority voting technique. Figure 9.8 shows the XGBoost algorithm tree. XGBoost classifier model is shown in Figure 9.9.

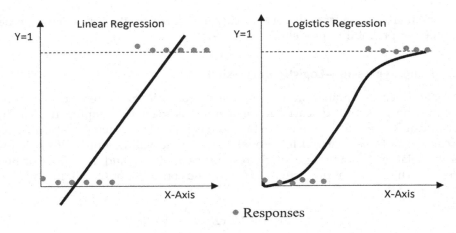

FIGURE 9.8
Extreme (XGBoost) trees.

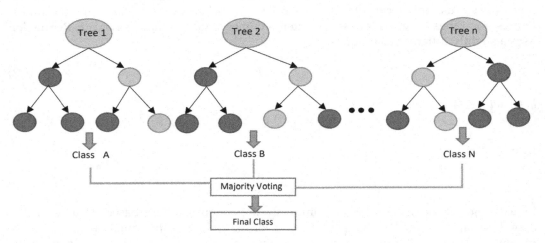

FIGURE 9.9
XGBoost classifier model.

9.9 Evaluation

This section assesses Dolle's manufacturing process's Overall Equipment Effectiveness (OEE). OEE determines how much of a company's production time is actually productive. As a result, it serves both purposes of being both a benchmark and a baseline. OEE is made up of three components: availability, performance, and quality (or scalability). When assessing availability, experts take into account any incidents that disrupt or stop the output as intended. When evaluating a manufacturing process' performance, look for factors that contribute to it moving at a slower pace than it should. Whereas, quality takes into account manufactured goods that do not meet quality requirements into considerations. One hundred percent on the OEE scale signifies that production is moving along smoothly, with no unexpected pauses, and only high-quality items are being produced. A typical morning shift lasts for 510 minutes, with breaks of 60 minutes, stop/down time of 80 minutes, and ideal production time of 60 seconds. These steps must be followed in order to arrive at an OEE figure. The first step is to determine the planned production time (PPT) and run time (RT). If you want to know how long your shift will last, you can use the PPT. This includes all of your scheduled breaks, including lunch and coffee. When calculating Run Time, keep in mind that it excludes both scheduled and unforeseen stops, such as job/product switches, stops due to bad string, screw machine errors, and other causes. After that, Good Count (GC) is computed by discarding the defective ladders. It is time to figure out availability (A), performance (P), and quality (Q). Availability measures the amount of time that a manufacturing process or machine is "OFF" due to a variety of factors. It accounts for unanticipated failures of the equipment, as well as the setup for the following work and/or alterations (planned stops). The process' performance is estimated, and quality issues about the quality standards of the products being produced are raised.

9.9.1 Methods and Modeling

Machine learning-based models are introduced in this part along with some of the main concerns like model sampling. This case study's primary objective is to forecast unplanned machine stoppage using historical repercussions and patterns. Supervised ML can be used to anticipate when a machine will shut down based on the type of data provided and the research question/goal. Learning algorithms that use supervised data, such as Machine is on "1" or off "0," train on previous data. The algorithm uses previous trends to determine which label should be applied to new data. NB, Logistic Regression, and XGBoost are the most often used classification algorithms in machine learning. As one of the most widely used machine learning algorithms for two-class binary classification, these classifier models are put to good use.

9.10 Result and Discussion

This segment measures the presentation of the chosen different classification method. The actual cases of "MachineOn = 0" (true negative), the classifier forecast correctly of them. Similarly, instances of "MachineOn = 1" (true positive), the classifier predicted correctly. And also the performance of the classifier model is identified by using different parametric as recall, precision, sensitivity, F-measure, and classification accuracy.

9.10.1 Performance Analysis

This work validates the performance of machine learning classifier using the different performance measures like accuracy, precision, recall, and F-Measure. These evaluation metrics are calculated from True Positive (TP), False Positive (FP), True Negative (TN), and False Negative (FN) values, which are constructed based on the performance of classifier.

Precision: Precision (Pre) is the fraction of retrieved instances that are related and is defined and calculated using Equation 9.4 as given below.

$$\text{Precision} = \frac{tp}{tp + fp} \tag{9.4}$$

Recall: It is the proportion of accurate class out of all the classes that are actually selected. Equation 9.5 is used below.

$$\text{Recall} = \frac{tp}{tp + fn} \tag{9.5}$$

F-Measure: This is a measure that combines accuracy and recall is the harmonic mean of accuracy and recall. It is calculated using Equation 9.6 as given below.

$$\text{F-measure} = \frac{tp}{tp + (fp + fn)} \tag{9.6}$$

Performances analysis of classifier without feature selection is shown in Table 9.2.

Accuracy: Accuracy is given as the proportion of the total number of TP and TN to the total number of data. It is determined using Equation 9.7.

$$\text{Accuracy} = \frac{tp + tn}{tp + fp + tn + fn} \tag{9.7}$$

Tables 9.3 and 9.4 represent the proposed model performance with the three classifiers. Table 9.3 shows the performance of analysis of classifier without feature selection. In this comparison analysis, Logistic Regression provides better prediction results; and another in Table 9.3 as performance analysis of classifier with feature selection. In this analysis, the same Logistic Regression classifier performs well than the other two classifiers.

Table 9.3 and Figure 9.10 show the performance analysis of prediction accuracy. In this analysis, we used feature selection method without feature selection scheme. This comparison analysis gives better results with feature than without feature selection. Also

TABLE 9.2

The Performances Analysis of Classifier Without Feature Selection

Classifier	Precision (%)	Recall (%)	F-Measure (%)
Naive Bayes	94.45	93.15	92.51
Logistic Regression	95.82	96.45	91.46
XGBoost	94.10	91.64	93.44

TABLE 9.3

The Performance Analysis of Classifier With Feature Selection

Classifier	Precision (%)	Recall (%)	F-Measure (%)
Naive Bayes	95.12	95.00	93.23
Logistic Regression	96.92	97.10	92.31
XGBoost	95.46	92.64	96.66

TABLE 9.4

The Prediction Accuracy Performance Analysis of Classifier

Classifier	Prediction Accuracy (%)	
	Without Feature Selection	**With Feature Selection**
Naive Bayes	97.11	97.91
Logistic Regression	98.38	99.04
XGBoost	97.68	98.42

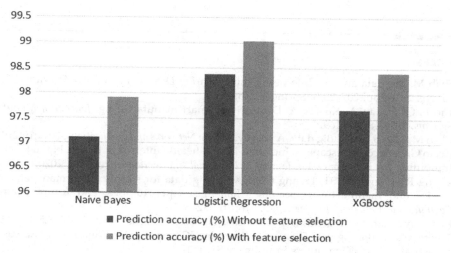

FIGURE 9.10
Graphical representation of prediction accuracy performances.

performance of three classifier models as Logistic Regression provides better results without feature selection of 98.38% and with feature selection of 99.04%, respectively.

9.11 Conclusion

With the development and implementation of machine learning techniques, it is necessary to have access to large amounts of data. This is because extracting knowledge is the most significant activity that leads to the realization of error-free processes. Furthermore, the continued development of ML applications allows the artificial/computational learning process. ML and its use in intelligent industrial environments by employing machine learning classifier will continue to be explored and developed further as a result of the work presented in this paper. The effectiveness of the equipment as a whole, as well as the forecast method's accuracy, were thoroughly examined. The findings have sparked interest in reducing machine downtime in order to improve production performance. But in terms of unplanned stops, the model's predictions are fairly good, as they are a major cause of poor production performance. There are three classifier models used: Naive Bayes, Logistic Regression, and XGBoost. The data is then sorted and analyzed. Lead and opportunity management can benefit from data-driven qualification support, which lowers the arbitrary nature of professional competence and experiences by integrating business analytics (in the form of machine learning). We applied the FA feature section approach to increase forecast accuracy. After all is said and done, it will be examined to see how predictive analysis, descriptive analysis, and a near-real-time dashboard can help smart manufacturing organizations improve their operational efficiency and productivity in general.

References

1. Shah M. Big data and the Internet of things. In *Big Data Analysis: New Algorithms for a New Society*. 2016 (pp. 207–237). Springer, Cham.
2. Tao F, Qi Q, Liu A, Kusiak A. Data-driven smart manufacturing. *Journal of Manufacturing Systems*. 2018;48:157–169.
3. Chen M, Mao S, Liu Y. Big data: A survey. *Mobile Networks and Applications*. 2014;19(2):171–209.
4. Aceto G, Persico V, Pescapé A. Industry 4.0 and health: Internet of things, big data, and cloud computing for healthcare 4.0. *Journal of Industrial Information Integration*. 2020;18:100129.
5. Zhong RY, Newman ST, Huang GQ, Lan S. Big data for supply chain management in the service and manufacturing sectors: Challenges, opportunities, and future perspectives. *Computers & Industrial Engineering*. 2016;101:572–591.
6. Kusiak A. Smart manufacturing. *International Journal of Production Research*. 2018;56(1–2):508–517.
7. Trentesaux D, Borangiu T, Thomas A. Emerging ICT concepts for smart, safe and sustainable industrial systems Computers in Industry 81, 1–10.
8. Merkt O. On the use of predictive models for improving the quality of industrial maintenance: An analytical literature review of maintenance strategies. In *2019 Federated Conference on Computer Science and Information Systems (FedCSIS)*. 2019 (pp. 693–704). IEEE.
9. McCoy JT, Auret L. Machine learning applications in minerals processing: A review. *Minerals Engineering*. 2019;132:95–109.
10. Ryzko D. *Modern Big Data Architectures: A Multi-agent Systems Perspective*. John Wiley & Sons (US); 2020.
11. Mustapha UF, Alhassan AW, Jiang DN, Li GL. Sustainable aquaculture development: A review on the roles of cloud computing, Internet of things and artificial intelligence (CIA) . *Reviews in Aquaculture*. 2021;13(4):2076-2091.
12. Nagorny K, Lima-Monteiro P, Barata J, Colombo AW. Big data analysis in smart manufacturing: A review. *International Journal of Communications, Network and System Sciences*. 2017;10(3):31–58.
13. Giudici P. *Applied Data Mining: Statistical Methods for Business and Industry*. John Wiley & Sons; 2005.
14. Valarmathi ML. An improved firefly heuristics for efficient feature selection and its application in big data. *Biomedical Research*. 2017:5(28).
15. Grolinger K, Hayes M, Higashino WA, L'Heureux A, Allison DS, Capretz MA. Challenges for Mapreduce in big data. In *2014 IEEE World Congress on Services*. 2014 (pp. 182–189). IEEE.
16. Rebentrost P, Mohseni M, Lloyd S. Quantum Support Vector Machine for big data classification. *Physical Review Letters*. 2014;113(13):130503.
17. Triguero I, Galar M, Vluymans S, Cornelis C, Bustince H, Herrera F, Saeys Y. Evolutionary under sampling for Imbalanced big data classification. *IEEE Congress on Evolutionary Computation CEC*. 2015:(5)715–722.

18. Raikwal JS, Saxena K. Weight based classification algorithm for medical data. *International Journal of Computer Applications*. 2014;107:21.
19. Mahmood SF, Marhaban MH, Rokhani FZ, Samsudin K, Arigbabu OA. SVM–ELM: Pruning of extreme learning machine with support Vector machines for regression. *Journal of Intelligent Systems*. 25 (4), 555–566.
20. Jimenez-Cortadi A, Irigoien I, Boto F, Sierra B, Rodriguez G. Predictive maintenance on the machining process and machine tool. *Applied Sciences*. 2020;10:224.
21. Luo W, Hu T, Ye Y, Zhang C, Wei Y. A hybrid predictive maintenance approach for CNC machine tool driven by digital twin. *Robotics and Computer-Integrated Manufacturing*. 2020;65:101974.

10

Principle Comprehension of IoT and Smart Manufacturing System

Maya Shankar Jha

School of Computer Science and Engineering, Galgotias University, Greater Noida, Uttar Pradesh, India

K. P. Arjun

Department of Computer Science and Engineering, GITAM University, Bengaluru, Karnataka, India

N. M. Sreenarayanan

School of Computer Science and Engineering, Galgotias University, Greater Noida, Uttar Pradesh, India

CONTENTS

DOI: 10.1201/9781003202776-10

10.1 Introduction to IoT

IoT which stands for Internet of Things is nothing other than a network that consists of many devices like sensors, software, and others [1]. In simplest word, we can term it as, "A group of physical devices which communicate and share data with each other over internet for some purposes or task." IoT devices are really smart and have access to Internet. They interact with each other over Internet and allow user for managing the network as per their need. The exact goal of IoT is to make every electronics and mechanical appliances used in our daily life "smart." Currently, there are many IoT electronic devices available in market such as Google Home, August Doorbell Cam, smart light switches, etc and as these devices are in great demand and helpful as well, we can assume it as a great invention for future [2]. Many industries and companies are using IoT for predictive analysis of their product, robots for mechanical works. These days IoT-based smart fans, bulbs, and rosters are also available in market. In future aspects, we can say that IoT is basically transforming our physical world into a dynamic network system of many communicating devices. As we are developing in technology, IoT is also getting a lot of opportunities to prove a strong position for them in technical world [3].

10.1.1 History and Evolution of IoT

Till 1830s, world was totally unaware of IoT. Between 1830s and 1840s, when first communication technique telegraph "The First Landline" was developed, it has given a small hint of possibility of communicating devices. On June 3, 1900, the first wireless radio transmission took place and this incident proved a possibilty of exchange of data without wired connection [4].

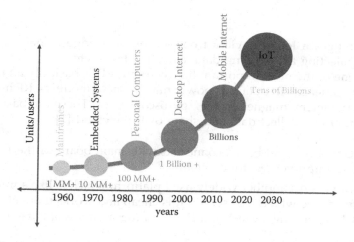

FIGURE 10.1
IoT evolution.

With the invention of computers in 1960s and Internet in 1990s, IoT was invented in 1999. The term IoT was stated by Kevin Ashton during his work Procter & Gamble in 1999. At that time, Radio Frequency Identifications (RFID) were considered essential for IoT.

This does not say that between 1840s and 1990s, scientists didn't work on communicating devices. With the limited possibility, there were many communicating devices and networks in 70s but at that time these things were pronounced as "embedded internet" and "pervasive computing" [5].

According to Cisco Systems, IoT was born between 2008 and 2009, and people and things were more connected during this period. Based on their states, things/people radio was 0.08 in 2003 while 1.84 in 2010 which is shown in Figure 10.1.

10.2 IoT Platforms and Operating System

In the current era of technologies, we are totally around the machines and devices which are IoT based. From air conditioner to smart fan and bells that we control from our smartphones or remote are designed with IoT. It is influencing our life totally from our reactions to our work cycle.

10.2.1 IoT Platforms

In normal English, platform is just a layer of surface. Similarly, here also, platform can be termed as the base for building the network or the system using development tools for constructing out the desired device/project. It makes the IoT system more capable for doing complex work and cheap as well. It provides a great value to businesses-target to lower the development price and accelerate the efficiency as well [6]. To understand the whole concept of platform, we have to go little deep and understand some common terms. Some common terms are explained briefly below.

10.2.1.1 Hardware

IoT hardware ranges a lot of devices from sensors to bridges. These devices manage functions like collecting and sharing data, detection tasks, etc.

IoT sensors, one of the most important hardware in IoT, is basically an input device. It consists of many other devices such as power management modules, RF modules, energy modules, accelerometers, magnetometers, gyroscopes, etc. These are basically input devices which gather and collect data and share over the cloud [7].

- Arduino Uno – A small board connected with main board of the IoT system to increase and improves the functionality.
- Raspberry Pi 2 – An another widely used platform which is like a mini computer that comprises the whole web server. It is cheap and works more efficiently with Windows 10 operating system and Python Programming language.

There are other alternatives as well such as BeagleBoard, STM32, PocketBeagle, etc.

10.2.1.2 Connectivity

As we deal with a number of devices at the same time, we must have to connect all the devices so that they can share data with each other and complete the desired task together. Connectivities such as WiFi, Bluetooth, and satellites are used to connect devices in IoT network [8,9]. Input devices like sensors collect data on the basis of instruction provided via programs and then they send it to the cloud or server. As per the instruction, output data is transferred to other device through the cloud. So we can conclude that connectivity works in a cycle of collecting and sending data over the cloud.

10.2.1.3 Best Communication Option

As the connectivity options are in numbers, sometimes user feels difficulty to choose which one is best for our project. Literally, this totally depends upon the need and the goal of our project. But there are some important things which should be kept in mind before confirming an option so that we can build a project with more efficiency in low price, etc. Some important parameters are as follows:

- Less power consuming.
- Can share data at high speed (bandwidth).
- Data sharing range should be long.
- Affordable.

10.2.1.3.1 IoT Connectivity Options

- **WiFi** – This with transmission frequency of 2.4 GHz or 5GHz is able to carry a large amount of data but over the short range only. This consumes more power as well. So it can be used in short-range applications such as home automation system.
- **Bluetooth** – Of course, this is a widely used option in electronics but it don't provide the facility of sharing a large amount of data. It uses low energy. It has been mostly used in indoor asset tracking where its limited range doesn't make an issue.

- **Ethernet** – It connects local area networks and allows the multiple systems or devices to connect at the same time. It provides high speed of downloading and uploading data. Video transferring devices such as cameras, robots, medical autonomous vehicles use Ethernet for data transfer due to its high bandwidth and low latency requirements.

- **Cellular IoT** – It provides the widest possible coverage as well as high speed for transferring data. It can handle high-definition data as well. Battery draining is a concern to care about. This can't be used where the system involves battery-powered remote sensors network.

- **Satellite** – When we talk about range, satellites come first. They always stand as an alternative for other types of connections. It can be used on global level in bigger projects. Fixed line Internet is an issue with satellite connection but with time it has also been solved as it is not a big issue.

10.2.2 Operating System

IoT network consisting of connected devices needs some sort of instructions to perform task. IoT operating systems, i.e., software are a type of embedded operating system which grant permission to user for performing functions of a computer in the Internet-connected devices [10]. Operating system is like a control panel for IoT network. It provides permission and security to the connected devices in network from vulnerabilities. It provides secure access to all devices for user as well as the option to manage all devices in productive and efficient manner. It processes and stores memory and data as well as runs the software over connected devices. Traditional operating systems running on Internet hosts as well as typical operating systems for sensors networks didn't seem much successful in fulfilling all the requirements and functionality of a wide range of connected devices. Therefore, we need a unique operating system for IoT to make things possible. There are a wide range of operating systems available for IoT but we are going to discuss only some of them which are more efficient in functionality.

10.2.2.1 Ubuntu Core

Ubuntu, a Linux distribution, is secure and lightweight operating system for IoT. As per the official declarations of Ubuntu core, it has been designed with "Security" as priority.

- A simple ecosystem with availability of secure app store.
- Temper-resistant.
- User can easily manage the permissions of devices.
- Support many default function.

10.2.2.2 Contiki

An open-source IoT operating system, invented in 2002, is famous for running IoT devices effectively using Internet protocol IPv4 and IPv6.

- Low power microcontrollers.
- Suitable for low-powered Internet connectivity.
- Easily run over 10kb of RAM and 30kb of ROM system.

- Core language is C.
- Provides a multitasking facility.

10.2.2.3 Android Things

It has been invented by Google and earlier it was named Brillo. As per the expert's opinion, "Brillo is derived from Android." It supports connectivity like Bluetooth and WiFi, and can easily run-on low power supply.

- Requires only 32–64 Kb of RAM and so called as lightweight OS.
- Open source, so users can operate it according to their own way.
- Google is trying to IoT app store as well.
- Devices can be detected using android smartphones.

10.2.2.4 RIOT

An open-source IoT OS, released under an unclonable GNU Lesser General Public Licence, has a huge development community. Experts term it as "The Linux" of IoT Ecosystem. Many famous companies are contributing in the development of RIOT operating system.

- Provides a reliable microkernel architecture.
- Adaptive network stack.
- Able to build the whole IoT ecosystem alone.
- Processors are 8 bit, 16 bit, and 32 bit.

There are many IoT operating systems as well in the market which are shown in Figure 10.2 but literally none of the available IoT OS is appropriate to serve the whole spectrum of the IoT ecosystem [11].

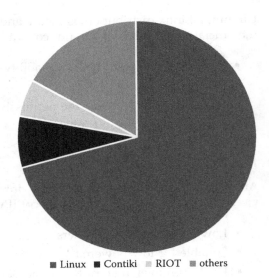

FIGURE 10.2
Uses statistics of different IoT OS.

■ Linux ■ Contiki ▨ RIOT ■ others

FIGURE 10.3
Different connectivity options in IoT.

10.3 Security in IoT Protocols and Technologies

Due to the number of devices connected together, there are always changes of vulnerability. Each and every device is connected with cloud, so if any of the connected device gets virus or any threat, it will cause defect in the whole IoT network. Figure 10.3 shows different connectivity options of IoT.

10.3.1 IoT Network Protocols

The mode of communication which establishes security for data that gets exchanged between connected IoT devices is known as IoT protocols. There are two networks used for connecting devices, i.e., Internet protocol (IP) and non-IP protocols.

10.3.1.1 Internet Protocol Network

In this network of communication, devices are connected via Internet. In this protocol, end-to-end data communication takes place within the scope of network. Some of the wisely used IP networks are discussed below.

10.3.1.1.1 HTTP (Hyper Text Transfer Protocol)

This has been considered as the best IP network which led the foundation of data communication over the Web. This is mainly used when there is large amount of data publication. The common issues are listed below.

- Battery life
- Cost
- Much constraints
- Not much energy saving.

Example: 3D printing uses HTTP protocols to connect printers.

10.3.1.1.2 LoRaWAN (Longe-Range Wide Area Network)

It connects battery-operated devices wirelessly with Internet. It consumes less power and provides a long-range signal transmission facility. Millions of devices get connected with a server at a time [12].

Example : Smart street lights in which lights are connected with LoRa gateway and gateway with the cloud using this protocol.

10.3.1.2 Non-Internet Protocols Network

In this network of communication, devices are connected via Bluetooth or RFID locally.

- **Bluetooth** – One of the most widely used protocols for short-range communication. The following are the features of Bluetooth:
  - Low-power consuming
  - Low cost
  - Wireless.

Example: Smart wearables like headphones, smartphones, etc.

10.3.2 Security

This section deals with security issue for both physical and network of IoT. Security impacts technologies and processes and takes major necessary actions to protect IoT devices and its ecosystem shown in Figure 10.4. There are four types of

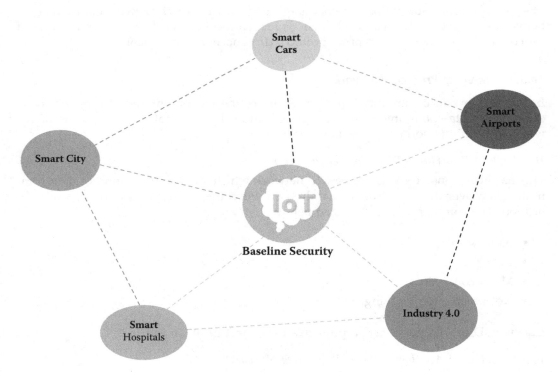

FIGURE 10.4
Importance of IoT security for sensitive data among different applications.

vulnerabilities which target from a broad spectrum of IoT security attacks. They are listed as follows:

- Physical attack (chip of the system gets attacked)
- Devices software gets attacked
- Lifecycle attack
- Communication attack.

IoT security provides protection platform for the devices connected and network from all types of vulnerability to the developer. Some of the points to conclude are as follows:

- Isolation measures can fend of software attack
- Tamper mitigation and side channel attack are suitable for protecting from physical attack.

10.4 Applications of IoT

Figure 10.5 shows the different application areas of IoT and the detailed explanation below.

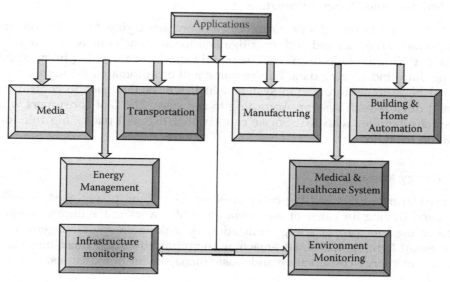

FIGURE 10.5
Applications of IoT.

10.4.1 Media

In this sector, IoT mainly recognizes the foot traffic of people at activities, i.e., visualizes the site pattern in real time how users are accessing and using it. Developers are trying to use it for big data journalism as this can easily filter and visualizes a large amount of data. It can also be used for manipulating advertisement. It will decrease the loading time for servers [13].

10.4.2 Transportation

In this sector, IoT is mainly targeted for higher efficiency, managing cost, fuel consumption, and response time increment of engines. It is also used in traffic lights. Assisted driving is future of transportation sector because in this, smart cars will be able to communicate with each other and this will promise a higher safety. Fleet management, expanded ridesharing, optimized maintenance, and dynamic navigation are the major projects where developers have to do more work.

10.4.3 Manufacturing

In manufacturing plants, IoT is used for monitoring the production flow, development cycles, and inventories as well. Predictive maintenance, supply chain management, product development, and asset utilization are the main applications of IoT in manufacturing field. Using devices build with retrofitting sensors, data about the whole production, working mechanism, and expected output can be gathered from each unit of the industry.

10.4.4 Building and Home Automation

Smart homes are future of our earth. Developers are trying to make maximum of gadgets, smart. From fan and bulb to fridge and toasters each one is turning into smart and efficient with the help of IoT. IoT is mainly used in controlling home appliances, collecting data, and sharing data. Future home will be automated through Internet and there will be a home automation system which will enable user to control over the connected devices with system. According to a survey, 22.5% of consumers who were surveyed are familier with IoT. So we can say that IoT will play a big role for home automation in India.

10.4.5 Energy Management

IoT is used in industries and big companies for controlling power used, boosting efficiencies, and finding the cause of inefficiency and also work in the improvement area. It can also be used for proper energy utilization by making energy management systems smarter. Smart lighting, machine-to-machine communication, and smart metering can be a big factor in energy conservation and waste management in industries.

10.4.6 Infrastructure Monitoring

Infrastructures such as railway tracks, bridges, wind farms, and many others use IoT devices for monitoring and controlling purposes. Connected charging stations at airports, bus stations, and parking also comes under smart infrastructure. IoT-enabled parking system can reduce crowding and driver stress. Connected streets can play a big role in efficient management of resource and people [14].

10.4.7 Medical and Healthcare System

It plays a major role in healthcare department. It collects data and helps in taking more better decisions for the treatment of patients. Using IoT-embedded devices, physicians can easily monitor patients' blood pressure, heart rate, and glucometer in less time. IoT devices can also play a big role for elder people as they can monitor their health condition at home. Not only for patients and physicians, IoT also plays a big role for hospitals and medical companies.

10.4.8 Environment Monitoring

IoT is getting used widely in this field. Monitoring air, water, soil, and forests for natural disasters, fisheries, and snowfall levels are the major uses of IoT devices. Weather apps which we use for precipitation prediction, air quality, and other updates uses IOT devices to get that all data. Low-power, wide area network has been considered perfect for environmental monitoring because it can connect a large number of devices over the wide area of network for a long time with less power consumption and data sharing [15].

10.5 IoT Application Fields

The above survey has been done by IoT ANALYTICS and is based on the 1414 projects taken in consideration in year 2020 shown in Figures 10.6 and 10.7.

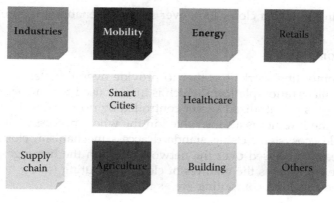

FIGURE 10.6
Top field of Internet of Things.

FIGURE 10.7
Survey analytics of IoT in global share.

10.6 IoT Enabling Technologies

There are a large number of technologies on which IoT relies. These technologies ensure the collection, storing, and analysis of data. The most common technologies are as follows:

- Cloud computing
- Big data analytics
- Wireless sensors network
- Web service
- Semantic search engines
- Internet
- Communication protocols
- Embedded system.

Here, we are going to take a closer look over some IoT-enabling technologies.

10.6.1 Cloud Computing

IoT and cloud computing works together to provide overall better service. Cloud computing is like a collaboration platform which is mainly used for data storage collected by IoT devices. It acts as a centralized server controlled by user or developer based on their requirement. As the Internet is also involved in the whole process so it becomes easy to handle the whole ecosystem. Using standard access mechanism, cloud computing resources can be easily accessed over the network through the heterogeneous client platform [16]. Figure 10.8 shows the features of cloud computing.

Services offered by cloud computing are as follows:

- IaaS (infrastructure as a service)
- PaaS (platform as a service)
- SaaS (software as service).

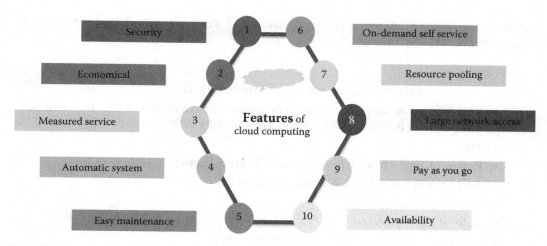

FIGURE 10.8
Features of cloud computing.

10.6.2 Big Data

In simple words, we can say that big data is nothing other than a tremendous amount of information collected from different connected devices. Measurement units used for big data are petabytes, terabytes, and exabytes. With the help of artificial intelligence and machine learning, collected data is compiled and predictions are made. This helps in making recommendations for the big companies. According to the data scientists from IBM, four "Vs" listed below play a major role in big data analytics. Figure 10.9 shows the

FIGURE 10.9
Illustration of collection of data from different sources using big data.

different electronics mediums generating structured, semi-structured, and unstructured data using big data technology.

1. Volume
   - Amount of data collected through connected devices
   - Based on some researches, the total accumulated volume of big data will be around 44 zettabytes or 44 trillion gigabytes by 2020.
2. Variety
   - Range of types from where data has been collected
   - Analytics software tackle unstructured data.
3. Velocity
   - Rate of data collected
   - Currently, it is 2.5 quintillion bytes per day.
4. Veracity
   - Accuracy of particular set of data
   - Some surveys suggest that the USA spends around $3.1 trillion per year over poor data.

10.6.3 Wireless Sensors Network

These types of networks are formed by a connecting number of sensor nodes to sense light, temperature, pressure, object, etc shown in Figure 10.10. A coordinator is provided in WSN with some scanning and storing units as well as radio interface communication units. These units scan transmitted data, and store information over the channel. There are three different channels provided: home channel, parent channel, and child channel. These channels operate with the requirement in active and inactive modes over hierarchical level.

10.6.4 Communication Protocols

Communication protocols sanction the network connectivity and coupling to applications. That is why it is considered the backbone of IoT networks. It is like a platform for

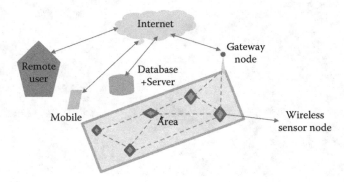

FIGURE 10.10
Working of wireless sensor network.

the connected devices to exchange data among them. According to some states, by the end of 2018, there were around 22 billion IoT-connected devices under use. Internet Engineering Task Force (IETF) publishes communication protocols. MQTT, COAP, and AMQP are some majorly used protocols in the market for IoT networks [17].

10.6.4.1 MQTT

- Stands for Message Queuing Telemetry Transport
- Ideal for M2M communication
- Designed for low bandwidth, high latency, and unreliable networks.

10.6.4.2 CoAP

- Stands for Constrained Application Protocol
- Client server protocol
- Methods are similar to HTTP.

10.6.4.3 AMQP

- Stands for Advanced Message Queuing Protocol
- Used for passing business message between applications and organizations
- Queuing, routing, message orientation, reliability, and security are features of it.

10.6.5 Embedded System

It is a part of IoT that consists of one more component like devices and gateway. It consumes less energy and is mainly used for controlling purpose, i.e., washing machines, remotes, microwaves, networking hardware, etc. it is controlled by real-time operating system (RTOS). Stat suggest that 98% of microprocessors that are manufactured are used as components in embedded system [18].

There are three components of it. They are as follows:

- Has hardware
- Has application software
- Has RTOS.

10.7 IoT for Smart Manufacturing

The biggest industry in the world is manufacturing industry. To deploy a technology to manufacturing is very expensive and time-consuming. But the introduction of Industry 4.0, the manual process in the manufacturing industries, is turned into smart manufacturing technology with a large number of advantages. The smart manufacturing reduces the human workload and increases efficiency and productivity. Here we are not replacing the human but reduce the load of human. Most of the work places are deployed with intelligent agents (machines) equipped with sensors and actuators. The new model of smart industries is the replacement of all the operations of old industries [19].

10.7.1 IIoT Impact in Manufacturing

The IIoT technology helps industries to automate all the processes and helps humans to reduce the complex and risky overload. A single click in a software can control all the processes of the industry right now because of the smart manufacturing implemented through IoT. The big machineries are embedded with sensors that sense like a human and give live report to the software, according to the software condition operations will happen normally. Every second data will send to the enabled technologies like cloud for further analysis of the data. Finally, all the results will display at the application in a different perspective, report and visualization for easily understanding the whole of the process in a simple way to take the next step for the business [20].

10.7.2 Supply Chain

IoT sensors are connected from the stage of raw material collection to the final product delivered at the consumer side. All the data collected, stored, and analyzed. The analyzed data is given to the system for taking a decision, for example, the manufacturers monitor the market, delivery of goods, and collect all the information like quantity of goods, quality, temperature, route, etc. If the goods are temperature sensitive, product should be kept accordingly to the particular room temperature.

10.7.3 Remote and Third-Party Operations

The industries not only belong to a single location, depending upon the size and type of industries, but it is distributed to different locations or even different countries. The process of these companies is almost same but the controlling and managing of these industries in each location depend on the manager or CEO of the branch. The invent of IIoT, all the branches of companies under one umbrella means it operates by one location [21–23].

10.7.4 Remote Production Control

IoT devices automatically configure and monitor their equipment accordingly. The employee can remotely get all the information about all the things related to industries like the machine status, stock, and raw material details. The staff can also check the future outcome, its display in the form of reports containing graph and visualization.

10.7.5 Predictive Maintenance

The human inspection is done by the intelligent machines. Here the problem is machines may cause the failure because of continuous working, heating, pressure, voltage, etc. These kinds of situations must identify and provide continuous maintenance, called predictive maintenance. This allows technical team to detect issues before some fault happens to the product. This identification we can make simple with the help of IIoT.

10.8 IoT Industrial Use Cases

IoT-enabled systems consist of different sensors, and M2M connected devices based on client desire. They have the ability to sense warming signals, share the collected data with the server and then server transmit required data to other connected devices so that the whole network works together. This thing makes it more efficient because we all know that if we are going to do a big job single handed, it can be good but not much perfect in a short interval of time while if same job is getting done by multiple people, it can be done in much less time. The same thing happens with IoT devices as they do a job together and perfectly. IoT makes it easier for industries to handle such a big workload easily and control over the network with these technologies. Here, we are going to discuss about some of the great inventions in the field of IoT for industrial uses shown in Figure 10.11 [24].

- ABB – Smart Robotics
- Airbus
- Asset tracking
- Smart metering
- AWS
- Connected vehicles.

10.8.1 ABB – Smart Robotics

ABB stands for Asea Brown Boveri which is a Swedish swiss that is multinational company famous for energy and automation. As robots communicate with each other, IoT plays a big role in robotics for its construction. IoT devices can monitor events and fuse sensor data collected from different scanning units. IoT is an end-to-end software

FIGURE 10.11
Illustration of IIoT.

framework which helps to do jobs using multiple inbuilt devices together from scanning, collecting, and taking action over data [25].

Smart robot has been considered as a substitute for human in many fields and for this robot needs higher efficiency. Artificial intelligence and IoT together make it possible for the technical world to replace human in many industrial works.

10.8.2 Connected Vehicle

It is an IoT technology built with wireless communication network. All vehicles are in bi-directional communication with each other which also help in traffic control and decrease accidents. This increases the safety for drivers as well. One of the old technology with which everyone is familiar is GPS. GPS helps connected vehicles to plan routes. One of the new trending technology, OnStar enables driver to get assistance whenever needed. Self-driving cars manufactured by Tesla are equipped with IoT devices which help artificial assistance to plan route, detect other cars, and provide security to people in car.

10.8.3 Asset Tracking

As the name reveals, it is a system used for tracking assets and components using antennas and wireless networks. It is used on industrial level for improvement of quality and components.

Use fields:

- Manufacturing
- Healthcare
- Law enforcement
- Education.

Issue:

- Network security risk
- Lack of standardization
- Privacy and compliance concerns.

10.8.4 Smart Metering

Smart metering is ok like a wide area network which works for addressing challenges like energy consumption and water uses with the help of city-wide smart grid system. Smart grid system connects building and makes things more efficient for smart city development. It is much secured and protected from cyberattacks.

Its features are as follows:

- It suggests a detailed feedback on energy consumption.
- It increases transparency.

10.9 Conclusion

From the above study, we can conclude that IoT is going to be the future of every smart object around us. As this allows transparent data sharing, constant feedback feature through applications, and higher efficiency in doing job, we are not much far away from a world dependent on IoT devices. From connected vehicles to smart robots, each of these is the future of our society. One day, IoT will transform our everyday physical objects that surround us into network of large cluster of information. IoT has developed a lot in last decade and the way developers are working, we can expect much more development in future. In 1960, there were 1 MM+ units per user while in 2010–2020 it increased to billions. Earlier security was also a big concern for IoT but with time developers made it possible to protect IoT devices and IoT inbuilt big companies' machines from vulnerability. Isolation measures, tamper mitigation, and side channel attacks have been concluded as best approaches to protect IoT devices in recent time. With time IoT entered in maximum technology-based sectors such as media, healthcare, home automation, manufacturing, and many more. Global share of IoT is around 22% in industries, 15% in transportation, and 12% in smart city projects. Technologies like cloud computing, big data, Internet, and wireless sensors network together make IoT as a trusted technology which can make human life more easy. The way IoT is showing involvement in transportation and home automation sector, we are not much far to see smartness in non-living things around us.

References

1. Shafique, Kinza, et al. "Internet of things (IoT) for next-generation smart systems: A review of current challenges, future trends and prospects for emerging 5G-IoT scenarios." *IEEE Access* 8 (2020): 23022–23040.
2. Wu, Qiong, Kaiwen He, and Xu Chen. "Personalized federated learning for intelligent IoT applications: A cloud-edge based framework." *IEEE Open Journal of the Computer Society* 1 (2020): 35–44.
3. Casado-Vara, Roberto, et al. "Distributed continuous-time fault estimation control for multiple devices in IoT networks." *IEEE Access* 7 (2019): 11972–11984.
4. Stoyanova, Maria, et al. "A survey on the internet of things (IoT) forensics: Challenges, approaches, and open issues." *IEEE Communications Surveys & Tutorials* 22.2 (2020): 1191–1221.
5. Singh, Ravi Pratap, et al. "Internet of things (IoT) applications to fight against COVID-19 pandemic." *Diabetes & Metabolic Syndrome: Clinical Research & Reviews* 14.4 (2020): 521–524.
6. Centenaro, Marco, et al. "A survey on technologies, standards and open challenges in satellite IoT." *IEEE Communications Surveys & Tutorials* 23.3 (2021): 1693–1720.
7. Chaudhry, Shehzad Ashraf, et al. "A secure and reliable device access control scheme for IoT based sensor cloud systems." *IEEE Access* 8 (2020): 139244–139254.
8. Hassija, Vikas, et al. "A survey on IoT security: Application areas, security threats, and solution architectures." *IEEE Access* 7 (2019): 82721–82743.
9. Alsaedi, Abdullah, et al. "TON_IoT telemetry dataset: A new generation dataset of IoT and IIoT for data-driven intrusion detection systems." *IEEE Access* 8 (2020): 165130–165150.
10. Al-Masri, Eyhab, et al. "Investigating messaging protocols for the Internet of Things (IoT)." *IEEE Access* 8 (2020): 94880–94911.

11. Chettri, Lalit, and Rabindranath Bera. "A comprehensive survey on Internet of Things (IoT) toward 5G wireless systems." *IEEE Internet of Things Journal* 7.1 (2019): 16–32.
12. Hassan, Wan Haslina. "Current research on Internet of Things (IoT) security: A survey." *Computer Networks* 148 (2019): 283–294.
13. Chaabouni, Nadia, et al. "Network intrusion detection for IoT security based on learning techniques." *IEEE Communications Surveys & Tutorials* 21.3 (2019): 2671–2701.
14. Meneghello, Francesca, et al. "IoT: Internet of threats? A survey of practical security vulnerabilities in real IoT devices." *IEEE Internet of Things Journal* 6.5 (2019): 8182–8201.
15. Boursianis, Achilles D., et al. "Internet of things (IoT) and agricultural unmanned aerial vehicles (UAVs) in smart farming: a comprehensive review." *Internet of Things* 18(2020): 100187.
16. Nižetić, Sandro, et al. "Internet of Things (IoT): Opportunities, issues and challenges towards a smart and sustainable future." *Journal of Cleaner Production* 274 (2020): 122877.
17. Adi, Erwin, et al. "Machine learning and data analytics for the IoT." *Neural Computing and Applications* 32.20 (2020): 16205–16233.
18. Neshenko, Nataliia, et al. "Demystifying IoT security: An exhaustive survey on IoT vulnerabilities and a first empirical look on Internet-scale IoT exploitations." *IEEE Communications Surveys & Tutorials* 21.3 (2019): 2702–2733.
19. Shafique, Kinza, et al. "Internet of things (IoT) for next-generation smart systems: A review of current challenges, future trends and prospects for emerging 5G-IoT scenarios." *IEEE Access* 8 (2020): 23022–23040.
20. Smys, S. "A survey on Internet of Things (IoT) based smart systems." *Journal of ISMAC* 2.04 (2020): 181–189.
21. ReyesYanes, A., P. Martinez Reyes, and R. Ahmad. "Towards automated aquaponics: A review on monitoring, IoT, and smart systems." *Journal of Cleaner Production* 263 (2020): 121571.
22. Aheleroff, Shohin, et al. "IoT-enabled smart appliances under industry 4.0: A case study." *Advanced Engineering Informatics* 43 (2020): 101043.
23. Somani, Arun K., et al., eds. *Smart Systems and IoT: Innovations in Computing: Proceeding of SSIC 2019*, Vol. 141. Springer Nature, 2019.
24. De Donno, Michele, Koen Tange, and Nicola Dragoni. "Foundations and evolution of modern computing paradigms: Cloud, iot, edge, and fog." *IEEE Access* 7 (2019): 150936–150948.
25. Ghazal, Taher M., et al. "IoT for smart cities: Machine learning approaches in smart healthcare—A review." *Future Internet* 13.8 (2021): 3–19.

Printed in the United States
by Baker & Taylor Publisher Services

Index